LIKE THE BOOK OF ACTS

LIKE THE BOOK OF ACTS

THE
BAPTIST CONVENTION
OF
NEW YORK STORY

KEITH L. COGBURN

PROVIDENCE HOUSE PUBLISHERS
Franklin, Tennessee

Printed in the United States of America

00   99   98   97   96   5   4   3   2   1

Library of Congress Catalog Card Number: 96–70444

ISBN: 1–881576–80–9

Photographs provided courtesy of Keith L. Cogburn, The Maryland Baptist, *the* New York Baptist, *and the Baptist Convention of New York. Photographs on pages 42, 88, 199, and 208 are reprinted from* MissionsUSA *and* Home Mission Study. *The Home Mission Board of the Southern Baptist Convention. Used by permission.*

Cover by Bozeman Design

PROVIDENCE HOUSE PUBLISHERS
238 Seaboard Lane • Franklin, Tennessee 37067
800-321-5692

TO MY PARENTS
JIM AND DOROTHY COGBURN

CONTENTS

Acknowledgments   9

Introduction—The Story in Context   11
1. A Foundation in Western and Central New York   17
2. A Foundation in the "Big Apple"   29
3. Advance on the Frontier   40
4. New Associations for the Heartland, the North Country, and the Southern Tier   53
5. The "Witness of All Things to All People"—the Expanding Ministry of the Manhattan Baptist Church   65
6. Mission Beyond the City Limits   79
7. Mission to the World   98
8. A New Convention "Born to Serve"   115
9. Getting Started, 1970–1979   133
10. Growth in Associations and Churches, 1970–1979   147
11. Coming of Age, 1980–1989   164
12. Growth in Associations and Churches, 1980–1989   183
13. A New Day for Mission Advance, 1990–1994   200
Conclusion—Like the Book of Acts   221

Appendix—The Historical Record of the Baptist Convention of New York   223
Endnotes   225
Index   243
About the Author   256

ACKNOWLEDGMENTS

This project would not have been possible without the enthusiastic cooperation of the large number of people I interviewed and consulted. It has been a joy getting to know many of the pioneers around whom the early chapters of this story revolve. Thank you for carefully and thoughtfully answering my questions, and for sharing some of your best memories of Christian service. The present New York Baptist family has also been quite supportive, helping me pull together a vast body of data. When I call next, it will be for a friendly chat, not to obtain some obscure name or date! Beth Ward in the convention office at Syracuse especially needs to hear this.

Several individuals have contributed directly to the successful completion of this history. My friend DeLane Ryals deserves a lot of credit for refining these pages. He worked diligently as an editor, making many beneficial suggestions for producing what we hope is a readable narrative. He also is an encyclopedia of information about the churches of the Metropolitan Association. Martha McGavic's strong suit is proofreading. I thank her for reading the manuscript with the exactitude of an eighth-grade English teacher. Terry Robertson read the text for balance—to make sure the Baptist Convention of New York story was viewed through a wide-angle lens. His observations were most helpful.

I also want to express my appreciation to the BCNY History Committee for offering me the honor and privilege of telling this important story.

Norma Pugh, chair of the committee, has been exceedingly patient awaiting the completion of this work. Even so, my pulse rate has jumped a bit over the last several months each time the phone rang—fearing she might be calling for a progress report. Norma—it is finally done! No kidding.

R. Quinn Pugh, recently retired executive director/treasurer of the Baptist Convention of New York, has affirmed and encouraged me since the first time we met—when he and DeLane Ryals visited Princeton Seminary in 1983 to welcome us few Southern Baptist students. I am deeply grateful for the confidence he showed in me in recommending that I write this book.

Finally, I owe an immeasurable debt of gratitude to my church members and family who have endured my preoccupation with this effort for so long. The dear people of the Raritan Valley Baptist Church have prayed me through this process, especially over these last months. I am glad I can again give them my undivided attention. And what can I say to thank my family for their patience, love, and support every step of the way? Laura, Emily, and John—let's go have some fun together! I love you.

Keith L. Cogburn
Edison, New Jersey
April 1996

Baptist Convention of New York

THE STORY IN CONTEXT

Last winter I spent a gray afternoon touring the exhibits and displays located at the old Ellis Island Immigration Station near the Statue of Liberty. At the height of its operation between 1892 and 1924, this station processed some twelve million immigrants. Among the displays I found most interesting was one that featured various types of carpetbags and wooden trunks these travelers used to store their meager worldly possessions. Not much, I thought, to hold one's investment in the future. But then I considered the words of the tour guide who assured us that while these sturdy souls brought little with them in the way of material goods, they brought a wealth of intangible assets to keep them in good stead—assets like fortitude, family devotion, and, in most cases, religious faith. I was reminded that from the earliest settlers in the 1620s, the story of religion in America has been a multifaceted narrative of "imported" faiths which rallied and succored immigrants of a common ethnic or regional origin in an unfamiliar land. And if the religious tradition happened to be of an aggressive missionary variety, or if it was amenable to the revivals and "awakenings" that swept across colonial America, then it tended to spill out of the cultural mold from which it was cast.

The story of Southern Baptists' northeastern expansion in the mid-twentieth century bears a curious likeness to this familiar seventeenth- and eighteenth-century pattern of denominational migration and growth in American religious life. "Immigrant faith," in fact, figured prominently in the history of Baptists in the South long before there was a Southern Baptist Convention.

When the convention entered its fiftieth state in 1963 with the establishment of a church in Vermont, the event ironically represented something of a New England homecoming for Southern Baptists. More than two hundred fifty years before, pastor William Screven and most of the members of the Baptist church at Kittery, Maine, migrated to Charleston, South Carolina, where they helped establish in 1696 the highly influential First Baptist Church, the first known Baptist church in the South.

The New England colonies also blessed the South with Shubal Stearns, Daniel Marshall, and Martha Stearns Marshall, all three passionate evangelists who brought with them to Sandy Creek, North Carolina, the revivalistic fervor of the First Great Awakening. In less than a generation after its organization in 1755, the Sandy Creek Church produced more than a hundred preachers and became a mother, grandmother, and great-grandmother to more than forty churches scattered throughout the Southeast.[1] Although quite different in significant ways, the Charleston and Sandy Creek Churches, along with their offspring, were the foundation for a stable and growing Baptist establishment in the South.

In the early decades of the nineteenth century, these "southern" Baptists joined their counterparts in the North in forming a fledgling national denomination to support an emerging missionary enterprise. The delicate concord of the so-called "Triennial Convention" was, however, soon disturbed by doctrinal and organizational disputes, and later was torn asunder by sectional hostilities over the slavery issue.

The vast majority of churches that birthed the Southern Baptist Convention in 1845 were centered in the southeastern states. The aftermath of the Civil War produced a change to this earliest detail of the Baptist landscape. Large numbers of southerners left their war-ravaged and politically chaotic homeland for places of brighter promise like Texas. Among the influx of new arrivals were a substantial number of Baptists, including many pastors and denominational leaders. With their migration the regional dominance of the convention began shifting toward the Southwest. By the early 1870s, B. H. Carroll and other visionaries like him were predicting that the Lone Star State would become an expansive Baptist Zion.

The final chapters in Southern Baptists' geographical expansion into a national denomination were written in the twentieth century. During the Great Depression of the 1930s, large numbers of forlorn "Oakies" and "Arkies" trekked from the "Dust Bowl" to the West Coast in hopes of finding jobs. Like the immigrants who sailed past Lady Liberty, these laborers carried little with them in the way of worldly goods. But they were sure to bring their religion, and the Southern Baptists among them organized churches from southern California to Washington State which by the late 1940s were organized into new state conventions.

The postwar years were a halcyon time for Southern Baptist expansion into new frontiers of growth. An industrial boom created employment opportunities in the Great Lakes region which attracted laborers from the South. A pattern of church growth and development similar to what had transpired in the West was repeated in this region.

Expanded domestic military operations following World War II also contributed to a growing Southern Baptist diaspora. Service personnel and their families stationed at posts in the upper Midwest and Northern Plains had a significant role in planting new Southern Baptist churches in places as unlikely as the Dakotas.

Closer to what then was considered "home," churches in states bordering the Old South formed new associations and conventions. Ohio Southern Baptists, for example, who had long enjoyed an affiliation with Kentucky Baptists across the Ohio River, organized their churches into a small state convention in 1954.

Between 1940 and 1955, the geographic area served by the convention and the number of people living within the convention's broadened territory almost tripled. Such dramatic denominational expansion was a phenomenon unparalleled in twentieth-century American church history. Many of the estimated 1.3 million Baptists who left the southern states obviously were taking their religion with them.[2]

This windfall of home mission opportunity and the challenges it posed caused many leaders to rediscover the convention's defining vision, first articulated in 1845: "It shall be the design of this convention to promote Foreign and Domestic Missions, . . . and to combine for this purpose, such portions of the Baptist denomination in the United States as may desire a general organization for Christian benevolence, which shall fully respect the independence and equal rights of the churches." Given the name they selected for the new body, the founders who endorsed this statement clearly were intent upon establishing a denomination demarcated along ever-hardening sectional lines. Might these leaders have been looking beyond the differences that divided them from their northern counterparts to a time of possible rapprochement? Or were they perhaps visionary enough to dream of a broadened geographic base beyond the South? Either thought is open to considerable question, but this much is certain: a century later when the reality of a truly national convention with churches north of the Mason-Dixon line began sinking in, these words were taken as prophetic for defining the denomination's destiny.

Messengers to the convention's annual session in 1951 went on record encouraging the Home Mission Board and all other boards and agencies to "serve as a source of blessing to any community or any people anywhere in the United States."[3] This mandate lent a new momentum to expansion efforts and set the stage for a denominational response to Baptists in western New York and along the northeastern seaboard who within a few years would be echoing the cry of the Macedonian: "Come over and help us."

In the pages that follow, I attempt to tell the story of Southern Baptists' advance into the territory now known as the Baptist Convention of New York (all of New York State, northern and central New Jersey, and south-western Connecticut). Although a formal state convention structure has been in place only since 1969, the history of SBC-affiliated churches in the region spans more than forty years.

The Baptist Convention of New York story began in the mid-1950s with a smattering of transplanted Southern Baptists who had resettled in the region. They arrived at a time when mainline denominations were experi-encing growth and when their own houses of worship were crowded on Sunday mornings. They came in the midst of what Courts Redford, then president of the Home Mission Board, called a "real Holy Ghost revival" with scattered flames that threatened to become a "consuming spiritual fire."[4] To their enormous credit, leaders like Redford and his associates galvanized Southern Baptists to seize the opportunities the times afforded for mission expansion into new areas.

Today a starkly different mood hovers over the religious landscape in America. Many of those who were led by the hand or carried into worship services in the mid-1950s now openly question the relevance of the church and demonstrate their apathy by sleeping late, or by massing at places other than church buildings on Sundays.

Fortunately, New York Baptists have negotiated the changing times over the last four decades with some measure of effectiveness. New models and strategies of mission are employed to confront the challenges posed for the church in these closing days of the second millennium. Whereas in the 1950s church extension in the region served mostly to gather southern white transplants into congregations which capitalized upon the appeal of a southern religious ethos, today's churches are more indigenous and reflective of the ethnic pluralism of the region.

Another important change has been the way in which churches and associations of the region have increasingly assumed a distinctive identity, no longer feeling obliged to import a template of church and denomina-tional life that works well elsewhere. Cooperation with the boards and agencies of the national convention remains a priority, but New York

Baptists stubbornly pursue methods and strategies that address the needs of churches in places like Bridgewater and Buffalo, not Nashville and Atlanta.

Much has changed, to be sure, since the first church in the region was gathered in 1954, yet some things have remained constant. Devoted, self-sacrificing, mission-minded laypeople still establish and sustain the churches of the Baptist Convention of New York. Another constant has been the visionary leadership and tenacity that pastors and their spouses have demonstrated over the last forty years. They often uprooted their families, taking children half a continent away from grandparents, and left the security of comfortable pastorates to venture out where the possibilities for total failure were greater than even imagined. One still finds these kinds of resourceful, pioneering spirits in leadership among the churches and associations.

I feel especially obliged at the outset to mention the contribution women have made to the churches and to the convention. Ava James (pronounced AH-va) was a missionary in her own right, aside from the fact that she was married to Paul James, the convention's "founding father." She often told young church planters that if they wanted to get their churches off the ground, they needed to start Woman's Missionary Union circles among their membership. June Andrews's recent book, *So Generations Will Remember*, attests to the impact women have made on the life and ministry of the Baptist Convention of New York. The book provides ample evidence to indicate how beneficial Mrs. James's advice must have been. If the WMU does not seem to occupy as large a place in this volume as it deserves, it is only because I have consciously tried not to duplicate Andrews's effort.

Despite my best efforts, I likely overlooked some people whose names ought to appear in the pages that follow. They are pastors and laypeople who built and nurtured churches—who did the real work of ministry for which others may have been given more credit than is due. Please accept my sincere apologies in advance. I also tried to mention at least once all of the existing churches listed in the 1994 Annual Church Profile. If through some oversight I failed to include your congregation, please forgive me.

One of the joys of this work has been the opportunity to speak first-hand with many of the people who helped bring the Baptist Convention of New York into being. Often their voices choked with emotion as they recalled their experiences. The faith, vision, and profound sense of calling these pioneers brought to their tasks have an almost palpable quality. Their legacy inspires me immensely. I hope that what follows conveys enough of their spirit that the reader will benefit similarly.

CHAPTER ONE

Baptist Convention of New York

A FOUNDATION IN WESTERN AND CENTRAL NEW YORK

Southern Baptists were fairly content in the early 1950s to remain a regional denomination. After all, were not their churches by definition supposed to be in the South, exceptions in the West notwithstanding? So what if the metropolitan centers of the Northeast with populations exceeding one million had not a single church affiliated with their convention? Was not the region really the territory and responsibility of those other Baptists—the ones from whom their forebears separated themselves a century before?

But while Southern Baptists had no official denominational presence as yet in the region, a diverse body of Southern Baptist people had arrived in upstate New York and New York City and its environs, and they were asking different kinds of questions. Could their pattern and program of church life "back home" be reproduced in a new locale to minister to their fellow transplants? Would it appeal to their neighbors whose lives were woven into the fabric of Yankee culture? Would it be okay to start a new Southern Baptist church up north?

One might think that Southern Baptists' earliest forays of ministry into New York and the northeastern seaboard states were prompted by the simple logic of mission to where the people were. One might also assume that mission efforts were initiated in the territory of the Baptist Convention of New York by the Home Mission Board, perhaps as part of a grand strategy for reaching the whole nation for Christ. Could there have been, in retrospect, a more compelling missionary challenge for Southern Baptists than that of pursuing the nation's most densely populated region with the gospel? Finally, one might suppose that state conventions in close proximity like Ohio and Maryland took an active interest in their neighbors to the north and initiated the task of church planting in strategic locations. All of these scenarios of missionary expansion were eventually played out to some extent in the development of new work in the region, but none was primary.

The impetus leading to the establishment of Southern Baptist churches in New York, New Jersey, and Connecticut was the same as it had been for denominational expansion into other so-called "non-traditional" areas: the presence of Southern Baptist people living in the new area. Southern Baptist transplants discovered one another, organized themselves into Bible study fellowships, prayed for God's direction, and asked their denomination for assistance in planting new mission chapels. Whereas "back home" they had experienced missions vicariously through educational programs and annual seasons of missions emphasis, these strangers in a strange land found that they were now the missionaries—called of God, in the words of Esther 4:14, "for such a time as this." From Niagara Falls to Syracuse to New York City and across the Hudson to northern and central New Jersey, this became a familiar pattern of church growth in the late 1950s and early 1960s. The "Pioneer Missions Movement," the formal designation for Southern Baptists' advance northward, was from the beginning a lay movement—a procession of followers leading.[1]

"Things Just Aren't the Same"

The Baptist Convention of New York story began in an unlikely place, with an unlikely candidate for home mission leadership. One of Ralph Zeigler "Zig" Boroughs's first tasks after graduation in 1953 from the New Orleans Baptist Theological Seminary was to lead his church in organizing its annual homecoming observance.[2] An important tradition like this for the Gantt Baptist Church, in the hamlet of Gantt, Alabama, called for careful preparations, like locating as many of the church's nonresident members as possible.

Much to the young pastor's surprise, almost two dozen members of the Gantt Church lived, of all places, in Niagara Falls, New York. The prospect of steady, high-wage jobs in the chemical plants of the region had produced a continuous stream of laborers from Alabama as brothers-in-law, cousins, and friends sent home the welcome word of job opportunities in the North.

Boroughs was pleased to address homecoming invitations to these economic emigrés, but disappointed to learn that few of them from his church or any other church in the surrounding county were actively involved in a Niagara Falls congregation. The Alabama pastor was particularly disturbed over what he heard from a former deacon who, after telling him all that the Gantt Church had once meant to him, confided that he had not been to church in three years.[3]

That summer those who made the long journey home explained to the pastor that northern churches just were not the same. The stereotypes that prevailed so strongly in the 1950s on both sides of the Mason-Dixon line were assumed and expressed. "Yankees" were considered cold and detached—a bit stiff and unfriendly. Southerners were self-conscious about being perceived as backward and racist—uncouth hayseeds with households full of rowdy, barefooted kids. These perceptions meant that much more than just geographical distance separated Covington County, Alabama, from western New York.

Understanding what southerners living "up north" actually meant by that little phrase Boroughs heard and which echoed throughout the 1950s—"the churches just aren't the same"—is a study in itself. Some expressed overall dissatisfaction with the mission, outreach, and evangelism programs of the churches they visited. For others, "singing the Lord's song in a strange land" was the problem. Worship patterns in northern churches were more structured and staid; what hymns southerners knew were sung at a different tempo; offerings were sometimes collected in funny little pouches; and inevitably the "Doxology" was sung at the wrong time in the order of worship. Moreover, no "invitation" was extended—a glaring, almost unthinkable omission in worship. But some considered that a few bars of "Softly and Tenderly" would not have mattered much anyway, since the sermons they heard seemed to lack the kind of revivalistic urgency typical of a Southern Baptist "preacher," not a robed "reverend" or "minister."

Interestingly enough, with the exception of communion practices, theological issues do not seem to have been a major factor in southerners' overall discontent with the churches they visited. Whereas many American Baptist Convention churches (now American Baptist Churches, U.S.A.) might have espoused ideas and subscribed to a social action agenda deemed "liberal" by some, still there were plenty of churches affiliated with the Conservative Baptist Association and a variety of other baptistic "independent" churches to which transplants could have turned. Yet even theologically conservative churches tended to irritate many transplants with their rigorous demands for pledges to eschew "worldliness" in the form of everything from chewing tobacco to adorning oneself with cosmetics and jewelry.[4]

These frustrations might have made church life more difficult and less satisfying, but they hardly would have been insurmountable obstacles for sincere believers who were Christians first, Baptists second, and Southern Baptists third. Yet these people were southerners, and southern culture and religion were still very much intertwined in the 1950s. Numerous studies of southern culture demonstrate the profound impact religion had in shaping and defining the character of the South well into the twentieth century.[5] Churches—especially those in communities like Gantt—were a foundation of unity and strength for the southern way of life. A powerful cultural "mystique" about Christian practice and the place of church in one's life was at work contributing to the discomfort southerners had with the churches they visited. Uprooted southerners could not escape their feelings of alienation and loneliness, even though churches in the North shared their Baptist name, part of their history, and much of their theology.

The churches were "just not the same" for another important reason: Southern Baptists did not tend to think of themselves as one convention in a larger denominational family of Baptists—they represented a faith and order distinct from that of their counterparts in the North. In a 1959 interview immediately after his election as president of the Southern Baptist Convention, Ramsey Pollard commented on his denomination's missionary activities outside the South. "The name, 'Southern Baptist Convention,'" he explained, "carries with it more than geographic meaning. It has a doctrinal and functional meaning."[6] Southern Baptists identified their way of doing things—their massive program of missions, education, and evangelism—with the Baptist way. Sunday School literature, mission education programs, seasonal emphases, sermon topics, and even preachers' jokes were of such a uniform character that people moving from one place to another in the South could expect to find almost the same pattern of church life duplicated in a new area.

"Southern Baptist" was, like Sears, a name you could trust. This program-oriented denominational loyalty and the effects of culture shock contributed to the widespread dissatisfaction with northern church life expressed by those who returned to the Gantt Church's homecoming in the summer of 1953. These factors also meant that Zig Boroughs's outrageous idea of organizing a Southern Baptist church in Niagara Falls was worth their consideration.

A Church "Home" Away from Home

The Niagara Falls opportunity stirred anew a calling Boroughs had experienced a few years before. After hearing a foreign missionary describe the challenge of his work in Nigeria, young Boroughs, then a schoolteacher, felt a calling to such a vocation. The Foreign Mission Board received his application for appointment shortly before graduation from seminary, but much to his disappointment the board did not accept him for an assignment. Boroughs was told he lacked experience in pastoral ministry and was counseled to get some stateside work under his belt before following his calling abroad.[7] Now Niagara was beginning to look more like Nigeria once had looked. Gantt, Alabama, which at the time of his graduation hardly seemed like an appropriate proving ground for mission work, was now the place of service through which his calling could be realized.

That fall Boroughs began a systematic effort to contact all the families from Alabama living in the Niagara Falls area. Most of the more than sixty families he tracked down expressed interest in being part of a Southern Baptist "church home away from home." The thirty-seven people who gathered in Richard and Faustine Williamson's living room to discuss the idea, while surely aware of the pioneering nature of the task they considered, could not have imagined the far-reaching implications of their meeting.

On that spring evening in 1954, the Alabamians compared notes about their frustrations with churches in the area, but mostly their conversation centered upon the faith and resources necessary for the unfamiliar task of starting a new church. Despite many questions that could not be answered at that point, the group voted to form the "Niagara Falls Southern Baptist Mission," under the sponsorship of the Gantt Church. Their decision to proceed with the venture was inspired by a positive missionary faith like that expressed by Ettie Jo Gilmer, who recalled the group's concluding sentiment as: "When God calls, you just do it!"[8]

On May 30, 1954, these unwitting people of destiny, these new "missionaries," held their first service. The Gantt Church gave their blessing to the group, put eighty-five dollars in John Hiott's pocket, and sent him north to help start the work. Hiott, fresh out of New Orleans Seminary, guided the mission throughout the summer months, welcoming twenty-seven new members. The congregation moved to the LaSalle YMCA during this time and changed its name to the LaSalle Baptist Mission. By August Hiott had determined to accept a call as a staff member in a southern church.

The highlight of the summer was a revival meeting which featured the preaching of Zig Boroughs. His concern for the long-term growth and stability of the LaSalle Mission brought him northward. He wanted to visit the community and extend warm handshakes to the many persons with whom he had become closely acquainted through correspondence and telephone calls. Boroughs wondered if the group shared the sense of calling God had given him for a new work in this out-of-the-way place for Southern Baptists. Was a Southern Baptist church in western New York feasible? Although he realized that the success of the church ultimately depended upon God's blessing, he also knew that grit and dogged determination would be needed to put the church on a firm foundation to reach "the Jew first, and then the Greek."

The Gantt pastor's burden for the group was plain for all to see, giving someone the temerity to put forth another crazy idea—that Boroughs resign his Alabama pastorate and trek northward for a new assignment as pastor of the LaSalle Baptist Mission. No arm-twisting was necessary. In Boroughs's words, he was by that time "rarin' to go!"[9]

In a scene worthy of Steinbeck's *Grapes of Wrath*, Zig and Mary Boroughs and their six children headed north, pulling a U-Haul trailer packed like a trick snake in a can. To supplement his meager fifty dollars per week salary, the pastor worked as a substitute teacher and later as a laborer in a chemical plant. His initial requests to the Home Mission Board for assistance were met with referrals back to the Alabama Baptist State Convention, which were met with referrals back to the board. Denominational leaders seemed in a quandary over what to do with this freestanding congregation located in unfamiliar territory.

Despite these frustrations and concerns, Boroughs expressed confidence in his calling. In a letter addressed to his mother, who apparently had taken on the role of official worrier for her son and the grandchildren he had taken with him, he wrote: ". . . The Lord sent me here, and will take care of us, as he always has and is doing now. Even if reverses come, which they will with or without help from the SBC or other sources, we will feel secure in knowing that we are in the work and in the place God wants us to be. Please pray for us. . . ."[10]

In June 1955, the LaSalle Baptist Church was constituted with fifty-four charter members and was welcomed into the Erie Association, affiliated with the recently organized State Convention of Baptists in Ohio. The "Ohio connection," often personified by the ubiquitous executive director of the convention, Ray Roberts, soon became an invaluable resource of fellowship, administrative assistance, and financial support for new Southern Baptist work in western New York.

Inspired by the prospect of new churches under the LaSalle Church's sponsorship, Boroughs challenged his brothers and sisters in the South with these words: "The Indians called the area of the Niagara River the 'gate.' LaSalle Baptist Church now stands in the 'gate.' Will you join us in prayer that the gate to New York State will swing wide, opening the way for the message and program of Southern Baptists to reach the 14.5 million people in this great state?"[11] Families like the Williamsons, the Mathisons, the Kevers, the Foors, and a host of other dedicated laypeople helped the LaSalle Church become an open gate for missions through which Southern Baptists entered the Empire State.

East to Syracuse

The LaSalle congregation's dream of helping plant a new church elsewhere in New York was realized sooner than anyone anticipated. Wilburn C. Ferguson was an engineer with the General Electric Company and a deacon in the First Southern Baptist Church of Tucson, Arizona.[12] During his church's annual home missions emphasis in March 1957, he taught the adult mission study. As his experience had usually borne out, he learned more in teaching the study book, *Home Missions U.S.A.*, than anyone else in the class. He was, in fact, intrigued and inspired by the stories he related of home missionaries carving out ministries in challenging and unlikely places.

The class sessions ended predictably with an admonition to remember the dedicated servants on the home front who needed the church's prayers and sacrificial gifts. Little did Ferguson realize that in just a short while his family would be the object of home mission interest. Two months after he taught the course, he was on his way to Syracuse for a special research project. Indicative of his commitment to a higher vocation, he and his wife, Beulah, felt that God had a special purpose for them in this unexpected and unwelcome relocation.

The Fergusons were disappointed to learn from the Home Mission Board that Syracuse was not among the challenging and unlikely places where new Southern Baptist work was beginning. Solomon F. Dowis, secretary of the cooperative missions division, offered little encouragement to them in a terse, businesslike response to their inquiry. He did, however, provide them with Zig Boroughs's address.[13]

Boroughs's reply was a direct challenge to the family to become charter members of a new church in Syracuse. Despite the more than two hundred miles that separated them from Niagara Falls, he was confident that his church could be a nurturing presence for a new mission in central New York. By the end of the letter, the LaSalle pastor practically had a new church constituted, asking the Fergusons to begin praying that God would prepare the heart of a mission-minded pastor to serve them.

In a subsequent letter, Boroughs outlined in a way that sounds amusing today what experience had taught him about gathering a core group to form a church. Among other things, he suggested carrying a notebook and pencil at all times for recording the names and addresses of anyone with a southern accent. And Boroughs had definite ideas about where such voices might be heard. "Most southerners," he wrote, "start off in the cheap rent areas of downtown. The Polish and Italian sections of this city are full of Rebels. They rent a third-story flat from an Italian or Polish family, or they live over bowling alleys, taverns, or stores. You will also find them in federal housing projects. Trailer camps usually have a good many southerners."

Finally, he counseled Ferguson, the southerners are "homesick and scattered, and suddenly they find in a Southern Baptist mission something that reminds them of the little country church down South, and their hearts are strangely warmed, and some catch fire for the Lord. . . ."[14] Boroughs acknowledged that his vision might sound rather circumscribed, but he insisted that a strong foundation of families with a Southern Baptist background was needed "to get things rolling."

Things got rolling for Ferguson in May 1957 when he followed the advice of Paul Nevels, area missionary of the Erie Association, about placing an ad in the Syracuse paper to help locate interested Southern Baptists. Among the first persons to respond was a man who, though not a Baptist himself, offered encouragement and mentioned that his son—a native of Syracuse—was pastor of the Broadway Baptist Church in Columbia, South Carolina. Ferguson immediately wrote the pastor, needing all the friends he could find for the new work. Meanwhile, he was finding new friends all the time in Syracuse. By June the engineer had in hand the names of ten families interested in forming a church.

Paul Nevels made arrangements to hold revival services and a Vacation Bible School in the area with the assistance of two summer missionaries from Ohio. Nevels proved to be a dependable source of help to the mission. Whatever resources the Home Mission Board and the Ohio Convention had to offer, he saw that Ferguson knew about it.

The final piece of good news proved to be the best news for the proposed mission. The young pastor from South Carolina, Paul Becker, was interested in returning to Syracuse to lead the mission if the group would have him![15]

In the early 1940s, Becker left Syracuse to leave behind the corrupting influences of his youth. Columbia Bible College in South Carolina was an important place for the young man to find himself. While there he felt a calling to "pioneer missions," which at the time he anticipated as overseas work. His early ministerial career, however, convinced him that "pioneer" must have meant the backwater of South Carolina. He majored in serving as a pastor to small, part-time country churches, which developed into thriving, full-time places of ministry. After more than a decade of fulfilling ministry in this setting, he had grown restless and eager for a new challenge.[16]

Wil Ferguson's letter could not have been more meaningful if it been canceled with heaven's postmark. Both Paul and his wife, Ruth, were delighted at the prospect of this new ministry. For years they had imagined the influence Southern Baptists could have in this area to which they had often returned for vacations. The Beckers expressed an eagerness to come north to the point of insisting that they work in secular jobs until the mission had resources to provide for their needs. Ferguson and the handful of families preparing for their first service in June were equally pleased at the thought of calling a seasoned pastor—a native New Yorker no less—to lead their congregation.

The Syracuse chapel was gathered on June 20, 1957, in a rented room of the downtown YMCA. Later, the group relocated to an abandoned Grange hall near Cicero. Zig Boroughs and four members of the LaSalle Church were among the eighteen on hand for this first prayer meeting and worship service. Just as one might have scripted the story, the Ferguson family stepped forward to present themselves for membership. During the revival meeting the next week, the Findsen family followed their example. From the first Sunday, the chapel subscribed to a standard Southern Baptist program of Sunday School at 9:45, worship at 11:00, Sunday evening Training Union at 6:00, and "preaching" at 7:00. All this was scheduled even if the Ferguson and Findsen families were the only ones present! By midsummer the mission had five families in regular attendance and an ever-lengthening list of prospective members.

With a lot of faith and the backing of the LaSalle Church, the mission called Becker as pastor. Much to everyone's surprise, he did not offer an immediate acceptance of the call. Two weeks went by before Ferguson received his "almost definite" positive response.[17] Had the South Carolina pastor's initial enthusiasm for the new project waned after more deliberate reflection? Did he have second thoughts about exchanging the temperate climes of the Palmetto State for relentless lake-effect snowstorms? His sense of calling remained certain—his concern was with his denomination.

A New Pastor and New Concerns

Word that Becker was considering the Syracuse pastorate brought a negative response from some associational and state convention leaders in South Carolina. Some felt that Southern Baptists had no place starting churches in territory staked out by Northern Baptists. Others considered the LaSalle Church and its offspring "maverick"—outside proper channels of the convention's mission program.

A more curious set of critics resented "Yankee" churches bearing the Southern Baptist name. Racism, not just provincial bigotry, was the issue with these detractors. Their fear was that northern churches in the Southern Baptist fold would integrate racially and prove to be a nasty leaven for the whole convention. They were relieved to learn that primarily white southerners were being gathered to begin the new works, even though it bears mentioning that the Syracuse church later had a racially mixed children's Sunday School, and took an open-door approach on the so-called "Negro question."[18]

Becker chafed under the criticism he experienced. He resented the New York churches being regarded as wayward stepchildren. Before he committed himself wholly to heading north, he wanted the Home Mission Board's blessing. He hoped to make it clear to his critics in South Carolina and to any other interested Southern Baptists that he was participating in their program of cooperative missions, whether or not he received any of their money. He intended for the Syracuse mission to become a thoroughgoing Southern Baptist church, fully subscribed to the Southern Baptist program.

In August Becker met with A. B. Cash, secretary of the Home Mission Board's pioneer missions division, and Solomon Dowis, who originally had greeted the Syracuse mission idea with a tepid response. Dowis was concerned at the rate with which Boroughs and Becker were proceeding in their mission endeavors without the supervision of his department. To prevent further "freelancing," the board issued a policy that paperwork be filed with the Atlanta office before anyone went to a new field to start a church. Failure to comply with this procedure would render a mission pastor ineligible for funding.

Dowis made it clear that the Home Mission Board had little money to support the work in upstate New York. Citing Southern Baptists' divided mind about church-starting efforts in the North, he told Becker that the lion's share of board funding would be channeled to New York City—a "pioneer" territory the convention could "swallow," perhaps even unite behind. Becker assured Dowis and Cash that he was not seeking financial assistance, but primarily moral support and approval for the mission task.

He told the board officials that God was calling him to Syracuse and that he intended to be obedient to that call. The two replied that they had no authority or desire to alter arrangements which had already been made. They furthermore commended Becker's desire to cooperate with them, and promised the board's "blessing." Cash suggested that, while no salary support would be possible in 1957, some help could be arranged for the following year. He promised to visit Becker that fall in Syracuse. Dowis later came to respect and admire Becker's devotion to the extent that he frequently referred to him in addresses as an illustration of the Southern Baptist missionary spirit.[19]

A Base for Mission Expansion

In October the mission welcomed Paul Becker and his family home to Syracuse. By the time he arrived, the congregation was meeting in a downtown Christian and Missionary Alliance church building for which a contract for purchase had been secured. The young church became more secure financially with the Ohio Convention's commitment to provide a pastoral salary supplement until Home Mission Board support began in 1958. Becker began his ministry where Ferguson and the others had left off—working hard to locate and gather transplanted Southern Baptists in the area. Knowing the appeal of a southern religious ethos, and sensitive to accusations about recruiting members from other churches, he suggested a slogan for the church, "A touch of the South in the heart of the North." This marketing tactic would "help the Yanks to realize we're after the southerners (primarily) and might make some homesick southerner curious enough to come around." He distributed hundreds of cards which read, "There is a Southern Baptist Church in Syracuse!" and touted First Southern as "the friendliest church in town."[20] Within a few months after his arrival, the church had nearly tripled its attendance, providing a foundation from which to reach out to the local community.

In a January 1958 promotional letter outlining the reasons his denomination was in New York, Becker wrote:

1st: because when Jesus said, "Go ye," he did not make any exceptions as to where we were to go. Wherever men are lost, there we have an obligation to preach!

2nd: because such a large proportion of these people are not actively associated with any church and feel that, "no man cares for my soul."

Pastor Paul Becker meets with Wilburn, Beulah, and Tommy Ferguson, founding members of the First Southern Baptist Church of Syracuse.

> 3rd: because there is no other concerted effort by any gospel denomination to promote church-sponsored missions in this, the most heavily populated state in the Union.[21]

The presence of transplanted Southern Baptists in the North had already taken a back seat in his vision for the church. The last thing Becker wanted the church to become was what he termed a "grits and fatback society." He believed that the effectiveness of the Southern Baptist program of solid Bible preaching and teaching, expansive missionary outreach, and evangelistic efforts on every front would transcend geographical boundaries.

Ernest J. Bowden, whose weekly "Pulpit to Pew" column appeared in the Syracuse *Post-Dispatch*, observed that while the First Southern Baptist Church appeared primarily to be a "rallying center for people from the South," the times were "propitious for what they have to give." The writer expressed gratitude for the church's bold expression of the faith which challenged people to live like Christians. He concluded: "I think you will hear more of Southern Baptists in Syracuse."[22]

CHAPTER TWO

Baptist Convention of New York

A FOUNDATION IN THE "BIG APPLE"

W hat caused southerners in the 1940s and 1950s to leave home for the industrial centers of the North? "The tractor," one Alabamian was quick to point out, "just put folks out of work." The widespread availability of modern farm implements resulted in a decreased demand for manpower in even the most rural and poor sections of the South. No longer could a young man provide for his family by sweating out a living on a farm. Factories in northern cities and in the growing urban centers of the South, offered an attractive alternative for these eager workers, many of whom had just returned from conquering the Axis Powers. In short, people were saying good-bye to the farm for the big city and its environs.

But while urbanization was underway in the South, the cultural ethos of the region remained unmistakably "down on the farm." Few things made a Southern Baptist prouder than to boast that his or her church was friendly and warm "just like a good old country church"—even if that church welcomed hundreds to the heart of downtown Dallas or Atlanta, or called itself the "First Southern Baptist Church" of a city far outside the South. All that was good and right in the world was identified with rural, small-town life. Mayberry was a Southern Baptist kind of town. An urban Goliath that nicknamed its baseball team "the Yankees" was not.

Increasingly, though, Southern Baptists were becoming convicted that while their support for sharing the gospel in the postwar world was an urgent priority, their commitments at home were shortsighted and regionally circumscribed. One leader who recognized this shortcoming was F. C. Tuttle, then serving in Ohio where a new state convention was carrying northward the banner for missions. "Like Paul," he declared, "Southern Baptists are obligated both to Jews and Gentiles, to Greeks and Barbarians. . . ." Apparently oblivious to the humor and regionalism inherent in the analogy, Tuttle urged his denomination to follow the example of Jonah and "carry the gospel to Nineveh."[1] Home mission leader Solomon Dowis began calling upon Southern Baptists to weep over the "pagan" cities of America—the "Ninevehs"—which were untouched by their witness.

Leaders across the Southern Baptist Convention were beginning to sense that they were entering a rich season of opportunity to "make America Christian." "The North," declared one speaker in a flourish of hyperbole, "with 50 to 60 million committed to no church, is our twentieth century frontier, and we are a frontier religion!"[2]

Southern Baptists called upon other Baptist groups across the United States to join them in a redoubled evangelistic effort that would culminate in 1964 with a sesquicentennial celebration of Baptist denominationalism in America. For their part, Southern Baptists launched the "Thirty Thousand Movement" in 1957, an ambitious campaign to start thirty thousand new congregations and mission points at home and abroad.

Unbounded confidence permeated the denomination in the latter half of the 1950s. Memphis pastor Ramsey Pollard, president of the convention from 1959 to 1961, embodied the optimistic spirit of his fellow Southern Baptists with these now famous words: "I am more tremendously convinced than ever before that the last hope, the fairest hope, the only hope for evangelizing this world on New Testament principles is the Southern Baptist people represented by their convention."[3] Still somewhat ambiguous, however, was the extent to which the cities of the Northeast were included in this aggressive "world vision" of mission.

By the mid-1950s, personnel at the Home Mission Board were confident that sooner or later transplanted Southern Baptists were going to start a church in a metropolitan area of the Northeast, likely New York City. It was a pattern the board was accustomed to in other pioneer areas, including, of course, upstate New York. Essentially a reactive approach to mission church extension, the normal procedure was for the board to acknowledge the new work, offer a modest salary supplement for a pastor ($50–$150 per month), and help the church become networked with the nearest association and neighboring state convention.

The northeastern work would be different, due in part to the broadening missionary vision of the convention, but also for purely administrative reasons. The densely populated cities of the northeastern seaboard were a mission field "white unto harvest" like none Southern Baptists had encountered in the twentieth century.

Visionaries like A. B. Cash recognized the need for an intentional development of churches and denominational infrastructures to support missionary advance in the region. Expansion could not be surrendered by default to a random, haphazard pattern. Cash, who became something of a "czar" of pioneer missions, advocated that the board adopt a strategy more characteristic of the Foreign Mission Board's approach to planting new churches—that fully supported missionaries be sent to develop churches that later would become self-supporting.[4]

The Home Mission Board waited in the wings for a group in the city to request help. Southern Baptists "officially" would enter the Northeast not as an invasionary force, but as an invited missionary partner providing for the needs of their own people. As anticipated, inquiries from a variety of families began surfacing about the possibility of Southern Baptist-sponsored mission work in New York City.

Families on Mission in the Big City

Educational pursuits brought James Aaron and his family to Manhattan, while Uncle Sam's orders for Master Sergeant Clarence Massey and his wife, Chlocile, reassigned them to Fort Tilden in Brooklyn. A proposed plastics plant in Port Reading, New Jersey, required the engineering skills of James Robb, who along with his wife, Pauline, and their two children, made the Garden State their new home. The concerns that brought these families to a common destination were inconsequential, however, compared to the larger missionary purpose to which they came to feel called.

The same mission study book which motivated Wil Ferguson to lead in gathering a church in Syracuse inspired the Aarons to pursue a similar course in New York City. It was, in Melba Aaron's words, "just the right thing to do at the time."[5] It was not, however, a convenient thing to do for this young family that lived in rented quarters under the subway tracks in Far Rockaway. The Masseys came to New York seasoned for a missionary task by several years of service to new churches in Washington and California. These native Georgians had such a strong sense of Christian vocation as "military missionaries" that they often thought of their transfer orders as coming not from the Pentagon but from the Lord.[6] "Transfer" had become such a familiar word for the Robbs that the family purchased a mobile home to facilitate their moves. They, too, arrived in the metropolitan area with experience in home missions, having been founding members of the First Baptist Church of Waverly, Ohio. The Robbs so distinguished themselves as lay missionaries that the Home Mission Board published a Royal Ambassadors study book about them in 1963: *James Robb—Pioneer*. A. B. Cash called them a real pioneer family "with a trailer for a covered wagon and eastern America for a frontier."[7]

Putting these families in touch with one another was Ray Roberts, the leader of the Ohio Convention, who had become the point man for new work developing in New York. He visited New York City in February 1957 in response to James Aaron's inquiry about the possibility of starting a church there. Aaron and John Moore, another young man interested in the proposed new work, met and prayed with Roberts about the matter at the Statler Hotel in Manhattan.

Although he was not able to gather all the interested parties for this initial prayer meeting, Roberts arranged for the Masseys, Robbs, and Aarons to meet the next month in front of the Madison Avenue Baptist Church following Sunday worship. How would they recognize each other, given the hundreds who worshiped at the Upper West Side church each week? Perhaps the men could wear flowers in their lapels like in the movies, Pauline Robb imagined. Somehow the families found each other without flowers, gathered in the Massey's Brooklyn apartment to enjoy lunch and began laying plans for a new church.

Was a Southern Baptist church in the heart of New York City possible? This question seemed to have been answered already in their minds. The issue most at hand was: How will it be done? As Baptists are wont to do, they took up an offering for the first New York City mission fund. They used the $19.56 they collected to buy advertising in local papers and to send letters to Baptist state papers across the South, encouraging readers to contact the group with names of friends and relatives living in the metropolitan area. Responses arrived daily with the names of bright prospects scattered throughout the five boroughs of the city and the suburbs of Long Island, the Hudson Valley, New Jersey, and places as distant as New Haven, Connecticut. Despite the expansiveness of the region, core families committed themselves to visiting each prospect personally.

Ray Roberts maintained close contact with these determined laypeople. The group saw promise in the Ohio leader for enthusiastic support from their denomination. Gatherings in cramped apartments grew by May 1957 into a small congregation sharing Sunday School and worship in the McBurney YMCA building on West Twenty-third Street. Professor Huber Drumwright of Southwestern Baptist Theological Seminary, who at the time was completing a year of sabbatical study at Princeton Theological Seminary, was secured as an interim pastor for the "Southern Baptist Chapel," as the group first called itself.[8]

All of the necessary components were now in place for Southern Baptists to make their move into the Northeast. A critical mass of laypeople with a keen sense of responsibility and dedication to the missionary program of their convention was gathered. Far though it was from the geographical and cultural base of Southern Baptist life, the chapel understood itself as integral to the denomination's program of mission advance. Being denominationally "tethered" ironically only reinforced the members' sense of belonging. The group's short-term prospect as a mission church, but more importantly, their future as a mission base for a larger denominational expansion into the region, was dependent upon the national convention's response.

A. B. Cash spent the summer of 1957 in New York City visiting prospects and helping the group gain momentum. Meanwhile, the Home Mission Board in July gave provisional approval for substantial aid to the new work. All seemed neatly in place, but obstacles and opposition lay ahead.

New Friends in Maryland

Charles Jolly remembers well the day a "big redhead with a grin and friendly word" pulled him aside to broach an idea that would lead to one of the most significant events of his life. Jolly, then pastor of the College Avenue Baptist Church in Annapolis, Maryland, encountered Ray Roberts as they were leaving the convention hall in Chicago where Southern Baptists had just held their 1957 annual meeting. His longtime friend brought him up to date on developments in the Buckeye state, and shared with him news about the young convention's missionary outreach into New York.

Roberts then confided to Jolly that the growing chapel in New York City was putting too much of a strain upon his time. His hands were full in Ohio overseeing the development of a new state convention. Demands were also placed upon him by the expanding work Ohio Baptists sponsored in Pennsylvania and upstate New York. Put simply, Roberts and the Ohio Convention could not adequately respond to the needs of Baptists along the northeastern seaboard.[9] Roberts then posed the question that initiated

Maryland Baptists' long and fruitful relationship with New York Baptists. "How about your church, Charles, sponsoring the new work in the city?"

Roberts had been told by A. B. Cash and Sol Dowis that while the Home Mission Board was ready to make as much as one hundred thousand dollars available for the northeastern work, the board's policy of local church sponsorship would have to be followed. "Local" was construed by the Ohio executive to mean a locale somewhat closer than his present territorial responsibilities. The College Avenue Church was closer, at least, than Cleveland, Dayton, or Columbus!

For people like Jolly who were reared in the rural South, New York City seemed a world away, even if it was a little more than two hundred miles up the road. He expressed interest, nevertheless, promising to discuss the idea with the Maryland State Convention leader, C. C. Thomas, and with Paul Bard, the associational director in the Annapolis area. Both men greeted the idea favorably. With their affirmation, Jolly shared the intriguing proposal for mission involvement with his congregation, while Ray Roberts approached the New York chapel with the idea. To Jolly's delight, the proposed arrangement received everybody's enthusiastic endorsement, or so it seemed. A disturbing phone call from C. C. Thomas caused the Maryland pastor to fear that the whole process was about to be scuttled.[10]

Thomas recounted that at a gathering in Baltimore, representatives of the Home Mission Board and the Maryland Convention leadership had entered into a spirited debate over the proposed mission in New York City. Some Maryland leaders were curt in telling Courts Redford, president of the Home Mission Board, that not everyone in Maryland believed Southern Baptists ought to insinuate themselves into New York City. "What would be next," critics sarcastically inquired, "an SBC church in Paris? London?" Even though such comments were far afield from the real issues at stake in the growing pioneer movement, the rancor left a sour taste in the mouths of many for the project.[11]

Thomas warned Jolly not to get himself out on a limb because respected members of the state's mission board had reservations about the Annapolis church's plans. But the pastor was already out on a limb. "Reservations" was Thomas' polite understatement for what amounted to hard-line opposition on the part of some.

Leading the opposition was Francis A. Davis, a Baltimore tobacco merchant, and lay leader in the state convention. His criticisms were later publicized in the *Maryland Baptist*: "Can Southern Baptists cooperate with American Baptists on the national level through the Baptist World Alliance if they cannot cooperate on a local level? Or is it not impracticable for a

New York City church to be out of fellowship with other Baptist churches in its own community and be in fellowship with another set of Baptists in another state"?

Davis wondered why the New York mission really needed to have a state convention and an associational affiliation to be a Southern Baptist church. He suspected that the Home Mission Board was attempting to foist a major responsibility upon the Maryland Convention that would strain its staff and resources. Jolly, in the businessman's mind, was the board's "patsy."[12]

Dejected, Jolly thought that the project was doomed. He did not think the congregation would press the issue against the wishes of their state leader, or if they thought it would cause contention in the convention. Or would they? The pastor went to a tailor shop in the community to speak with H. T. Pike, a leader in his church and in the Maryland Convention. Jolly tells the story: "I had no idea how he would feel about this drawback. He was standing, sewing on a garment. I told him the story and said, 'Mr. Pike, what do you think we ought to do?' He kept sewing, prayerfully thinking. In a moment he looked at me with that characteristic smile and twinkle in his eye: 'Why pastor, we'll just go right ahead!' . . . I've often thought what the outcome would have been if that layman had not said those words."[13]

Pike's sentiments exemplified the spirit and conviction of the College Avenue Church. On July 21, 1957, the church voted to adopt the Southern Baptist Chapel of New York City as its mission. Later, the mission church was accepted into fellowship with the Southern District Association. Membership in the association proved to be tantamount to membership in the Maryland Convention, according to an obscure clause in the state body's constitution. Thus a potentially divisive floor fight at the annual session of the Maryland Convention was averted.

With the Manhattan congregation related to the Maryland Convention, the Home Mission Board voted to channel support for the entire northeastern seaboard region through the state body. Within a short time amicable arrangements were worked out between the board and the Baptist Convention of Maryland to facilitate the ambitious missionary partnership.[14]

A Shepherd for the Flock

Who would lead the Southern Baptist Chapel in Manhattan? By the middle of 1957, still only about twenty-five people were carting hymnals, literature, and cribs into the rather dingy McBurney YMCA for worship each Sunday. The group did not have much with which to lure a pastor. Perhaps a recent seminary graduate, full of idealism and lacking a better offer, could be convinced to venture into the city. But leaders like Ernest Mayo and John Moore, and others mentioned previously, were people of uncommon vision who sought a "pastor-missionary"—an aggressive leader who would lead their little flock to establish at least six missions in the metropolitan area.[15] They could not have dreamed that an erudite pastor in mid-career, serving a congregation of three thousand in the heart of Atlanta, would be the right leader for their humble church. Absurd as it sounds, Paul S. James, pastor of the Baptist Tabernacle, was indeed the one to whom the Home Mission Board turned for leadership of the New York mission.

Born the son of a Northern Baptist pastor, James spent most of his childhood in the village of Hartford, New York, near Glens Falls. In the mid-1920s, he left home for Wheaton College to prepare to be a pastor. The young man's introduction to Southern Baptist life came when he enrolled with classmates Wally Amos Criswell and Herschel H. Hobbs in the Southern Baptist Theological Seminary in Louisville.

After succeeding his father in the pastorate of the Second Baptist Church of Auburn, New York (1934–1941), James was called at age thirty-three to the Baptist Tabernacle in Atlanta. For the next fifteen years he distinguished himself as a local leader. He served as chairman of the 1950 Billy Graham Crusade in the city and as president of the Atlanta Baptist Pastors Conference.

Of all his commitments, however, none was more rewarding than his extended tenure as a local trustee of the Home Mission Board. For a time James served as chairman of the "Pioneer and Western Missions" committee of the board, which put him in touch with what was happening on the cutting edge of SBC growth into new areas. He had a front-row seat to watch the unprecedented territorial expansion of the convention. Discussions about ministry in Chicago, involvement with the Motor Cities Association in Detroit, reports about Ray Roberts's work in Ohio—Paul James knew what his denomination was attempting in frontier areas, and he was touched by the spirit of the movement.[16]

A bona fide Yankee with a Southern Baptist education and a solid record of church experience; a knowledgeable, respected leader with a missionary heart; urbane and gregarious—Paul James was a natural for the challenge of the Big Apple and the whole Northeast if he could be persuaded to go. His invitation came on a warm July evening in 1957 when Courts Redford called him out of worship in the chapel of the Glorietta Conference Center in New Mexico. Outside on the patio the Home Mission Board president asked him to consider a calling to New York City. James remembers the flood of emotions and shock that rushed through him to hear the proposal. His decision depended in large part on the response he would get from the one who was standing at his side in the chapel.

As he returned to the service, the chapel was reverberating with the familiar refrain from "Footsteps of Jesus":

Footsteps of Jesus,
that make the pathway glow;
We will follow the steps of Jesus,
wher'ere they go.

Paul James then whispered to his wife Ava, "Do you really mean what you're singing?" Wearing a puzzled look on her face, she replied, "Of course I do." He then pressed further: "Suppose those footsteps led to New York. . . ." No verbal reply followed. Inwardly, though, her heart sank as she thought, "Anywhere—anywhere in all the world, dear God, except New York City."[17]

If ever a person was born with missions in her genes, it was Ava Leach James. Her parents were Northern Baptist missionaries who spent their honeymoon sailing to Burma on a vessel called the *Ava*. Ava was also a city in Burma where the first Baptist missionary from America, Adoniram Judson, was once imprisoned. At age four Ava contracted such a severe case of rheumatic fever that doctors thought she would never fully recover. Her family consequently returned to the States where her father enjoyed a long career as a pastor in Hackensack, New Jersey, among other places. It was at Wheaton where she pursued studies in music that she first met her future husband.

Ava felt a calling to ministry that she carried out faithfully wherever the couple served. She took a remarkable personal interest in people, especially seeking out those who drifted to the edge in church life. And she was "always talking about missions," her husband remembered. In fact, Paul credited Ava's influence with awakening his own heightened missions awareness.[18] Would she leave the "wonderful Southland from which she had hoped the Lord would never take her?" She would, but only because the Master's footsteps led northward.

The Lighthouse Made Brighter

Paul and Ava James responded favorably to the Home Mission Board's call after the Southern Baptist Chapel gleefully expressed its concurrence in the calling. "I am prepared today to say 'yes' to your call," Paul James wrote. "Believing as we do that the hand of God is in all of this and that it is His will for us at this point in our ministry . . . surely all of us sense that there is something of historic proportions in what Southern Baptists are undertaking in New York. I often think of the one hundred and twenty Spirit-filled Christians who made such a tremendous impact on the city of Jerusalem in the early days. I come as a member of a great team, and all of you are on it."[19]

The pastor's auspicious-sounding duties included overseeing all mission efforts in the metropolitan area, but at the time "all mission efforts" consisted of thirty people huddled in a rented hall. He anxiously pondered what the transition would be like to oversee thirty congregants instead of three thousand. Ava "watered her roses with tears" for the remainder of the summer, yet she was confident that the new calling was right. She even chided her husband for suggesting that the risk of total failure for their endeavor was great. "Who are we, after all, to start something in New York?" he questioned her privately. She sensed that the Lord's hand was in this new direction of ministry and, if so, she reasoned, it would not fail.

The couple was surely answering a higher calling to lead Southern Baptists in their greater New York mission advance. They left much behind. On

The Maryland
BAPTIST
July 12, 1962

Paul and Ava James were featured on the cover of the Maryland Baptist *in July 1962.*

a November Sunday evening, some fourteen hundred members tearfully bade them good-bye. Their Atlanta farewell was a stark contrast to the chilly reception messengers afforded the Jameses two days later at the annual session of the Maryland Convention. The New York mission question was still very much a sensitive subject for the gathering.[20]

Once the Jameses set up housekeeping in New York, they remembered as though in a dream what a spacious house had been like—one "surrounded by trees, lawns, and gardens in a sprawling neighborhood; where family life was relaxed and congenial." Instead, they found themselves "wedged into three and a half rooms fourteen floors above the ground. There [were] only two windows, opening on a street lined with apartment houses as alike as ditto marks. There [were] no lawns, no flowers, no songbirds; nothing but a few dwarfed trees to break the monotonous vista of an endless flow of traffic."[21]

The warm embrace they received from their new family of Baptists, however, more than compensated for the initial shock of inconveniences and hardships they encountered. The Jameses were buoyed by the optimism and esprit de corps they found among their new congregation, small in number though it was.

The New York congregation experienced an immediate surge of growth following the arrival of its new leader. Individuals whose commitments were held in abeyance pending the calling of a pastor stepped forward to be counted. Members of the Home Mission Board were so gratified by reports from New York City that in December they voted to double their investment in the project to two hundred thousand dollars for 1959.[22]

Membership increased dramatically to a total of ninety-nine who gathered at the Hotel New Yorker on January 10, 1958, to constitute themselves as the Manhattan Baptist Church. They were joined by Charles Jolly and a busload of members from the College Avenue Church, leaders from the Home Mission Board, A. B. Cash and Solomon Dowis, and representatives from other evangelical church groups in the city. The Manhattan Baptist Church was, according to the *New York Times*, the first new church to be organized in the borough in forty years![23]

American Baptists took cognizance of the proceedings, and graciously invited the new pastor to address their New Jersey Convention later that same year. In his remarks James sought to allay fears that his coreligionists were arriving on the scene as competitors. Southern Baptists were, instead, allies seeking to promote the cause of Christ. He then invoked a metaphor that became one of his favorites in downplaying the rivalry between Baptist groups: "There can be no competition between lighthouses."[24] The lighthouse in the Northeast was a little brighter.

CHAPTER THREE

ADVANCE ON THE FRONTIER

In the summer of 1959, R. G. Puckett traveled northeast from Columbus to the farthest reaches of the Ohio Convention of Southern Baptists. The young editor of the *Ohio Baptist Messenger* wanted to provide his readers with a firsthand account of what was happening among the handful of new churches in western New York. For months he had carried reports of missions and home fellowships rapidly springing up throughout the region. He had heard about the spirit and missionary zeal of pastors like Zig Boroughs, Paul Becker, and others arriving on the scene.

Puckett's weekend in the Empire State included a Sunday morning stop at the Downtown YMCA in Rochester, where he preached to a congregation of fifteen dedicated souls who had begun meeting that spring for Bible study and worship. From Rochester it was back to Buffalo where that afternoon he enjoyed watching a television program produced by the Southern Baptist Radio and Television Commission: *This is the Answer.* New SBC congregations in western New York were identified following the program. That evening he preached at yet another new mission fellowship, this one just outside Buffalo at Orchard Park. There he had the joy of seeing a young woman profess her faith in Christ.

Puckett's trip home offered him an extended opportunity to reflect upon events of the weekend. So touched was he by the experience that he wrote, "Lord, thank you for all this! May I live to see what fifty years will bring to Southern Baptists in this area."[1]

Mission Leadership on the Expanding "Frontier"

The five years that had passed since the founding of the LaSalle Baptist Church in Niagara Falls already had brought considerable development to Southern Baptist work in the region. Like Puckett, Arthur L. Walker was deeply impressed by what he heard of mission efforts in western and central New York and two locations in northern Pennsylvania. He was so favorably impressed that when Ray Roberts approached him about serving the region as an area missionary, he agreed to go, sight unseen.

In May 1958, Walker left a comfortable pastorate in Miamisburg, Ohio, to become area missionary for what four months later became the Frontier Baptist Association. The "area" part of his title referred to an expansive territory that extended east from Buffalo to Albany, south into parts of Pennsylvania, and north to the Canadian border. Although the Ohio Convention was not yet five years old, Southern Baptist work there seemed well established compared with what Walker found on the "frontier." He felt fortunate to be a co-laborer in the work, and to join the ranks of those "making history in a glorious way" for mission advance.[2]

By the time Walker assumed his duties, a third congregation had been gathered in upstate New York. The Erie Baptist Chapel in Buffalo joined the LaSalle Church and First Southern Church in Syracuse, in welcoming their new leader.

The Erie work was begun in August 1957 when members of the LaSalle Baptist Church held a revival meeting and a Vacation Bible School in the Buffalo area. Paul Nevels, the area missionary of the Erie Association, conducted the services. His ministry was complemented by the efforts of students Vol McFadden, James Partin, John McKelvey, and Bob Wright.

Once a core group was established of persons interested in forming a church, weekly worship was held at the Delaware Avenue branch YMCA in Buffalo, where the group met for the next four years. Bob Wright completed the summer as preacher for the Erie Baptist Chapel.[3]

The new work in Buffalo differed in important respects from its "mother" church in Niagara Falls. Whereas the LaSalle Church consisted primarily of laborers transplanted from Alabama, the Erie Chapel included junior corporate executives newly arrived from metropolitan areas across the South. The LaSalle Church had relative strength in numbers, while the Erie Chapel benefited from a more secure financial base provided by its largely white-collar constituency.

The Erie Church was also considerably slower in growth than its sponsoring church. By the time the chapel was ready to call a pastor in November 1957, only eleven people had formally united with the group as members.[4]

Those who had committed themselves to the chapel were confident, however, that with pastoral leadership this meager statistic would steadily improve.

Walter Heilig was convinced as well that the Erie Baptist Chapel was destined to grow. The Greensboro, North Carolina, native was intrigued by what fellow New Orleans Seminary graduate Zig Boroughs shared with him about the expanding New York mission field. Heilig knew upon meeting with the group that his calling was to leave his staff position at the First Baptist Church of Palatka, Florida, for the challenge of pioneer missions. His wife, Esther, admitted to having "cold feet" about the move, which seemed appropriate, given the New Year's Day blizzard in 1958 that welcomed the Heilig family to their new home![5]

The next several months brought substantial growth. In September 1958, the Erie Baptist Church was constituted with forty-five members. Like the LaSalle and First Southern Churches before it, the Erie congregation quickly

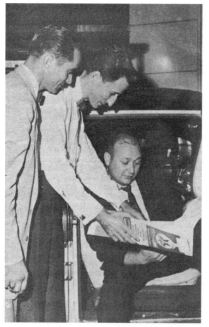

demonstrated its commitment to starting new churches. Within a year new works were planned for Orchard Park and Rochester.

In 1961 the church purchased prime suburban property in the Amherst section of greater Buffalo. In anticipation of their relocation to the site, the congregation changed its name to the Amherst Baptist Church. Two years later, the church distinguished itself by erecting the first Southern Baptist church building in the Northeast. Walter Heilig, an electrician by trade, supervised the project with the help of leaders like Bernard Foor, Tommy Densmoore, and Henry Fink.[6] The days of "setting up church" at the YMCA gave way to a new, joyful time of being at home in New York in a way Southern Baptists had not been previously.

On the road to Columbus: Walter Heilig and Arthur Walker check the map with Zig Boroughs (seated), founding pastor of the LaSalle Baptist Church—New York Baptists' first church.

Arthur Walker was thus welcomed by three New York congregations solidly committed to mission expansion, and by a trio of

In 1963 the Amherst Baptist Church dedicated the first church building constructed by Southern Baptists in the Northeast.

talented and resourceful home missionaries. In his first two months on the field the area missionary logged almost five thousand miles preaching, teaching, and visiting in the churches. He also worked closely with summer missionaries and other volunteers in surveying potential new church sites. Walker came to be characterized by his tiny Renault Dauphine that provided transportation and doubled as a mobile office.

The "Frontier" Organized and Commissioned

When the Frontier Association was organized in September 1958, Ray Roberts was on hand to offer a challenge. The executive of the Ohio Convention reminded his listeners of three "blessed" facts: they had a "command that is clear"; an "opportunity unequaled"; and a "savior unlimited."[7] His words were a mandate for the churches to reproduce—to "sow down" the associational territory with new congregations as Baptists in Ohio had done and were continuing to do at a blinding pace.[8]

The Niagara Falls, Buffalo, and Syracuse congregations were keenly sensitive to new opportunities for church starts. Pastors and lay leaders alike envisioned denominational growth akin to what had transpired in Ohio. At the organizational meeting of the Frontier Association, Ray Roberts awarded each New York church with a certificate of appreciation either for sponsoring, or being organized as one of the thirty thousand new works in Southern Baptists' Thirty Thousand Movement.

Expansion to Rome, Utica, and Orchard Park

Inquiries about Southern Baptist work from persons living anywhere in western or central New York were met with an enthusiastic response. Walker typically provided the initial contact, which was followed by a visit from the pastor nearest to the potential new site. If the inquirer sensed a calling to help start a new work, and was reasonably confident that a cadre of others interested in a Bible study fellowship could be gathered, a "mission" was usually launched. The church nearest the new work then "extended an arm" to help, which meant, as the saying went on a pioneer mission field, that the church raised a hand to wave![9]

Realistically, more than just friendly greetings were offered from sponsoring churches. Financial resources were tight, to be sure, but often money was not the most pressing need for missions. Leadership and encouragement were critical. The ten or twelve people gathered in a living room, a Grange hall, or a YMCA building needed to be infused with a sense of divine purpose. They needed to recognize that their own seemingly meager efforts were part of a much larger movement. The area missionary, pastors, and key leaders of the churches were poised to meet these kinds of needs.

Perhaps the most valuable assistance rendered to these small mission groups came from pastors who recommended colleagues they thought had the "right stuff" to serve effectively on a pioneer mission field. Those already in western New York were well acquainted with the hardships and joys of such service and with the types of communities that needed new churches.

One of the best examples of this kind of "match-making" occurred in the summer of 1959 when John Thomas (J. T.) and Bertie Mae Davis traveled from Ruston, Louisiana, to Niagara Falls for a visit with Zig and Mary Boroughs. Pastor Boroughs's former classmate from New Orleans Seminary came expecting to preach in a revival meeting for the LaSalle Church. Zig had in mind a slightly different plan.

J. T. Davis's assignment that week was to make a geographical triangle across the Frontier Association, preaching for the Orchard Park, Massena, and Rome Chapels. In his mind, "chapel" was too ostentatious a word to describe what he saw as he preached to small "clusters" of earnest Southern Baptists scattered about the region. The prospects were fair for new churches at Orchard Park and Massena, Davis thought—but Rome was a different story. There, two or three short-term service families from nearby Griffiss Air Force Base and one transplanted executive and his family were meeting together.[10]

The Rome Chapel was gathered in July 1958 after summer missionaries conducting a door-to-door survey discovered a couple willing to open their home for weekly fellowship meetings. Shortly thereafter, Phil Bryant, a summer missionary working with the First Southern Baptist Church of Syracuse, became a pastor to the group. So committed was he to this calling that he transferred his college credits to Syracuse University so he could remain for the year ministering to the group.[11] Davis's encounter with the Rome fellowship came at the conclusion of Bryant's ministry, just after the young man left to pursue seminary studies.

Bryant's departure dealt a blow to the morale of those gathering near the air base, but Davis's visit brought renewed vitality. To lay leaders Raymond and Sharon Monk, and others in the group, the chemistry seemed right between the Louisiana pastor and the fellowship. They were convinced he was the one to shepherd their small flock. J. T. Davis did not share their opinion.

Responsibility for communicating the call to Davis belonged to the pastor of the Rome fellowship's sponsoring church. Paul Becker, pastor of the First Southern Baptist Church of Syracuse, concurred with the group's sentiments, but was not surprised to hear a firm "no thank you" from Davis. Common sense dictated that a man not bring his family of six half-way across the country to become a pastor to less than twenty people. The whole idea seemed ridiculous to Davis, but Becker continued to press the issue, calling almost weekly.

Fear, more than anything else, held J. T. Davis back from a commitment to New York—fear he would be unable to provide for his family. When he finally confided to Bertie Mae his feelings that God might be calling him to the home mission field, she called his fears ridiculous: "If the Lord wants you in New York," she counseled, "then he'll take care of us."[12]

The Davis family arrived in Rome in November 1959. From the day he arrived, the pastor never had to seek outside employment to meet the needs of his wife and children. Under his leadership the Rome Chapel was constituted as the Grace Baptist Church in April 1960, with sixty-five charter members. J. T. Davis began a missionary career in New York that culminated almost twenty-five years later with an entire association being named in his honor.[13]

One of Davis's first missionary assignments was to supervise a developing work in Utica. Like the Rome church, the Utica mission was begun with the sponsorship of the First Southern Church in Syracuse. Davis's closer proximity in Rome gave him an opportunity to provide hands-on leadership for the group, but little was needed, due to the gifts of Charles Barron, a lay preacher in the Grace Baptist Church who joined the Utica group.

While working in Montana as a geophysicist, Barron was a deacon in the first Southern Baptist church established in the state. His rewarding experiences there led him to pursue studies at Southwestern Baptist Theological Seminary to prepare himself better for ministry in pioneer mission areas.[14] When the Utica Baptist Chapel was formed in January 1960, Barron was asked to serve as pastor for the group until a full-time pastor could be called. He remained as pastor into the mid-1960s as the congregation sought a permanent location. Under the leadership of pastor Clifford Matthews, the mission was constituted in 1968 as the Clinton Road Baptist Church.[15]

The Erie (Amherst) Church began a rich tradition of church planting by sponsoring a mission in a community close to home: Orchard Park. Mike and Katie Michael, leaders in the Erie congregation, began hosting Sunday evening fellowships in their Orchard Park home in February 1959. They and two other families, the Kirkbys and Beshears, were confident that Providence had brought them together to form the nucleus of a new church.

The group determined by early summer that a new meeting place was needed if their informal fellowship was to become a mission. They secured the village Grange hall for Sunday Bible study and worship. With help from members of the Erie Church, the couples placed announcements in mailboxes throughout Orchard Park heralding the beginning of something new on the Fourth of July weekend—a Baptist church!

No fireworks greeted the event. In fact, only one person besides the three core families attended that morning: Shirley Bove. She was amused that Sunday School and worship were carried out regimentally as if three hundred were present, but she was also touched by the faith and commitment she recognized in those starting the church. A month later it was she who professed her faith when editor R. G. Puckett preached for the chapel.[16]

Shirley Bove later almost single-handedly kept the Orchard Park mission alive for a time. After several services in which she was the lone worshiper present, someone broached with her the possibility of disbanding the mission. "If Southern Baptists hadn't come here," she replied, "I wouldn't know the Lord. I aim to help keep them here."[17]

During the next several months the chapel grew modestly. Orchard Park had never had a Baptist church, so the presence of one took some getting used to for the community. With the help of a generous benefactor and the Ohio Convention, the church called a pastor in January 1960—H. Garland Sparks from the Welsh Neck Baptist Church in Society Hill, South Carolina. A little more than a year later, when the chapel was constituted as the First Baptist Church of Orchard Park, the membership of the congregation had jumped from ten to almost forty.

Reaching to the Rochester Area

Arthur Walker's earnestness in pursuing leads for new missions proved especially fruitful in Rochester. A pastor from Tampa, Florida, contacted the missionary in November 1958 about a couple in his church who recently had moved to the Rochester area. The pastor was concerned that Calvin and Irene Rickman, both young Christians, find a church that would nourish their growing faith.

The Rickmans were delighted to greet Walker, but disappointed to learn that the nearest Southern Baptist church was seventy miles away. They longed to find a church with the kind of warm fellowship and worship they had grown accustomed to in Florida. "Have you thought about starting one?" Walker inquired as he considered the strategic significance of a new work in the city.[18]

The Rickmans and Arthur Walker agreed to work together in preparing for a new mission. Later, the Amherst Baptist Church became a sponsoring partner with them in the venture. Several months of advertising in local papers and running notices in Baptist state papers for help in locating prospects culminated with the mission holding its first meeting in May 1959. Despite a rather inauspicious beginning with only ten present, the group vowed to continue meeting weekly for Bible study and worship at the Downtown YMCA with Walker as their preacher.[19]

By the spring of 1960, the group had garnered sufficient strength to call a pastor. Among the eighteen members who extended a call to William H. Raper, pastor of the Southside Baptist Church in Columbus, Ohio, were a music teacher, a professor working on his doctorate at Rochester Institute of Technology, and the director of Eastman Kodak's portrait department.[20] Under Raper's leadership the Rochester Baptist Church was constituted in May 1961 with sixty-five charter members. One year later, the congregation moved to a large church building it purchased with a loan from the Home Mission Board.

The Rochester Church endured some difficult years in the early 1960s after it assumed a mortgage payment, and its supplement of aid from the Ohio Convention expired. Pastor Raper became bivocational, doing odd jobs from carpentry to delivering telephone directories.[21] By the mid-1960s, however, the church was on a firmer financial footing, ready to extend itself to other locations in Monroe County.

In September 1966, three families from the church helped form the core group for the Bayview Baptist Chapel in Webster. Jim Jones, a lay preacher from the Rochester Church, served as pastor for the mission. With the promise of special assistance from the Home Mission Board under "Project

500," a program devised in the late 1960s to provide additional funds for establishing five hundred new churches in areas entered by Southern Baptists since 1940, the church called Royce Denton as its first full-time pastor in July 1967. The following year the Bayview Baptist Church was constituted. After relocating in the mid-1970s, the congregation renamed itself the Jackson Road Baptist Church.

The Rochester Church next reached out to Henrietta, sending more families and lay pastor Jim Jones as "missionaries" to the area to establish a new church. In 1968 Joe Oliver came to be pastor of the Henrietta Baptist Chapel, which was constituted the next year as the Caulkins Road Baptist Church. The church later relocated to become the Pinnacle Road Baptist Church.

New Leadership and the Struggle for a New York Identity

The commitment to "sow down" western and central New York with new churches often led to gratifying results as described above. The record of growth in the early years of the Frontier Association was not, however, that of unmitigated success in church planting. For every new church successfully begun, there were two fellowships or missions that failed to take root as churches.

Between 1957 and 1963, efforts were made to start churches at Fredonia, Mohawk, Canandaigua, Ransomville, Olean, Penfield, and Ithaca—all of which were short-lived. Chapels like Lockport and Grand Island were begun with more sustained efforts in the late 1950s. Pastors J. C. McKinney and Donald Bennett, respectively, served the chapels and the Frontier Association as early leaders. Both were handicapped, however, in their efforts to minister effectively by having to devote too much time to outside employment.[22] Occasionally, tenuous fellowships dissolved before pastoral leadership ever arrived. The departure of a visionary lay leader who held the core group together could also prove so demoralizing that the group would disband.

Whatever the reason, hardship, or combination of factors that led to their demise, all of the new works were begun with the conviction that Southern Baptists needed a witness in communities throughout western and central New York. In many of the earliest targeted communities where missions were attempted, strong churches eventually were established.

Charles Magruder, who in January 1962 succeeded Arthur Walker as area missionary for the Frontier Association, was sensitive to the struggles endured by mission pastors and churches. Contrary to the notion that seemed at times to prevail at the state convention headquarters in

Columbus, New York was not Ohio. The mission fields were different in many important respects, as Magruder, a native Ohioan, quickly observed.

Whereas industry and postwar military operations brought an influx of Southern Baptists to many parts of Ohio, only small pockets of transplants could be gathered in New York to provide core groups for new churches. Southern Baptist work in Ohio was also strengthened by a spill-over effect from neighboring Kentucky, where a state convention had been in place since 1837. New York Baptists had no such neighbor on which to rely for help. Finally, Ohio Baptists did not have to contend as much as New York Baptists with what Magruder called, "old-world ethnic cultures." Inroads into the predominantly Roman Catholic culture did not come easily. People who worshiped in homes, under tents, and in storefront quarters were not afforded much credibility.[23] The new leader stressed these realities in advocating a formula for mission pastoral aid that provided a more generous supplement over a longer period of time.

Since the mid-1950s, the Ohio Convention had channeled salary support from the Home Mission Board to mission pastors as follows: $150 per month for six months; $100 per month for three months; and $50 per month for three months. Only under special circumstances could support be extended beyond one year. Mission churches were expected to become self-sustaining within that time, regardless of where they were located within the expansive four-state region of the Ohio Convention of Southern Baptists. As early as June 1961, the Frontier Association went on record asking the state convention to reconsider its plan for mission pastoral support.[24]

Ray Roberts stood firmly behind the formula. On at least one occasion when a New York church was seeking to extend assistance for a mission pastor beyond twelve months, he openly questioned the effectiveness of the man's work. Perceiving that the mission had made little progress toward self-sufficiency in the first year, the state leader doubted that another year of support for the pastor would lead to such. "I'm not too good at math," he quipped, "but I think nothin' times two still equals nothin'!" While Roberts was by no means as stingy with mission funds as this statement might suggest, neither was he easily convinced that more money was the instant solution for a struggling mission.

By the mid-1960s, however, the Ohio leader was becoming more aware of the differences between Ohio and New York. His own relative ineffectiveness in revival meetings held in New York churches no doubt contributed to a more enlightened stance toward mission support in the state. In one protracted meeting he held in a leading New York congregation, not a single decision was registered—certainly atypical of Roberts's usual success with evangelistic efforts.[25]

"I believe this is a new day for our work," Magruder joyfully announced to pastors in February 1963, upon returning from the Gulfshores Conference on Associationalism in Mississippi. He offered this optimistic assessment for two reasons. First, A. B. Cash, director of the Home Mission Board's pioneer missions division, had confided to him that the Ohio Convention leadership was "looking with favor" upon a new format for mission support. This new format, implemented in 1964, called for monthly mission pastoral aid in the following amounts: $400 for twelve months; $350 for six months; $300 for three months; and $200 for three months. Clearly, the call for more generous and extended support had been heard in Columbus and Atlanta.[26]

Second, Magruder was encouraged by the fresh winds of change he felt regarding the role of associations within the Southern Baptist Convention. The Gulfshores conference proved to be a watershed event for helping Southern Baptists recapture the vision of the association as a "fellowship of churches on mission in their setting."

In a sense, Magruder's work was that of watering the seeds his predecessor had helped plant. Church extension remained a priority for the new leader, but he also worked to help the Frontier Association mature as a local denominational body with its own fellowship and mission agenda.

He assisted the churches of the Rochester area similarly, organizing "Baptists in Western New York"—a quasi-executive committee to coordinate work across a broader area. With meetings in Batavia, the necessity of time-consuming travel to Buffalo was eliminated for leaders in Rochester. Moreover, the internal organization required in electing area members to the board provided the groundwork for what became the Greater Rochester Baptist Association in 1969.[27]

"The easy fruit has been plucked," Magruder observed after one year in New York. "Breaking the fallow ground and cultivation are called for. . . . Long, arduous labor must be expected and expended by our existing work in reaching out to new areas."[28] This became the theme of his ministry.

Further Growth in Western New York

The "arduous labor" that Charles Magruder spoke of for furthering mission expansion in New York brought a growth spurt to the Frontier Association in the mid-1960s. The Amherst Baptist Church, with the leadership of pastor Curtis Porter who arrived in 1964, helped start the Sheridan Park Baptist Church (now, Calvary New Covenant Church) which was constituted in 1966. Robert Craig was the church's first pastor. A mission at North Tonawanda was begun in the mid-1960s through the joint efforts of the

LaSalle and Amherst Churches. Summer missionary Ross West helped get the mission started through survey work and leadership in worship. Jim Bullis was called as pastor for the mission in 1966. The North Tonawanda Baptist Church (now, Abundant Life Baptist Church) was constituted in 1967.

Since Donald Bennett's departure in February 1964, the Grand Island mission had been scattered, meeting only sporadically in fellowship groups. The North Tonawanda Church sponsored a Vacation Bible School at a Grand Island funeral home in July 1966, leading to the reestablishment of the mission. Stanley Bullis, Jim Bullis's father, became pastor of the mission the following year, and in April 1968 the group was constituted as the First Baptist Church of Grand Island.

Non-English language ministry was initiated in the Frontier Association area in 1964 after the Home Mission Board purchased a church building in inner-city Buffalo, previously occupied by a Polish congregation. Even though the former occupants of the building were relocating because of the changing demographics of the Fillmore Avenue community, board leaders and Charles Magruder felt that significant ministry among the city's Polish population could still be undertaken at the sight. Michael Odlyzko, a recently arrived immigrant from Warsaw, was appointed by the board in March 1964 as pastor of the Fillmore Avenue Baptist Chapel.[29]

Within three years the need for a bilingual ministry at the chapel became clear to associational and Ohio Convention leaders. Second-generation Poles, and even some "old country" immigrants who were becoming more proficient with their new language, preferred to worship in English. Byron Lutz of Indiana was appointed by the board in 1968 to serve as English pastor and to develop weekday ministries at the chapel.[30] The Fillmore Avenue Baptist Church was constituted one year later.

The formation of the Fillmore Avenue Church signaled the beginning of a multicultural ministry for the churches of western New York. Negotiations that led to the development of the church, however, suggest that some denominational leaders still had limited expectations of what Southern Baptists could become in the state.

In a May 1967 letter to Elias Golonka, assistant secretary for the department of language missions at the Home Mission Board, Charles Magruder noted, "In the foreseeable future, we do not plan any additional Southern Baptist witness within the city of Buffalo." The first among four reasons he cited for this was "the loss of the white population" in the city. No further "white" churches were apparently needed, given that the Fillmore Avenue Church was "in the most strategic location in Buffalo in regards to other white Baptist churches."[31]

Magruder's comments were in no way meant to express a racial bias, but they illustrate the extent to which Southern Baptists in the mid-1960s still thought of themselves primarily as a white denomination sent to start white churches, even in the multicultural, urban melting pots of the North. Frontier Association churches ministered to racial minorities, to be sure; yet it seems remarkable with hindsight that no one envisioned starting an African-American church, given that the black population in Buffalo was expanding as the white population diminished. The paradigm for a predominantly Anglo ministry was still very much intact.

As the decade of the 1960s drew to a close, a burden for a new church that was first felt ten years before was finally realized. The Bill Beshear family—charter members of the Orchard Park mission, sponsored a home fellowship in Fredonia in 1959. After two years of struggle, the effort was abandoned. Frank Norton, a plant manager with the M. Wile Suit Company who was transferred to the Fredonia-Dunkirk area in the mid-1960s, also dreamed of seeing a church established in that strategic area of the state.

With encouragement from Charles Magruder and Dan Connally, pastor of the Orchard Park Church, Norton contacted a number of pastors asking them to seek God's will about investing their lives in an area Southern Baptists had not yet entered. Gene Fant took Norton's inquiry with utmost seriousness. The Mississippi pastor traveled northward and found the prospective families that summer missionaries had discovered "hungry for the gospel." In December 1967, he became pastor of the Fredonia-Dunkirk Chapel.

After several years of meeting in the cafeteria of the M. Wile Company and later in a large farmhouse, the congregation was eager to construct its own building. Their dilemma was in deciding between two equally desirable locations: one on East Main and the other on West Main in Fredonia. When the congregation split evenly over which property to acquire, a woman suggested a novel solution—casting lots! By lot, the congregation settled upon the West Main property, and became the West Main Baptist Church.[32]

The West Main Church lived up to the strategic importance placed upon it as a Project 500 church. The congregation quickly moved to start a mission at Silver Creek (1968), which five years later was constituted as the First Baptist Church of Silver Creek. The church began ministries to alcoholics, nursing homes, college students, and the Hispanic population of Dunkirk, among whom a mission was established several years later.

By 1969 the churches of western New York were realizing the highest ideals of associationalism. From what were scattered and isolated missions a little more than a decade before, a meaningful denominational infrastructure emerged which provided fellowship, nurture, and ministry opportunities for churches. The western, or "Ohio," bloc of a nascent state convention was in place.

CHAPTER FOUR

Baptist Convention of New York

NEW ASSOCIATIONS FOR THE HEARTLAND, THE NORTH COUNTRY, AND THE SOUTHERN TIER

If New York was not Ohio—then what was it? What were the unique needs of the state that could be addressed with fellowship, training, and ministry provided by local associations? Southern Baptists' shift in their perception of the association, as evinced by the Gulfshores conference, was no doubt influenced in part by the needs of churches in pioneer areas. Scattered and isolated, tethered across hundreds of miles to the geographical, cultural, and ideological center of Southern Baptist life, New York congregations needed a nurturing denominational presence close at hand.

Pastors in New York certainly recognized the value of an association for providing fellowship and training opportunities for the churches. Whereas in the South their associational involvement might have been minimal (due to the distances separating churches within a county!), Southern Baptist pastors in the North were willing to travel as far as two hundred miles for a meeting.[1] Few laypeople were able to avail themselves of training opportunities in distant areas.

As the churches became scattered farther across the state, Frontier Association leaders recognized the need for a new association to serve the growing number of congregations beyond western New York. Ray Roberts shared their sentiment, recognizing that the development of new associations was a healthy outgrowth of church extension. The process of forming a new association was set in motion in June 1961 when pastors from central New York gathered at the First Southern Baptist Church in Syracuse for what was scheduled as a "planning meeting." More than just establishing calendar dates was on the pastors' minds. In addition to petitioning the Ohio Convention for a more equitable formula of mission pastoral aid, they took the bold step of requesting an additional area missionary for their region.[2] Their request was viewed favorably by the Ohio leadership, who suggested that the area missionary for the Frontier Association divide duties between the associations until a new leader was called.

The Central Baptist Association was organized in September 1961 at the First Southern Baptist Church of Syracuse. Three churches—First Southern, Grace Baptist Church (Rome), and the Massena Baptist Church—along with their eight missions, constituted the new body. Paul Becker was elected the first moderator of the association.

When Charles Magruder arrived in January 1962 as area missionary for the Frontier Association, he also received the endorsement of the Central Association to act as its missionary. Such an arrangement ostensibly supplied both associations with leadership, but it represented no real progress toward providing congregations in the northern, eastern, and southern parts of New York with someone to minister exclusively to their needs.

The following year an arrangement was worked out between the two associations, the Ohio Convention, and Magruder, where he would relocate to the Central Association area to serve only that association. A new area missionary would then be sought for the Frontier Association. When the move failed to materialize after several months, the Central Association terminated its agreement with Magruder and chose to function without an area missionary.[3]

From the beginning of their relationship with Ohio Baptists in the mid-1950s, New York pastors enjoyed good-natured humor directed at their "mother convention" and its founding father, Ray Roberts. They teased about being the "redheaded stepchildren" of the Ohio Convention, but avoided the line in the presence of Roberts, who sported a generous shock of red hair. One group of pastors even cheered themselves on lengthy trips to Cleveland and Columbus with spontaneous choruses of "Glory Be to Ohio" (to the tune of the "Gloria Patri"). With the accompaniment of a harmonica, they sang:

Glory be to Ohio,
Ray Roberts, and Darty Stowe [state missions leader].
As it was in the beginning,
is now and ever shall be,
Ohio without end. Amen. Amen!

The lighthearted interstate rivalry reflected in these anecdotes had by the early 1960s become a growing dissatisfaction with the "Ohio connection." The state convention's failure to provide associational leadership in a timely manner produced feelings of neglect and alienation that could not be assuaged by promises of a new day for associational vitality and increased mission support.[4]

Central New York pastors voiced their concerns to A. B. Cash, who reminded them that the Home Mission Board worked directly with state conventions, adhering to their guidelines for mission support and the placement of personnel. When questioned about the board's seemingly more generous support of the northeastern seaboard work, he explained that the kind of funding that work received was the result not of the board's priorities, but of the Maryland Convention's more liberal mission support policies. He suggested that the pastors contact Paul James in New York City, and Roy Gresham, the Maryland Convention executive, about the possibility of realigning the Central Association with the Maryland body.[5]

With encouragement from James and Gresham, and with the blessing of Ray Roberts, the churches of the Central Association affiliated with the Baptist Convention of Maryland in 1964. Press reports indicated that the move was in no way intended to reflect negatively upon the Ohio Convention, but to enhance the developing work in New York by uniting a large bloc of upstate churches with the churches of the Metropolitan New York Baptist Association.[6]

That same year the Central Association turned to one of its own for leadership, pastor John Tollison of the Central Baptist Church of Syracuse (formerly, the First Southern church). The South Carolinian's interest in pioneer missions was awakened after hearing Zig Boroughs describe the New York work in a conference. Tollison traveled northward in January 1961 to visit mission sites where pastors were needed. At Paul Becker's encouragement, he preached for First Southern's mission at Elmira, but came away feeling as though he might have been mistaken in his sense of calling to pioneer missions. Only a very positive experience of preaching and fellowship at First Southern that evening salvaged his trip.

Three months later, Becker called Tollison to suggest why he had sensed no calling to the Elmira work—Becker felt the call to leave Syracuse for ministry in the Southern Tier city. He then asked Tollison's permission to recommend him as his successor.[7] In June 1961, Tollison became pastor of the First Southern Baptist Church of Syracuse, soon to be renamed the Central Baptist Church. After three years of effective ministry there, which included the development and oversight of five missions, Tollison was a natural choice as area missionary for the Central Association, a post he held until 1968.

Continued Growth to New Areas and Neighboring Communities

By the mid-1960s, total membership among the churches of the Central Association doubled that of the Frontier Association. This rapid growth was due in large measure to the ongoing missionary outreach of the Central Baptist Church in Syracuse and the Grace Baptist Church in Rome. Together, these congregations continued to reach into different parts of the state and to add new works in neighboring communities.

The Central Church in 1962 extended sponsorship to an independent Baptist congregation in nearby Phoenix. Pastor Charles Lingelbach of the Community Baptist Chapel was impressed with the missionary programs and fellowship he saw among Southern Baptist churches. Renamed the Bethel Chapel in 1964, the church deepened its associational ties throughout the 1960s and was constituted as the Bethel Baptist Church in 1968.

The Northside Baptist Chapel was formed in 1966 by a group of families from the Central Baptist Church who lived in the Liverpool area. With John Tollison's encouragement and guidance, the group held its first worship service in a furniture store building that the church called home until its sanctuary was completed in 1973. Robert Craig of Tonawanda, New York, arrived in 1966 as pastor, and led the congregation to constitute as the Northside Baptist Church two years later.

Just as churches in western New York experienced numerous setbacks in their efforts to plant new missions, so in central New York not all missions became thriving churches. And even a few that did were eventually lost when they later renounced their Southern Baptist affiliation. This kind of loss had an almost devastating effect where new associations were formed by a handful of churches. The Mallory Baptist Church was an early case in point.

The so-called "Miracle at Mallory" occurred in May 1962 when South Carolinian Ansel Gambrell led a revival meeting in the rural village of Mallory that yielded forty professions of faith. With the assistance of the Central Church in Syracuse and support from the Home Mission Board, the church was constituted in 1964. The Mallory Church later erected a building and became one of the stronger Southern Baptist congregations in central New York.[8] But by the mid-1970s, the church had begun drifting away from its denominational moorings. Pastor A. J. Gibson led the church to adopt a charismatic approach to ministry. The church became independent and eventually disbanded.[9]

In 1965 Paul James suggested to John Tollison that the Central Association could provide more of a nurturing presence to the Mohawk Valley Chapel in the Albany area than could the New York City work. The chapel was begun in 1959 as a mission of the Manhattan Baptist Church. Ben Cowell, a Navy officer who served as the chapel's first pastor, was licensed to preach by the New York City church in 1960.

Recognizing the strategic importance of new work in the Capital District of the state, Tollison responded favorably to James's suggestion. Howard and Francis Watt of the Mohawk Valley Chapel found J. T. Davis and members of the Grace Baptist Church in Rome eager to help them. With the Grace Church's guidance and the support of the Home Mission Board, the mission was soon able to move to a more favorable location and to call Donald Knapp of Grove City, Pennsylvania, in November 1965 as its first full-time pastor. Knapp was appointed by the board as pastor director to oversee other anticipated work in the Albany area. In January 1968, the chapel was constituted as the Trinity Baptist Church.[10]

The Grace Baptist Church also reached out to the community of Floyd in 1967, commissioning five of its member families to start a new work there. With a generous gift from the First Baptist Church of Jena, Louisiana, the Floyd Baptist Chapel purchased a five-bedroom home that provided a living room for a sanctuary and bedrooms for Sunday School classes. Pastor Davis divided his duties between the Grace Church and the Floyd Chapel until the latter called its first pastor, Darrell Coble, in January 1969. Under his direction, the church was constituted nine months later as the Floyd Baptist Church (renamed One Heart Church in 1994).

Although the Central Association was conceived in part out of a frustration with the status quo of the Ohio Convention, too much should not be made of this factor in assessing the formation of the new body. Cordial relations were maintained with the Ohio Convention and the Frontier Association, and friendships among leaders remained securely intact. More than anything else, the churches' struggle for a unique New York identity and penchant for local autonomy were responsible for the development of the association. No longer were they satisfied to be a far-reaching extension of a distant state convention. The Maryland Convention was somewhat closer to home, but most importantly, it offered an opportunity for fellowship and cooperation with a growing sister association in the metro New York area which shared their sentiment for self-direction. An important link was forged for the broader autonomy of a new state convention.

A New Light on the Northern Border

By the end of the 1950s, Zig Boroughs was coming to feel that his work at the LaSalle Baptist Church was completed. In the four years he had spent at Niagara Falls, the congregation had grown from its humble beginnings to a point where in 1959 almost three hundred worshipers jammed the church's sanctuary on Easter Sunday morning.[11] Another region now beckoned—the so-called "North Country."

In the upper Adirondack and St. Lawrence Valley regions of New York, Baptist churches were in short supply. Nineteen congregations provided ministry to the area's 250,000 residents, with no Baptist churches found in a surprising number of towns.[12] Throughout the late 1950s, the regions experienced considerable development due to the massive St. Lawrence Seaway project which connected the Great Lakes with the Atlantic seaboard. The aluminum industry promised to bring further growth with the Reynolds Company and General Motors initiating construction projects valued at over one hundred million dollars. Boroughs looked northward and saw the snow-covered villages "white unto harvest."

Robert Jacks, a building superintendent with the Reynolds Metals Company, provided the initial impetus for the formation of the Massena Baptist Chapel in June 1959. The son of a pioneer Southern Baptist mission pastor in the Northwest, Jacks felt he "had no choice" about whether his family would help form the nucleus of a new church. He understood his higher purpose in moving to Massena as that of "raising another witness for Christ."[13] The layman gladly cooperated with Paul Becker and the First Southern Church in Syracuse in establishing the new mission.

The Home Mission Board recognized the strategic importance of the new work, designating Massena as a "pastoral mission point." Boroughs was appointed by the board in October 1959 to serve as pastor to the mission and to oversee the development of other Southern Baptist churches anticipated in northern New York.[14]

By the time the Massena Baptist Church was constituted in May 1960, another new work had been formed at Plattsburgh, consisting primarily of military personnel from the Strategic Air Command base located there. Boroughs divided duties between the Massena Church and the Champlain Valley Baptist Chapel in Plattsburgh, even though the latter congregation was sponsored by the Grace Church in Rome. When the home missionary was not in these two communities, he was cultivating new churches in Alexandria Bay, Potsdam, and elsewhere in the North Country.

The Alexandria Bay Chapel was developed in November 1960. Zig Boroughs again turned to J. T. Davis and the Grace Baptist Church for sponsorship of the new work. In a move reminiscent of that which helped bring Davis to New York, Boroughs invited several South Carolina pastors to preach at mission sites. Coley Harrison drew the Alexandria Bay assignment and became pastor there in 1961. More than anything else, his seven-year tenure "at Bay" was marked by tenacity in the face of difficult odds. The church was constituted in 1969.[15]

Another of Boroughs's guest preachers was Norman Bell, who spoke at Utica and at Potsdam in the home of Maurice and Florence Lindsay. The Potsdam gathering consisted largely of members from the Massena Church who wanted a church closer to their homes. The work began in the summer of 1960 with the aid of summer missionaries Sonny Wilkinson and Kenneth McLeod, who led Vacation Bible School and a revival service. After the Lindsays' two oldest daughters made professions of faith during the revival services, Zig Boroughs had no trouble convincing the family of the need for a strong, evangelical church in their community.

Harriet Christy was also impressed by the spirited witness of Southern Baptists. She had been praying forty years that "God would raise up a church in Potsdam that would preach the word of God unashamedly." "I believe," she later declared, "that Southern Baptists coming to Potsdam [were] a direct answer to my prayers."[16]

Members like Christy and the Lindsays helped to create an atmosphere in the mission conducive to evangelism. They found a kindred spirit in Norman Bell. He assumed his ministry at Potsdam in June 1961 with only the Lindsay family formally united as members. When the church was constituted six months later as the Emmanuel Baptist Church, twenty of the thirty-one charter members had been baptized into the congregation. This pattern persisted over the next several years, with roughly three-fourths of the church's new members uniting by baptism. Moreover, the vast majority of the members were New Yorkers.[17]

Norman Bell provided a commendable example for Southern Baptists seeking to establish indigenous churches outside "traditional" areas. Others before him had begun making inroads among local New Yorkers, but none appear to have been quite as effective in this endeavor as he was from the beginning of his ministry. The die was cast in upstate New York for churches to move beyond taking pride in counting a few "natives" among their membership to a ministry more firmly rooted in the communities.

Few churches were more rooted in a community than the First Christian Church of Brushton, an independent, evangelical congregation founded in 1841. Members of the church were inspired by the gospel Norman Bell proclaimed over the radio each Sunday from nearby Potsdam. After the Brushton Church dismissed its pastor in 1964, members turned to Bell and a deacon from the Emmanuel Church for a pulpit supply. Soon Bell was pastor to both congregations. He negotiated an agreement with Brushton

Church to break with its time-honored tradition of independence and become affiliated with Southern Baptists, if the membership liked the direction the church was taking after one year.

In February 1966, the First Christian Church of Brushton became a Southern Baptist congregation as a "mission" of the Emmanuel Baptist Church. Later that year, Bell resigned from the Potsdam Church to devote his full-time efforts in Brushton.[18]

Although the Massena Church enjoyed an auspicious beginning with excellent lay and pastoral leadership, the congregation survived only two years. Serious personal problems within the congregation contributed to the church's disbandment. Zig Boroughs resigned in December 1962, completing a brief, though distinguished career as a pioneer home missionary in New York. The state's northernmost church left a proud legacy as best put by Norman Bell: "Any time a church dies in giving birth to other churches, it has not lived or died in vain."[19]

The Adirondack Association Formed

By the mid-1960s, pastors and lay leaders in the North Country were pondering the idea of an association for their region. The east/west partitioning of the Frontier Association to create the Central Association in 1961 had provided a more workable arrangement where churches could realize more benefits from their mutual affiliation. Yet even as a part of the central New York family of churches, the northernmost churches felt isolated. Laypersons had difficulty attending training events and meetings that usually were held several hours away in Syracuse, the designated "nerve center" of the association. Pastors wanted to develop a

Norman Bell was among the guests returning for the BCNY's twenty-fifth anniversary observance in November 1994. Seated behind him is John Edwards. To his left is Judith Richards, missionary to Taiwan.

closer-knit fellowship to help them cope with the piercing loneliness they often felt in their work.

In October 1967, the Emmanuel and Champlain Valley Churches joined the missions at Alexandria Bay and Brushton to form the Adirondack Baptist Association. Soon, missions at Richville and Saranac Lake were added to the growing fellowship of churches in northern New York. Like the Central Association, the churches of the Adirondack body chose to affiliate with the Baptist Convention of Maryland, and they looked to John Tollison for leadership as area missionary. Robert Jacks, by then a member of the Emmanuel Church, wielded a solid aluminum gavel as the first moderator of the association.[20]

The Adirondack Association became a rallying point for fellowship and service among laypeople, many of whom were new to Southern Baptist life. Leaders like Jacks, Florence Lindsay, and John Edwards helped make "Southern Baptist" a term less associated with geography and more related to a program of cooperative missions, education, and evangelism.

Southern Baptists Along the Southern Tier

Like his colleague at Niagara Falls, Paul Becker came to feel that his initial church planting effort in New York was complete after almost four years. The First Southern Baptist Church of Syracuse was firmly established as a "mother" of churches in central and northern New York. With the building full almost every Sunday with more than two hundred worshipers, Becker felt a bit too "established" himself. The church's struggling mission at Elmira beckoned with a challenging new opportunity.

The Elmira mission was begun in the fall of 1960 after Arthur Walker and a team of summer missionaries who surveyed the area demonstrated to Becker and the First Southern Church the need for a new work in the city. A small home fellowship was formed in September 1960 that later met in the Birchwood Tabernacle in Elmira Heights. Beset by numerous frustrations—most importantly, difficulty in calling a pastor—the local group and the Syracuse Church were ready to disband the mission by early 1961. The Elmira mission required leadership that Becker could not provide, unless, of course, he was willing to go there himself.

At Paul Becker's request, the Syracuse Church called him as pastor of its fledgling Elmira work in March 1961. Difficulties persisted even for the veteran church planter. The congregation sojourned in four different locations over a span of eighteen months. For a time the group crowded into the Becker home after being evicted from rented quarters. In the fall of

1962, the congregation culminated two years of struggle by entering a newly restored Presbyterian church building it purchased with assistance from the Home Mission Board and the Laurel Baptist Church in Greenville, South Carolina. The bell atop the handsome meetinghouse tolled for services in November 1962.[21]

As expected, the visibility provided by the building brought an immediate increase in attendance. By the following autumn the mission was constituted as the Southport Baptist Church, with more than a hundred worshipers in attendance each week.

Paul Becker completed a decade of remarkable service to New York Southern Baptists in 1967 when he left Elmira to follow his home missionary calling to Wisconsin. Under his leadership Southport distinguished itself as a church that reached local people. Of the 225 members on the church rolls at the time of his departure, 175 were persons Becker had baptized.

Simultaneous with the development of the Elmira Church was the emergence of yet another mission along the Southern Tier. In the early 1960s, IBM was drawing people like a magnet from all over the United States to its headquarters in Endicott. Among the new arrivals were Alabamians, Virginians, Texans, and Oklahomans—many of them Southern Baptists eager to find a local church.

Truett Thompson took the initiative in the summer of 1961 to contact fellow IBM employees about gathering a Southern Baptist fellowship. When Paul Becker heard of these developments, he put the group in touch with the First Southern Church in Syracuse. This contact brought assistance from Bob Finnis, chairman of the church's missions committee, and leadership from lay pastor Glen Dick. A new mission was soon established in the area: the Tri-Cities Baptist Chapel.[22]

The growing network of SBC churches in his home state piqued the interest of Roger Knapton. He and his wife Mary returned to New York in August 1961 for a vacation from his duties as pastor of a growing church in Bethel, Kansas. While in New York, Knapton preached several times for the new congregation, which came to ponder the value of having a native son as their pastor. The transplanted southerners who comprised the mission anticipated that a New Yorker would challenge them to move beyond the comforts of a southern enclave to reach out to their neighbors.

Roger Knapton returned home to become pastor of the Tri-Cities Chapel in March 1962. Two months later the mission was constituted with thirty charter members as the First Southern Baptist Church of Endicott.[23] Knapton remained as pastor of the congregation (renamed Lincoln Avenue Baptist Church in 1965) for more than thirty years.

Mission Expansion and the Southern Tier Association

By the mid-1960s, the Southport and Lincoln Avenue Churches were firmly established, and beginning to dot the Southern Tier of New York with chapels. New growth came quickly.

The Southport Church became involved in a rather unusual mission project with the First Baptist Church of Wellsburg, an independent church established in 1789. After a suspicious fire destroyed its historic sanctuary, the church was divided and dispirited. News of a vibrant new church in the neighboring Elmira area brought several members to visit the Southport Church. Rather than join his congregation, Paul Becker suggested that the guests unite as a remnant to form a mission church. The resources and inge-nuity of Southern Baptists in starting churches could then be applied in their situation.[24]

The Wellsburg Baptist Chapel was formed in 1966, with Glen Dick as pastor. Two years later, Coley Harrison was called from the Alexandria Bay Church to become pastor at Wellsburg. With Harrison's leadership the church built a new sanctuary and became more assimilated into associa-tional life. The tradition of almost two hundred years of independence, however, proved difficult to overcome. Within ten years the church was only nominally related to Southern Baptists, later dropping its affiliation altogether in 1979.

The missions of the Lincoln Avenue Church were begun by more tradi-tional means, with summer missionaries conducting surveys and Vacation Bible Schools in outlying areas of Endicott and to the north in the Geneva area. Families from the Endicott Church formed the core groups for missions at Windsor and Johnson City.

The Windsor Chapel was organized in 1965, but languished without pastoral leadership until 1970 when it was constituted as the Trinity Baptist Church. Within five years the church disbanded. The Ackley Avenue Chapel in Johnson City was begun in 1968. The Endicott Church provided the mission with a building, and in 1969 called Waylen Bray as pastor. This mission was also short-lived, disbanding within two years.[25]

New work in Geneva was initiated in 1965 when William Johnson, a transplant from Cincinnati, began seeking a Southern Baptist church in the area. After consulting with John Tollison and Roger Knapton, he began hosting fellowships in his home to seek support and direction for a proposed new church. Among those most interested in being a part of the mission were Knapton's parents, the Warren Knaptons.

In October 1965, the Geneva Baptist Chapel called R. M. Forbes as its first pastor. His leadership placed the mission on a firm footing for sustained growth. A generous loan from Warren Knapton enabled the chapel to purchase a vacant church building in the heart of Geneva. The congregation was constituted in 1969, and three years later became a part of the Greater Rochester Association.

Such rapid growth in mission starts led once again to a parceling of the Central Association into another new association—the Southern Tier Baptist Association, formed in 1968. In contrast, however, to the ground-swell of local sentiment that produced the Adirondack Association, the decision to establish the Southern Tier body was motivated by the desires of a growing network of statewide leaders to cover each section of New York with a formal associational structure.

With the Geneva Church far removed to the north, and with the demise and weakness of missions in the region, the Southern Tier Association realistically was an association of two churches. In 1969 it became part of the Central New York Area—a structure through which the new area missionary for the Central Association, Eldon Jones, attempted to coordinate the ministries of three associations.

CHAPTER FIVE

Baptist Convention of New York

THE "WITNESS OF ALL THINGS TO ALL PEOPLE"—
THE EXPANDING MINISTRY OF THE
MANHATTAN BAPTIST CHURCH

The establishment of the Manhattan Baptist Church caught the attention and imagination of Southern Baptists nationwide. Baptist Press heralded the event with full-page photographs and articles for state convention newspapers across the country.

By any ordinary measure the chapel represented a humble denominational beginning in the city. Yet for a people infused with a sense of divine purpose, it meant that the "urban Goliath" would be confronted with the evangelistic and missionary program of Southern Baptists. It meant also that a "beachhead" had been established in the Northeast for further mission expansion. The prospect of evangelizing America's largest and, by popular perception, most "pagan" city became a part of the convention's enlarged sense of destiny.

One can easily see why Paul James might have lain awake at night wondering what qualified him to become a kind of "founding father" for the work in New York City and beyond. Those who called him made it clear that they expected their new leader to be more than just a shepherd to a small flock. They wanted a missionary who could lead in the development of several chapels in bedroom communities adjacent to the city. A. B. Cash speculated that the prospect of mission starts was so promising in the metropolitan area that five or six new works could be launched in a matter of months.[1]

Paul James approached his new assignment more soberly and realistically. He considered that while Southern Baptists might loom large in the divine scheme of mission advance, the danger for total failure in the metropolitan centers of the Northeast was real. His coreligionists were unfamiliar with the complexities and intractable difficulties of urban life. Southern Baptists populated the growing urban areas of the South, but there many churches represented the last bastion of a simple, rural way of life that new city dwellers recalled nostalgically.[2]

The Manhattan pastor's resolve was to embrace the city with all its bewildering contrasts: enormous wealth within blocks of grinding poverty; gleaming skyscrapers towering above crowded tenements; and exquisitely refined cultural and artistic expression juxtaposed with the depths of moral degradation. Unlike so many of his brothers and sisters who were inclined to associate all things urban with "pagan" and to declare—"New York's an interesting place to visit, but you couldn't pay me to live there"—James was drawn to the city by the example of Jesus' compassion for Jerusalem and Paul's decidedly urban strategy for mission.

Paul James was confident that his denomination could have an effective ministry in the metro area by capitalizing on its "time-honored methods of getting the job done for Jesus." "'Southern Baptist,'" he said prior to leaving Atlanta for New York, "means something great and wonderful all over the world. It means a Bible-centered ministry of preaching and teaching; warm-hearted evangelism; and missionary fervor."[3] With Ava at his side as a full partner in ministry, James set his hand to the difficult task with workmanlike determination and persistence.

Competing with the Devil

The Manhattan Baptist Church brought a new level of visibility to the Home Mission Board's program of pioneer missions. Despite the fact that Southern Baptists had been forming churches in the North for more than a decade—even to the point of organizing a state convention in Ohio—it was not until the New York City congregation was gathered that the northward advance of the denomination became an issue of national religious significance. American Baptist leaders were by no means disinterested onlookers.

Paul James was afforded a polite welcome from his Baptist colleagues in the metro area, but some like W. B. Lipphard, editor of the American Baptist magazine, *Missions*, wondered if James's arrival was foreboding for the American Baptist Convention. His coming confirmed in the editor's mind Southern Baptists' intentions to entice churches out of the ABC with the promise of generous financial support. Lipphard believed this was how Paul James would achieve expansion in the New York City area.[4]

At the annual meeting of the American Baptist Convention in 1958, Porter Routh explained what was transpiring in New York City and other areas new for Southern Baptists. The head of the SBC Executive Committee dismissed the notion that something sinister was afoot. Routh assured his audience that they did not need to be concerned about churches realigning themselves. "Southern Baptist expansion," he pointed out, "is a forward surge to make America Christian. . . . The Thirty Thousand Movement is not a church-stealing escapade."[5]

Routh's words may have calmed fears of a hostile denominational takeover, but other things about Southern Baptists' "invasion" remained troubling for American Baptists. Some charged that a "program" and statistical gains were more important in the SBC than Christian ethics.[6] Was it proper to start new churches in communities already served by Baptist congregations? Was it fair to lure out of American Baptist churches former Southern Baptists—members who were among their best stewards and Bible study leaders?

The controversy reached a crescendo in the summer of 1959. Blake Smith, pastor of the University Baptist Church in Austin, Texas, joined two American Baptist scholars on a panel at the annual meeting of the ABC to discuss the subject: "The Southern Baptist Invasion: Right or Wrong?" His address before the Des Moines, Iowa, gathering was in sharp contrast with the apologia delivered the year before by Porter Routh.

With an eloquence and incisiveness typical of the Texas pastor, Smith conceded that Southern Baptists had been insensitive toward their brothers and sisters in the North. He discounted the hyperbole that led the rank and file of his denomination to believe that the region to their north was "one vast territory of spiritual destitution." Parts of the North were surely heathen, he asserted, "as heathen, almost, as Arkansas, Mississippi, and Texas." Smith also labeled as "preposterous" and "absurd" the frequent charge that American Baptists were not doctrinally sound and were not preaching the gospel.

Not all of Smith's criticisms, however, were leveled at his own denomination. He acknowledged that new works had been launched in close proximity to existing Baptist churches only because those churches had failed to extend an understanding and compassionate hand to the "strangers in a strange land" from the South. He chided the northerners for not being more intentional in their outreach to newcomers.[7]

One thing was certain, he told the audience: Southern Baptists were in the North to stay. Baptists in the North and South needed to discover a means for reconciliation, dialogue, and cooperation, lest whatever unity existed between the two communions be wrecked beyond repair. The

Texan was given a standing ovation.

Smith's comments raised the ire of many in the SBC. Editors like R. G. Puckett of Ohio, who considered the witness of American Baptists in his state "mediocre," suggested that Southern Baptists not waste their time responding to someone who did not know the situation firsthand.[8] He was joined by others in denouncing Smith as one who was more concerned about sensitivities and perceived territorial rights than the Great Commission. "Southern Baptists will not face in judgment a council on comity ethics," wrote J. Kelly Simmons of California, "but they certainly will be responsible before the Eternal Judge for an accounting of their New Testament stewardship."[9]

Over the next few years, the issue continued to surface periodically. In 1961, for example, after *Newsweek* correspondent Karl Fleming published an article describing Southern Baptists' "bare-knuckled" approach to missionizing in the North, the furor over the matter was renewed. When an expanded version of the article appeared in the Home Mission Board publication, *Home Missions*, American Baptists filed an official protest.

R. Dean Goodwin, director of the ABC's communications division, suggested to Arthur Rutledge, president of the Home Mission Board, that the language of the article was "more fitting for a ruthless corporation that is out to 'get its competitors' than it is for a dedicated missionary organization." Rutledge apologized for the harsh language of the article, emphasizing that it did not represent the attitude of Southern Baptists toward their northern counterparts. In the board leader's thinking, the devil was his denomination's only real competition.[10]

While most of Paul James's relationships with American Baptists were cordial, he encountered some hostility over the invasion issue. A layman from the historic First Baptist Church of Morristown, New Jersey, allegedly was unable to speak of Southern Baptists without cursing. James discerned what he thought to be the root cause of the controversy when he shared lunch with the man. As the layman unburdened himself, he spoke of his own congregation effectively serving a broad area encompassing several communities. James perceived that the man subscribed to a "parish" understanding of the church. The model was based upon an antiquated notion of a society thoroughly "churched," with Baptists, Methodists, and other members of the Protestant family supporting the respective church bearing their denominational label in each "parish" or territory. Nearly three centuries of ministry in the area had produced in the northern New Jersey church an "established" church mentality.

James explained that Southern Baptists subscribed to a church-centered mission strategy in new areas, wherein congregations organize to reach out to the vast sea of unchurched persons regardless of the specific community in which they live.[11] As it turned out, not a single member of the layman's church lived in Madison, where a new mission affiliated with the Manhattan Church was forming.

Joseph Heartburg, executive minister of the American Baptist Churches of New Jersey, warmly greeted Southern Baptists as partners in ministry. He expressed neither suspicion nor resentment but gratitude for the ministry of his fellow Baptists. His example of openness led to a dialogue group between SBC and ABC pastors. Glenn Igleheart, who arrived in the Northeast in 1968 as a missionary of the Home Mission Board for "Work Related to Non-Evangelicals" (which later became the department of Interfaith Witness), facilitated group discussions of joint ministry and sponsorship of new churches. During this time the First Baptist Church of Montclair, where Harry Emerson Fosdick began his ministry, reconstituted itself as a dually aligned ABC/SBC church through a merger with a Southern Baptist mission at Cedar Grove, New Jersey.[12]

An Extraordinarily Gifted Fellowship

Creating a dynamic, visionary Southern Baptist presence in America's largest city was a daunting task, rife with obstacles and distractions, but it was in no way a challenge Paul James undertook alone. Standing with him and Ava was an extraordinary concentration of gifted and resourceful laypeople. Young executives, lawyers, artists, airline pilots, fashion designers, military personnel, writers, and students were among those who grasped the significance of their church and embraced their calling as "missionaries."

The Manhattan Church initially consisted almost exclusively of upwardly mobile southerners. Except for the formal ambience provided by the Gothic-style auditorium at 311 West Fifty-seventh Street, where the congregation began meeting in March 1959, the church was hardly distinguishable in its worship and program from an upper-middle-class congregation in the South. The editor of the Oklahoma *Baptist Messenger,* who visited the church on Easter Sunday 1959, happily reported to his readers that he could have closed his eyes in worship and imagined himself in Atlanta, Dallas, or Oklahoma City.[13]

Warmhearted, informal fellowship also characterized the Manhattan Church. New arrivals were pleasantly surprised to find a setting where their thick drawls blended in with everyone else's. The congenial atmosphere was powerfully appealing—almost as appealing as the church's fellowship dinners which were touted as "just like home except for the red bugs."

The joy these members experienced in discovering and socializing with one another was tempered, however, by an ongoing, and at times distressing, concern that their church and the missions they planned be more than just colonies for transplants from the South. Their intentions were far more visionary, in keeping with the tradition of mission concern in which they had been nurtured.

When Buryl Red stepped through the doors of the Manhattan Church in the summer of 1960, he felt as though he had entered a time and culture warp. The accents, the hymns, and the language of Zion reminded the young musician of his religious heritage in Arkansas. Since his arrival at Yale University in 1958, his aunt Maggie Leece Holiman, the pastor's secretary, had encouraged him to come for a visit. Now he knew why.

Upon meeting the members and the pastor, Red knew that this was far more than a cultural enclave. He sensed the group's depth of commitment to broader missionary purposes. Paul James's rare combination of erudition, devotion, and hospitality was irresistible. When he later moved to New York City and was asked by James to develop a music program for the church, he enthusiastically accepted the opportunity.

Something of the uniqueness of the Manhattan Baptist Church can be seen in the impact Buryl Red's creative energy had upon the congregation. He, perhaps more than any other member at the time, was interested in giving the church a cosmopolitan flavor. He had the audacity to ask "heretical" questions like, "Is it sinful to do something besides Training Union and evening worship on Sunday nights?"

A lengthy Sunday morning commute into the city discouraged many members from returning on Sunday evenings for services. Some worshipers were also involved in evening fellowship groups across the metropolitan region. One segment of the membership, however, was available only on Sunday nights: music students and professional musicians who performed in other churches for morning worship. The potential for a strong music program in the church was actually better on Sunday evenings than on Sunday mornings.

Buryl Red thus capitalized upon a remarkable pool of talent in producing concert series and other special events on Sunday nights that featured such talents as Norman Treigle, a leading baritone in New York City opera circles. With cooperation that was unusual among classical musicians, Broadway singers, and actors, Red took on avant-garde projects utilizing special projection effects and rock-style gospel music. One of the drama students with whom he worked, Ragan Courtney, later collaborated with him in producing one of Southern Baptists' most popular and enduring musicals, *Celebrate Life.*

Out-of-town guests sometimes asked—"are you really doing this here?"—and the pastor raised an occasional eyebrow at a Sunday evening event. Yet the congregation recognized that music and the arts were a legitimate way of reaching a segment of New York that otherwise would not be reached by a more traditional program of ministry. The Manhattan Church's choir achieved considerable acclaim, producing demonstration recordings for the music department of the Baptist Sunday School Board, and performing at such venues as the 1964 annual session of the Southern Baptist Convention in Atlantic City. In 1970 the choir performed before a national television audience as a part of CBS's Christmas Eve programming.[14]

Visionary and Progressive Deacons

In the late 1950s, most of America's largest oil companies and financial institutions had corporate addresses in New York City. The city was also headquarters for the nation's apparel industry and a home for businesses involved in international trade. For the young, upwardly mobile executives of these companies, exposure to New York's commercial environment was a rite of passage on the way to regional management positions in other parts of the country. Some spoke of "doing time" in the corporate jungle.

A transfer to New York City was hardly a delight for most southerners, even if it was a necessary stepping-stone for a career promotion. For transferees who happened to be Southern Baptists, the move had implications beyond secular employment. A junior executive's stint in the metropolitan area was given new meaning by the presence of the Manhattan Church. The compelling mission of the congregation elicited in many a level of dedication and participation in church life they had not known before. Seeing oneself as missionary on a mission field, while fulfilling one's secular vocation, was easy for a member of the Manhattan Baptist Church.

Paul James had confidence almost to a fault in the leadership ability of corporate executives. For him, the management skills, imagination, dedication, and hard work that produced high levels of achievement in the business world were the stuff of which church leadership was made. With an East Side address and a Mercedes-Benz automobile, the pastor left some with the impression that his ministry was directed primarily at an upscale constituency. The early history of the Manhattan Church, however, suggests that James was not an elitist and that his confidence in the men who became leaders in the church was well placed.

Deacons and mission pastors of the Manhattan Baptist Church often met in corporate board rooms. Norvell Jones chairs this session under the watchful eye of Paul James (standing). Seated from left to right are: Bob Bell, Norman Watson, Clayton Day, Carroll Reeves, Herb Maher, Howard Hovde, and Sam Sorrell. Across the table are: Hardy Denham, unidentified, Earl Hollis, and Thad Williams.

Deacons of the Manhattan Church were, as a rule, corporate executives or men of considerable accomplishment in other fields such as medicine or the military. Their meetings were held not in the church basement, nor in a cramped Sunday School space, but in the plush board rooms of oil companies for which some of them worked. The pastor teased about having the "highest deacons' meetings in the Southern Baptist Convention"—forty-two floors above the streets of Manhattan![15] Given the "lofty" subjects they discussed, such a venue seemed poetically apropos.

One of the first issues the deacons took up was the matter of starting new churches. James and the deacons determined that a deliberate course of action was needed to help ensure the long-term prospects of Southern Baptist work in the area. Accordingly, the men made a careful study of the matter throughout the spring and summer of 1958. What resulted from their efforts was a veritable manifesto for mission advance, noteworthy not so much for the strategy it prescribed as for the ideals it embodied—ideals that inspired a generation of churches in the metropolitan area.

As a preamble, the deacons affirmed that the Manhattan Church subscribed fully to the Home Mission Board's program of pioneer missions. In so doing, the church committed itself to becoming the "mother church" for new works throughout the region just as its "investors"— Southern Baptists across the nation—expected.

First, fellowship groups would be established in the homes of church members who knew the Southern Baptist program, and who demonstrated the "sacrifice, vision, dedication, loyalty, persistence, passion, and patience" demanded for pioneer work. When a fellowship grew to a sizeable and stable number, it would become a chapel, and a mission pastor would be called to serve the fledgling congregation. For the foreseeable future all members of chapels would maintain their membership with the Manhattan Church, with their financial contributions forwarded to the church's treasury. The deacons recognized the necessity of safeguarding the well-being of the mother church.

Although the document did not specifically address the issue of chapels constituting as churches, the assumption seems to have been that when a congregation was able to provide for its own meeting place and pastor, it was ready to become a church. But, as Paul James observed elsewhere, "the trolly didn't stop there." All new churches were expected to become regional centers for mission advance—to repeat the above process with daughter churches of their own.

Finally, the deacons called for an aggressive evangelistic effort in the proposed new works. "It is not for the convenience of Southern Baptist families that chapels are started," they declared, "but rather that we may minister to whole communities through the planting of New Testament churches. . . . Let all of us who have a part in this glorious ministry prove ourselves to be zealous and tireless missionaries worthy of Christ and our Southern Baptist people."[16]

Crossing the "Bridge" on the Racial Question

The deacons also grappled with another critically important issue early in the church's history: race relations. When Paul James arrived in New York City in the fall of 1957, one of the first questions a reporter asked him was: "What are you lily-white Southern Baptists going to do when people of color come around?"

Such a question was not at all surprising, given that the crisis at Central High School in Little Rock was still fresh on the American public's mind. Southern white churches stood in the vanguard of opposition to school integration. The probability of blacks "coming around" to a white church in the South was remote, but in the isolated cases where they did, trouble usually followed. As late as 1962, blacks were arrested for trespassing when they tried to enter an Albany, Georgia, Southern Baptist church. In 1965 a Nigerian student was admitted to membership in the First Baptist Church of Richmond only after an acrimonious four-hour business meeting.[17] Closed doors, certainly controversy, typically could be expected of a Southern Baptist church if and when blacks came around.

"We'll cross that bridge when we get to it," the pastor cautiously replied to the reporter. He was unable to predict how the new church would respond if a person of color sought membership. The New York congregation was anything but a typical Southern Baptist church, yet among its membership were those who had been taught since childhood that segregation was God's will. Would the social mores of the Old South dictate the church's policy, or would a different standard be applied? Paul James was unsure what to expect.

The Manhattan Church arrived at the "bridge" of racial concern much sooner than anyone expected. A few weeks after Chris Oswampke, a Nigerian student, began attending the church in the fall of 1958, he approached the pastor about uniting with the congregation. Oswampke had become a Christian through the influence of Southern Baptist missionaries who encouraged him to come to the United States for his education. While a student at Georgetown (Kentucky) College, he was denied membership in a local church. Bitterness over the issue resulted in the congregation's division. The young man expressed a desire to identify with Southern Baptists, but assured James that he did not wish to cause another firestorm of controversy.[18]

What would Southern Baptists in New York City do when people of color came around? Sam Sorrell, a young oil company executive from Mississippi, helped answer that question when the pastor put the matter of Chris Oswampke's membership before the deacons. Sorrell observed that the Manhattan Church was attempting to be a New Testament church—a congregation not unlike that which developed at Antioch. The churches there and elsewhere evidently observed no racial distinctions. The deacon then reminded the group: "This is New York, not the South . . . and you can't draw circles here."[19]

The deacons heartily embraced Sorrell's rationale as their official stance for the young man's inclusion in the church. The Manhattan Baptist Church warmly received Chris Oswampke, becoming one of the few churches in the Southern Baptist Convention at that time where black people, or people of any non-Anglo race, were freely welcomed for membership. Paul James gave Sorrell and the other deacons much of the credit for helping the church make such a bold move, but leaders like Norvell Jones and Norman

Watson recalled that they would have been ashamed to have done anything less, given what they knew of their pastor's feelings about openness to all people.[20] Little did they realize what implications their open-door policy would hold for the future of Southern Baptist work in the region.

Ministry Among Students

Among the more than two hundred thousand students on fifty campuses in New York City were bright young men and women whose faith had been nurtured in Southern Baptist churches. Nothing comforted their anxious parents quite so much as knowing that a new church awaited their sons and daughters in the city—a congregation with accustomed patterns of worship and ministry which would provide their young people a gracious welcome. From a half-dozen to fifteen students attended worship regularly at the Manhattan Baptist Church. Many of them caught the congregation's pioneering missionary spirit.[21]

When Gene Maston arrived at Columbia University in 1959 as a graduate student, he came interested in continuing the kind of Baptist Student Union work he had started while studying at the University of Chicago. A young lawyer in Chicago, Paul Pressler, encouraged him to investigate the possibility of reorganizing an informal "evangelical" fellowship he had gathered a few years before at his alma mater, Princeton University.

Since the late 1940s, Southern Baptist students at Princeton Theological Seminary like James Leo Garrett, Ralph and James Langley, and Cecil Sherman had been organizing and leading student groups in the Princeton area. With Sherman's leadership in 1954–1955, the "Baptist Students of Princeton" welcomed as many as two hundred members of the seminary and university communities for Sunday morning worship. Not all of those who crowded into the seminary's Miller Chapel were Baptists. Many were students of other denominations who found the warmly evangelical, biblically based ministry of the group a refreshing contrast to the stuffiness they often felt in the borough's churches.[22]

In the years after Sherman's departure, the "Baptist Students of Princeton" floundered without leadership and eventually disbanded. Sherman tried to no avail to convince the Home Mission Board to make a modest investment in the Princeton ministry. When Maston visited the Princeton campus in 1959, he found no Baptist student organization, nor did he find any Baptists associated with the evangelical fellowship Pressler had helped organize several years before. In consultation with Paul James, he determined that his time could best be spent working with students attending the Manhattan Church.

Southern Baptist campus ministry in New York City was begun in November 1959 when Gene and Freda Maston hosted a gathering for students from the Manhattan Church. When he saw that they shared his enthusiasm for a new ministry, Maston encouraged the students, most of whom were enrolled in graduate and professional schools in the city, not to impose familiar patterns upon their setting, but to draw up their own plans for a nontraditional, distinctively urban campus ministry.

In February 1960, the students launched a citywide Baptist Student Union with the goal of providing a monthly meeting that was spiritually and intellectually stimulating, and that met their fellowship needs. New York campuses did not need a kind of Baptist "club," they concluded, but an organization through which the gospel could be shared in a reasoned, articulate fashion. Paul James agreed. "We have in our midst at Manhattan church," he wrote, "a group of young adults who have been taught by their education to question authorities, weigh evidence, investigate assumptions, challenge conclusions, and maintain aesthetic standards." He commended Maston for "projecting a ministry that is Christ-centered and yet is relevant to the kinds of questions" students are taught to ask.[23]

S. H. Frazier, a deacon of the Manhattan Church and head of research psychiatry at Columbia Presbyterian Hospital, and professor Wayne Oates of the Southern Baptist Theological Seminary were among the early guest speakers for the New York City BSU. They and others of similar expertise were adept at addressing the kinds of questions students like William Pennington Vann, a senior at Columbia University, found compelling.

Elected the first president of the BSU, "Penny" was a young man full of questions, but the greatest value of the group for the young Texan was the support it afforded students, most of whom were like him—far from home. The Manhattan Church and the Baptist Student Union were like home inasmuch as they recalled for students the warm fellowship and mission concern so much a part of their Southern Baptist heritage.[24]

The New York City BSU functioned outside "official" chaplaincy programs where they existed at city universities. Columbia University, for example, was "singularly unenthusiastic" about affording recognition to any organization associated with Southern Baptists. Gene Maston had no reason to believe that the United States Military Academy at West Point would be any different, given its long-standing tradition of mandatory chapel with chaplains assigned for Protestant, Catholic, and Jewish cadets. And given the tight regimentation of the academy, he doubted if an organization could function on post without the explicit endorsement of the commandant. The New York campus leader nevertheless promised cadet Odus Elliot, who visited the Manhattan Church en route to West Point in August 1960, that he would accompany him to the chaplain's office that fall to investigate the possibility of starting a Baptist student group there.

As expected, Chaplain Theodore Speers was reluctant to allow a denominational group on campus. He was inclined instead, interestingly enough, to ask Maston to consider coordinating the Officer's Christian Union, an evangelical fellowship already in place. While West Point had a tradition of civilian chaplains, commissioned officers had always overseen the ministry of the OCU. Ostensibly, the opportunity seemed to nudge open the door for a Baptist witness on campus, yet Maston was wary. He suspected that in reality the chaplain was seeking to replace the officer in charge of the OCU with whom he had difficulties. Rather than "pull someone else's chestnuts out of the fire" and operate a Baptist campus ministry somewhat surreptitiously, he chose a few weeks later to decline the offer. Then something remarkable happened—something that Maston called a miracle. At this august institution so steeped in tradition, a place where for more than 150 years denominational organizations had not been allowed to work directly with cadets, Speers asked, "Okay . . . what would you folks like to do?"[25]

Maston was so astonished he could hardly answer. Fully expecting to be rebuffed, he was unprepared to lay out a formal proposal for a West Point Baptist Student Union. All he knew was that the Protestant chapel services, which had a distinctive Episcopalian flavor, were not meeting the spiritual needs of students like Elliot and Art Webb. Webb, whose spiritual roots were in a Southern Baptist church in rural Tennessee, thought he had mistakenly fallen in with the Roman Catholic cadets his first Sunday on post. He did not know what to make of assistant chaplain Gooch's frequent references to a "Paul" he did not know—one surnamed Tillich.

Baptist cadets needed fellowship, a time to open their Bibles and consider the words of Paul the Apostle, an opportunity for a more informal service of worship, and a chance to pray for one another.[26] Chaplain Speers granted Maston and the cadets permission to organize a Baptist Student Union that could meet in his office each Sunday evening beginning in February 1961. Within a year the group received the formal endorsement of the commandant and was granted permanent standing as a campus organization.

Through the cooperation of the Baptist Sunday School Board and the Maryland Convention, Gene Maston was appointed in July 1962 as director for the New York City and West Point Baptist Student Unions. That fall his responsibilities were expanded to cover the entire Northeast. Over the next few years he helped develop campus ministries at Harvard University, Massachusetts Institute of Technology, the United States Coast Guard Academy, Yale University, and Vassar College.

With the help of Lomita Hudnall and other student members of the Central Baptist Church in Syracuse, Maston formed a BSU at Syracuse University in 1965. Albert and Betty Jo Bell came to the campus in 1968 as US-2 missionaries to direct the ministry.[27]

In 1966 the Home Mission Board appointed Caby Byrne as a second full-time campus minister in the metropolitan New York area. His primary responsibility was the West Point ministry, though he also gave time to cultivating work at the United States Merchant Marine and Coast Guard Academies. Byrne resigned in August 1970.

Gene Maston resigned in 1968 as regional director of campus ministry for the Northeast. In less than a decade, he had helped establish a Southern Baptist presence at almost a dozen schools, traveling from campus to campus like a circuit rider. Through networking campuses and students with retreats and other special events, he also had laid the groundwork for state convention student work in New York/New Jersey and in New England.

The Manhattan Baptist Church was more than just a new church in a new city for Southern Baptists. It was a rallying point for an enormously talented and dedicated group of laypeople to share their personal gifts in mission. With their creativity, openness, and broad vision for ministry, members of the church set an example that subsequent generations of leaders in the metropolitan area sought to emulate.

CHAPTER SIX

Baptist Convention of New York

MISSION BEYOND THE CITY LIMITS

M embers of the Manhattan Baptist Church had no difficulty making an application of Jesus' command to share the gospel "in Jerusalem, in all Judea and Samaria, and to the ends of the earth." These words resounded in their midst as if they had been spoken in the late 1950s to Christians in New York City. The congregation was eager to extend its witness beyond "Jerusalem."

The church's first opportunity to support a new work developed not in a suburb of New York City, but in the far reaches of New England. Members of the South Hill Baptist Church in Roswell, New Mexico, were among a large number of personnel transferred to Pease Air Force Base in Portsmouth, New Hampshire, in the summer of 1958. Under sponsorship by their former church, and later by the Manhattan Church, the members created a Southern Baptist fellowship that was constituted in February 1960 as the Screven Memorial Baptist Church.[1] The Manhattan Church subsequently sponsored churches in Springfield, Massachusetts; Hartford and New London, Connecticut; and Plattsburg, New York—all of which became charter members of the New England Baptist Association formed in 1962.

Mission to Madison

At the same time the Aarons, Robbs, and Masseys were discovering each other in Manhattan in early 1957, three families in Morris County,

New Jersey—the McCarters, Styerses, and Dukes—were getting acquainted and discussing the idea of a Southern Baptist fellowship. Although the families chose not to create a formal New Jersey fellowship, opting instead to merge with others in the metropolitan area to start the Manhattan work, they never lost their sense of regional identity and resolve to begin a chapel on their side of the Hudson. Forty of the ninety-nine charter members of the Manhattan Baptist Church were New Jersey residents.

The McCarters' home in Chatham became the earliest gathering place for New Jersey Southern Baptists. Wednesday evening prayer services were held there from the inception of the Manhattan mission. Bedrooms were transformed into makeshift nurseries, and the basement provided space for Matrel McCarter's vibrant "Sunbeam band." Women within the fellowship organized a WMU which brought them together each week for prayer, study, and outreach.[2]

In April 1958, the New Jersey "contingent," as they described themselves, took an important step toward becoming a church. With the leadership of Army chaplain Charles Meek of Fort Slocum, New York, the group initiated Training Union and evening services at the Ridgedale Avenue School in Florham Park. Chaplain Meek's dedicated efforts throughout the summer helped the emerging new work rebound from the loss of several families due to transfers. Summer missionary Gladys Hardy, who conducted surveys in the area and organized Vacation Bible School, also helped the New Jersey group maintain its momentum entering the fall of 1958.

Less than a year old as a fully constituted church, the Manhattan congregation was prepared by Thanksgiving to bid farewell to almost half its membership to begin the first Southern Baptist church in New Jersey. The New Jersey Baptist Chapel was launched on November 28, 1958. Chaplain Meek divided pastoral responsibilities with Columbia University graduate student, C. W. Kratz, a former SBC foreign missionary.[3]

Despite their relatively small membership, the congregation acted quickly to secure a full-time pastor. Members no doubt recalled the positive impact Paul James's arrival had made on their mother church the year before. Howard Hovde was a bright, energetic pastoral intern at the South Main Baptist Church in Houston, Texas. The search committee recognized in the young Wisconsin native the kind of vision, missionary zeal, and personal skills necessary for building a church in a bedroom community of New York City. In February 1959, the chapel called him as pastor.[4]

"A Little More Religion Can't Hurt"

Morris County, New Jersey, was one of the nation's fastest growing suburban areas in the late 1950s. When prime property became available in Madison—a college town of sixteen thousand adjacent to Chatham—the chapel selected a site on Green Avenue at Shunpike Road as its future home. The realization that no new church had been organized in Madison since 1897 led one interested resident to opine to the township zoning board that "a little more religion in this world can harm no one."

With a loan from the Home Mission Board and generous gifts from large churches across the South, the chapel purchased the property and laid plans for a colonial style building which was dedicated in June 1963. The Madison Baptist Church, constituted in May 1960, subscribed fully to pastor Hovde's far-reaching vision for Southern Baptist work in New Jersey. The church grew quickly even in the face of frequent transfers of members from the area. Net increase in membership amounted to an almost four-fold growth in just three years. Even so, Hovde was cautious about ascribing success to the mission venture too quickly: "Give us twenty-five years," he advised, "before attempting to pass judgment."[5]

The Madison Church sought to integrate itself fully into the religious life of the community. The congregation saw ecumenical cooperation as important for its witness. Missing was the usual reserve shown by Southern Baptists in relating to other denominations. In 1961, for example, the church joined Lutheran and Presbyterian congregations in sponsoring a week-long evangelistic emphasis. Madison member Wallace McCormick served as chair of the steering committee for the event. Pastors of area churches and faculty members from nearby Drew University were invited to preach for special Sunday evening events. Women in the church partici- pated as "observers" and later in a more official capacity in the Madison chapter of Church Women United, an organization related to the National Council of Churches.[6]

"A little more religion in this world . . ."—the citizen's offhand remark was more significant than he realized. Southern Baptists' newest congrega- tion in the Northeast was destined to touch the world through its stewardship and witness in the culturally diverse metropolitan area. Paul James came to characterize the church's generosity, cooperation, and mission concern as "the Madison spirit."

Howard Hovde resigned as pastor in June 1966. Having completed his doctorate at Columbia University, he and his wife Carole were appointed missionaries to Liberia, where he taught at Rick's Institute. His immediate successor, David C. Hall, served only a brief time. Charles A. Jolly, who led the College Avenue Baptist Church in Annapolis, Maryland, to sponsor the Manhattan Church more than a decade earlier, resigned his pastorate at the Pittsburgh (Pennsylvania) Baptist Church to become pastor of the Madison Church in January 1969.

The Madison "Family Tree"

The Madison Baptist Church was not yet a year old when word came that a home fellowship in central New Jersey was in need of a sponsoring church. When the church voted in July 1961 to adopt the new work as a mission, it set in motion a series of genealogical "begats" which in less than ten years produced four churches in Middlesex and Monmouth Counties.

The vision and impetus for beginning a church in central New Jersey were provided by Paul James at a fellowship event sponsored by the Manhattan Church in early 1961. Edison resident Vivian Cochran asked the pastor when he and the New York congregation were going to begin a church close to her home. James responded by turning the question around—"When are you going to begin one?" It had not occurred to her that she and her friends were free to initiate the work.[7]

With James's encouragement, the sponsorship of the Madison Church, and the moral support of a growing network of Southern Baptists in the Northeast, four families from Virginia, Texas, Alabama, and Missouri formed the nucleus of what became the Raritan Valley Baptist Church in March 1963. John Killinger served as the church's founding pastor, while pursuing postdoctoral studies at Princeton Theological Seminary. Walter Heilig, founding pastor of the Amherst Baptist Church in the Buffalo area, came as full-time pastor of the Edison Church in 1963.

The Raritan Valley Church adopted a "child" of its own in the spring of 1963—a fellowship of military families from Fort Monmouth, organized in the home of Ralph and Lena Mauriel. The mission enjoyed excellent leadership from Air Force Sergeant Bill Prather and Army Sergeant Joe Culpepper, who guided the congregation to its constitution as the Lincroft Baptist Church in 1964. The church called Marvin Haire as its first full-time pastor in September 1965, and soon thereafter changed its name to the Monmouth Baptist Church.[8]

In the late 1960s, financial support through the Home Mission Board's Project 500 enabled both the Raritan Valley and Monmouth Churches to reach out with additional mission chapels. In 1968 the Edison Church formed a chapel with five of its families in neighboring East Brunswick.

The following year the chapel called Alvin Cox as part-time pastor. In June 1970, the congregation was constituted as the East Brunswick Baptist Church. Dennis Malone became the church's first full-time pastor in 1971.

The Monmouth Baptist Church extended its ministry to two different Monmouth County locations. Jesse Dilday, the church's missions committee chair, opened his home in 1967 as a meeting place for church members living in northern Monmouth County. The fellowship organized itself as the Calvary Baptist Mission and began meeting at an Aberdeen elementary school. Jack Kinney provided part-time leadership until the congregation called Jon F. Meek Jr. in the summer of 1968 as its first full-time pastor. Under Meek's leadership the Calvary Baptist Church was constituted in September 1969.[9]

Members of the Monmouth Church who lived in the western part of the county developed a home Bible study in February 1967. The group remained informal and loosely organized until Army officer Darwin Bacon came in April 1969 as a part-time pastor for the group. Bacon, who was stationed in the Washington, D.C., area, traveled almost five hundred miles round trip each weekend to serve the mission and to court pastor Marvin Haire's daughter, whom he eventually married. The Freehold home fellowship became the West Monmouth Baptist Chapel one month after he arrived. In March 1970, DeLane Ryals became the church's first full-time pastor. The church was constituted in December 1972.

Further New Jersey Branches Extended

The year after the Madison Baptist Church assumed sponsorship of the Raritan Valley mission in central New Jersey, another opportunity arose to assist a group in the northwest New Jersey community of Succasunna. After three months of prayer and deliberation, four families united to rent a local school for Sunday services. Seven families organized the Roxbury Baptist Chapel in January 1963 and called R. P. Liesmann as part-time pastor. Upon his graduation in 1966, the Drew University doctoral student assumed full-time responsibilities. He led the chapel to be constituted as the Hope Baptist Church in September 1969.[10]

By the early 1960s, few Southern Baptists in New Jersey still maintained a direct affiliation with the Manhattan Baptist Church. Only the Carteret Fellowship, organized in the home of Manhattan Church members Elmer and Hazel Ammons, remained within the church's mission oversight. When members of the fellowship learned in the summer of 1963 that the Madison Church intended to initiate a mission in the nearby Clark area, the group decided to lend its strength to that effort. In September 1963, the Clark Baptist Chapel began gathering for Sunday evening worship in a neighborhood school. Bill and Mildred Boisture led in organizing a Sunday School and a WMU the next month. When Sunday morning worship was begun in November, the chapel called James Brooks, a graduate student at Princeton Theological Seminary, as part-time pastor.

The chapel changed its name in 1965 to the Terrill Road Baptist Chapel after purchasing property on Terrill Road in the community of Scotch Plains. The new work grew rapidly under the leadership of Brooks, who was pastor until 1966. He was succeeded by Kenneth King who led the chapel to be constituted as the Terrill Road Baptist Church in April 1967.[11]

Madison Baptist Church continued adding to its family of missions in 1964 when Pastor Hovde agreed to Elizabeth Thurston's request for assistance in beginning a new work in the Bernardsville/Basking Ridge area. Missions committee leader Bob Bell and James Strange, a theological student at Drew University, joined several couples in the Thurston home for prayer, worship, and the organization of a new mission in November 1964. The group called Strange as part-time pastor, and shortly thereafter began meeting in the local Masonic hall where the congregation gathered for almost twenty years. Bennett F. Hall became the Bernardsville Chapel's first full-time pastor in 1967, and led the church to constitute as the Somerset Hills Baptist Church in July 1969.[12]

Completing five years of new mission starts, the Madison Church assumed sponsorship in 1965 of a fellowship consisting of Raritan Valley Church members and other families from the Kendall Park, Princeton, and Belle Mead areas. The chapel was constituted in September 1969 as the Twin County Baptist Church.[13] Pastor Chris Ammons, who served the church from 1983 to 1985, was later appointed along with his wife Pam for missionary service in Spain and Peru. The church disbanded in 1991, directing that its assets be used in forming a future mission in the area.

Mission to Bergen and Passaic Counties

Like Morris County, Bergen County, New Jersey, was a growing area in the late 1950s that welcomed a large number of Manhattan commuters to its shady, comfortable suburbs. For men like Norvell Jones, Bob Jordan, Ira Adams, and Norman Watson, the weekly round trips across the George Washington Bridge numbered six rather than five. Sunday worship at the Manhattan Baptist Church was a priority.

With the growth of the New York City church, however, the priority of mission expansion led the men and their families to form a fellowship near their homes. In 1960 they began sharing Sunday evenings together in Bible study and worship. The group asked Army chaplain Clayton Day to lead them as a part-time pastor. Day was assigned to First Army Headquarters on Governors Island from 1958 to 1961. A charter member of the Manhattan Church and chair of the congregation's missions committee, Day was instrumental in the beginnings of several other churches in the area as well. In February 1961, the fellowship organized as the Bergen Baptist Chapel and began meeting in a Seventh-Day Adventist church building in Westwood.[14]

In the spring of 1961, Clayton Day traveled to Atlanta for training in a Home Mission Board evangelism event. While there, he ran into a fellow Palestine, Texas, native, Quinn Pugh, who had long known of "Happy" Day's gifts as a preacher. Pugh, then pastor of the Jackson Hill Baptist Church in Atlanta, had heard of the mission work in the Northeast through his acquaintance with Paul James. When he told Day of his intention to be in New Jersey that summer for the Theological Institute at Princeton Seminary, the chaplain insisted he preach for the Bergen Chapel while there. The young pastor was eager to see firsthand this ministry on the frontier of home missions.[15]

Quinn and Norma Pugh thoroughly enjoyed their visit with the Bergen people. A letter from Paul James in December 1961 indicating the chapel's interest in his coming as pastor came as a surprise but also as an intriguing possibility he could not ignore.

In February 1962, Pugh returned to New York to discuss the idea with members of the Bergen group and Paul James. "Does the Lord really want this?" he asked himself as he walked along a crowded avenue in the city. "Should I bring my wife and baby up to this place I know so little about?" "Am I capable of working with these people?" he prayed. Then, in a moment, he offered an apology to the Lord for "asking so many human questions," to which the Lord seemed to reply: "Those are the only kind you can ask!" Arriving back in Atlanta and sitting in the sanctuary of the Jackson Hill Church, he knew his work there was complete.[16]

Quinn Pugh became pastor of the Bergen Baptist Chapel in March 1962. Six months later the congregation was constituted as the Bergen Baptist Church. Under his leadership the church began a ministry of resettlement for refugees fleeing Castro's Cuba. The ministry led to the sponsorship of two Hispanic churches: the Nazareth Baptist Church in West New York, New Jersey (1965); and the Central Spanish Baptist Church in Paterson,

New Jersey (1967). In February 1969, the Bergen Baptist Church moved from its Westwood home to newly acquired facilities in Waldwick.[17] The church changed its name in 1991 to Christ Community Church.

In the late 1950s, the Manhattan Church was also successful in establishing a chapel in the Passaic County township of Wayne. The Suburban Baptist Church, originally sponsored as a mission in March 1959, was constituted three years later. Under the leadership of J. Herbert Bidgood, the congregation grew and purchased property near the community of Pompton Lakes. By the mid-1960s, however, Bidgood had grown disaffected with Southern Baptists over what he perceived as liberal tendencies. Citing concerns over the SBC's growing ecumenical involvements, epitomized in his mind by the denomination's membership in the North American Baptist Fellowship, he led his church to withdraw from the convention in 1965.[18]

Mission to Long Island

In much the same way the Madison and Bergen Churches were begun in New Jersey, new work was initiated on Long Island by members of the Manhattan Church who commuted to the city regularly for worship. Midweek prayer meetings and a Woman's Missionary Union were begun in Wantagh in the winter of 1958. With the help of student summer missionaries, the group sponsored a Vacation Bible School that July which attracted more than two hundred children. Numerous prospects were discovered for a new "Sunday evening" church anticipated in the fall.

A Seventh Day Baptist Church in Hempstead provided worship space for the Long Island Baptist Chapel, organized in October 1958. For the next several months, many of the families in the chapel continued to pack their lunches and journey into Manhattan for Sunday School and worship, but they eagerly returned to the island each Sunday night to support the ministry of their growing fellowship under the leadership of Navy chaplain Lonnie Knight. The mission launched a full program that included Sunday School and morning worship in March 1959.[19] Following Knight's transfer in the summer of 1959, Clayton Day assumed pastoral responsibilities.

The Long Island Chapel's search for a permanent home led them in the summer of 1959 to a small gladiola farm. With the help of the Home Mission Board and the Manhattan Church, the congregation purchased the property and began the arduous task of converting the property's bulb-drying barn into a sanctuary! The hours and energies expended in transforming the building impressed upon the members an agricultural metaphor for defining themselves: "Where once flowers and bulbs were grown physically," they explained, "souls would grow spiritually as a witness was provided by the surrounding area."[20] Open rafters, bare light bulbs, and noisy heaters did nothing to dampen the spirits of those who gathered for the first worship service in "the barn" in November 1959.

By the next summer the congregation was ready for a full-time pastor. The Home Mission Board and the Maryland Convention assisted the chapel in calling Don Miller as pastor-director for Long Island. The Pennsylvania native left a large Dallas pastorate in August 1960, hearing what he described as a calling to modern-day Macedonia—the Northeast.[21] Five months later on January 1, 1961, Farmingdale Baptist Church was constituted as Southern Baptists' first congregation on Long Island.

Miller brought with him a fervent evangelistic and missionary spirit, inspired by his own adult conversion experience. He introduced the slogan: "In the heart of Long Island for the hearts of all people." In the winter of 1961, he taught the church's twelve deacons that year's January Bible Study, and then dispatched them in teams to teach the material in six home fellowships. DeLane Ryals was mission pastor of the new Baldwin Chapel from 1962 to 1964, and assisted emerging groups in East Meadow and Westhampton Beach. Three of the "seedling" fellowships begun by the deacons were subsequently organized as churches: Emmanuel Baptist Church in Riverhead (July 1963); Central Nassau Baptist Church in Westbury (September 1963); and North Shore Baptist Church in Kings Park (January 1966).

In addition to these efforts, the Farmingdale Church also ministered to migrant farm workers who passed through Long Island every summer and fall. Don Miller arranged for the Home Mission Board in 1962 to appoint Osbern Clerk as camp pastor for the Cutchogue Labor Camp.[22]

Miller's tenure at Farmingdale was brief (1960–1963), but he returned to Long Island in 1966 as pastor of the North Shore Church,

A. B. Cash (left), who directed the Home Mission Board's program of pioneer missions from 1955 to 1967, discusses a mission strategy for Long Island with Farmingdale pastor Don Miller in 1960.

Kenneth Lyle (left), pastor of the Central Nassau Baptist Church, helped organize a youth center on Long Island in 1968.

where he remained for ten years. In reflecting upon his effective ministry in New York, the pastor stated that his church's "conservative theology and antipathy toward the National Council of Churches" had given it a "sounding board" with conservative Long Islanders.[23]

Larry Walker succeeded Don Miller at the Farmingdale Church in 1964. His leadership, charisma, and fervent evangelistic approach led to dramatic growth. The congregation which had tolerated crude facilities for worship not many years before entered a beautiful four-hundred-seat sanctuary in December 1967.[24]

As noted above, the Farmingdale Church's commitment to growing new churches bore early fruit. The Emmanuel Baptist Church, known originally as the Eastern Suffolk Baptist Chapel, was initiated in February 1962 in the home of Henry Suzukawa. Sunday School and worship were begun that summer in the Masonic Hall of Westhampton Beach through the assistance of Edward and Sandy James, summer missionaries. Under the leadership of pastor James S. Wright, who arrived in 1963, the church sponsored missions in Centereach and in Medford. In 1968 the congregations were constituted, respectively, as the Grace Baptist Church, with Jerry Scruggs as pastor; and as the Calvary Baptist Church, with Clifton E. Barnes as pastor.[25]

Kenneth Lyle came as pastor of the Central Nassau Church in 1963. Through his leadership the congregation became a center for ministry to Westbury and its surrounding communities. "What I'm driving at," he said in a 1968 interview, "is this: if the Christians are not ministering, and every person in the church is not functioning as a minister of Christ, it's not what the body of Christ ought to be."[26]

In 1967 the youthful, bright-eyed pastor applied his affinity for working with teenagers toward creating a youth community center in Westbury called "The Arena." In addition to its youth work, the Central Nassau Church focused upon the needs of alcoholics and neglected senior adults in their community, and created a weekly hospital visitation ministry. Said Lyle, "These ministries have a twofold focus: meeting needs of non-Christians to bring them into a closer relationship with Christ, and strengthening the laymen of the church."[27] The opportunities for ministry on Long Island, demonstrated in large part by the Central Nassau Church, led the Home Mission Board in the late 1960s to appoint Jerry Scruggs as director of Christian social ministry for the Long Island area.

Mission to the Hudson Valley

Southern Baptist work to the north of New York City in the Hudson Valley was initiated by Manhattan Church members Harry and Betty Watson, who in July 1959 opened their Wappingers Falls home for a Bible study fellowship. The "official" membership of the fellowship consisted only of the Watsons for several months, even though numerous persons interested in forming a chapel met with them in their home and in gatherings at Poughkeepsie and Newburgh. With the help of Tom Sims, an Air Force chaplain stationed at Stewart Air Force Base in Newburgh, the group began the Newburgh Baptist Chapel in January 1960, a mission of the Manhattan Church.[28]

Chaplains Francis Knight of Fort Slocum, New York, and Tom Sims provided pastoral leadership for the mission, which almost immediately attracted a large number of military families. In early 1960, several families brought to the Poughkeepsie area by IBM crossed the Hudson River to unite with the mission. In the summer of 1960, these families formed a fellowship of their own, and were later adopted as a mission of the Manhattan Church. Chaplain Charles Meek of Fort Slocum, who was instrumental in the beginnings of the Madison Baptist Church, became interim pastor of the group in August 1960.[29]

The Newburgh Chapel suffered through a restless beginning in 1960, losing almost half its membership to another new mission and meeting in six different locations. Bob Hildreth's arrival as pastor in April 1961 brought the mission some stability, but the young man was asked to divide his responsibilities between both congregations. In September 1961, he led the Newburgh mission to constitute as the Ridgecrest Baptist Church. "Vigorous" though he was described, Hildreth was unable to meet the needs of two full-time missions located several miles apart. One year after his arrival at the Ridgecrest Church, he resigned to devote his full energies to developing the Poughkeepsie mission.

Frank Venable, a native New Jerseyan, came as pastor of the Ridgecrest Church in September 1962. Inheriting a congregation with something of a vagabond reputation and a less than desirable location in downtown Newburgh, he focused his energies upon securing a permanent home for the church. He led the congregation that year to purchase and refurbish an abandoned grocery store building in New Windsor.[30]

The Ridgecrest Church flourished with the leadership of Venable and his successor, Howard Taylor, who arrived in 1968. The growth of the church, however, was heavily dependent upon an influx of transplanted Southern Baptists associated with Stewart Air Force Base. By 1969 membership stood at more than three hundred. The following year brought near disaster to the church. The closing of the air base resulted in the loss of thirty-six families, representing more than half of the church's income and three-fourths of its leadership.[31]

The Poughkeepsie mission was constituted as the Vassar Road Baptist Church in May 1962, one month after Bob Hildreth began devoting his efforts to that work exclusively. A year later the church was ready to enter a large new sanctuary—large enough to accommodate almost all the area's Southern Baptist transplants employed by IBM, should the church be able to enlist them. The pastor made no pretensions about the nature of the church: "IBM built Vassar Road," he stated in 1963.[32] By the end of the decade, the church was approaching a membership of three hundred and had planted a new church in Kingston, New York: the Southside Baptist Church (1968–1988).

Mission to Connecticut and Westchester County

In the summer of 1960, two newcomers to the Manhattan Church, Jack Skelton and Charles Boyer, discovered they were practically neighbors in the distant suburb of Greenwich, Connecticut. The Skeltons and Boyers soon began working together to establish a Sunday evening fellowship in the community. Two families had grown into five by November 1960, when the effort was launched—first in the Boyer home and by early 1961, in the Greenwich YMCA. The group was heartened and confirmed in its vision for a new church by steady growth throughout the year. Sunday School and Sunday morning worship were begun in hopes of soon attaining full church status under the Manhattan Church's guidance.

But in the spring of 1962, hopes for a new church began to fade when several families—including the Boyers—were transferred from the area. The group reverted to a Sunday evening program only. By the summer morale was so low that the few remaining attendees voted to give up on the idea of a new Southern Baptist church in Greenwich—all except Jack and Beverly Skelton, who were away on vacation at the time.[33]

The Skeltons believed wholeheartedly that God had called them to help start a new church and that he had not changed his mind in such a short time. The couple encouraged the group to reconsider their decision and not to give up hope. Hope arrived almost immediately in the persons of Benton and Pat Patterson, who had been instrumental in starting a church in Pennsylvania. The *Saturday Evening Post* journalist and his family were just the inspiration the group needed to rebound and to reclaim their vision.

That fall the fellowship secured Forrest Neal Pack to provide pastoral leadership. The retired Southern Baptist pastor living in the area led the families to resume Sunday School and Sunday morning worship. By January 1963, the group had achieved chapel status. Jack Skelton's ads in Baptist state papers indicating that he was "searching high and low in Connecticut and Westchester for church members" produced results.[34] The Greenwich Baptist Church was constituted in March 1963.

H. Lawrence Martin came in January 1964 as the church's first full-time pastor. He sought to involve the new church in the religious affairs of the community, joining the Fellowship of Greenwich Clergy, and leading an interfaith religious survey that involved Protestant, Catholic, and Jewish congregations.[35] He also worked diligently to find a permanent location for the church. The sophisticated, upscale community tended to look askance at Southern Baptists and even more so, given that the local chapter called the YMCA home. Martin's prospect for a new "home"—a dilapidated configuration of buildings last used as an alcoholic rehabilitation center— did not at first inspire confidence among the membership, nor did it endear the church to the neighbors who feared a new church would upset the peace of their community.

Martin nevertheless convinced the congregation that fifty-seven thousand dollars for the five-acre site was an ideal investment in the church's future. The town zoning board was less amenable, but after negotiating the proposal over several months, the church was given a green light. The Greenwich Baptist Church entered its new home in November 1965. Five years later the church completed a five-hundred-thousand-dollar multi-purpose building on the property.

In December 1966, Lawrence Martin resigned to become a Navy chaplain. A Canadian, Fred Boehmer, was called as pastor in September 1967. He led the congregation in following through on its commitments to chapels in neighboring communities, and later became one of Southern Baptists' most respected leaders in the Northeast.

The Greenwich Church drew a portion of its membership from Westchester County, New York. With a new home and a growing membership, the congregation was ready to explore mission possibilities in 1966. That winter Jack and Mary Wilson and James and Edith Robinson began hosting Sunday evening fellowships in their homes. In early spring the group relocated to the White Plains YMCA and asked Forrest Neal Pack to serve as their pastor as he had done before for the Greenwich Church. Over the next several months as growth continued, the congregation became a chapel, and relocated to rented quarters in a small Methodist church building in Hartsdale.

The new year opened with the Hartsdale Chapel regularly welcoming thirty to forty worshipers each Sunday. The congregation was constituted as the Westchester Baptist Church in November 1967. In April 1968, the church welcomed its first full-time pastor, Robert Fling, whose wife Helen was national president of Woman's Missionary Union. The young congregation advanced steadily under the couple's mature leadership, sponsoring a chapel in neighboring Rockland County, and initiating a ministry to international women in 1969.[36]

At the same time the Greenwich Church was birthing a new congregation in Westchester County, it also was reaching out to the community of

The Greenwich Baptist Church worships in its newly refurbished sanctuary in the mid-1960s.

Wilton, Connecticut, where Carlos and Jean Burns, and six other member families resided. The group formed the Wilton Baptist Fellowship around the Burns' coffee table in January 1967. The next month the fellowship began Sunday evening services in the community's American Legion Hall. Growth came rapidly for the Wilton congregation, allowing it with the help of the Home Mission Board to call a pastor, Edward James, in April 1967. The Wilton Baptist Church was constituted in December 1967.[37] Thomas Bourne became the church's second pastor in July 1969.

Mission to Rockland County

Following a brief tenure as pastor of the Manhattan Baptist Church, Maurice Fain relocated to Rockland County, New York, in August 1967. He came with names in hand of four prospective families who had expressed interest in forming a new Southern Baptist chapel in the area. Previously, these families had driven considerable distances to worship in neighboring counties. With Rockland County designated as a Project 500 new work site, Fain arrived with the firm backing of the Home Mission Board in his intention to plant a new church.

In September the families began gathering for Sunday evening fellowship in the home of Marion and Juanita Ray. By the middle of October, the group had secured the West Pomona Community Center for Sunday morning Bible study and worship. The Westchester Baptist Church assumed sponsorship of the new chapel in January 1968. In September 1969, the congregation was constituted as the Rockland Baptist Church. Fain remained as pastor until his retirement in 1989.[38]

Mission to Staten Island

Although the Borough of Staten Island cannot be considered a suburban area outside the city limits of New York, its neighborhoods function as bedroom communities of the city like those in New Jersey. After the completion of the Verrazano Narrows Bridge in 1962, linking the island conveniently with Brooklyn and adding to the accessibility of Manhattan, the area experienced a population boom that lasted several years.

Not unexpectedly, a number of Southern Baptists were among the newcomers to the island. In the mid-1960s, they sought the help of the Manhattan Church in organizing a mission. The Staten Island Chapel was gathered in 1964, and over the next few years benefited from an innovative telephone survey process through which many new prospects were discovered.[39] With the leadership of Richard Ridgeway and, later, pastor Lewis Lowe, and with financial support from the Bethsaida Baptist Church in Atlanta, the congregation was constituted as the Richboro Baptist Church in May 1968. A succession of pastors, many of them assisted by the Home Mission Board, led the church in various community ministries. The church disbanded in 1994.

Uniting in Fellowship and Mission

Some of those in Maryland who originally opposed the idea of sponsoring a chapel in New York City were concerned that a new congregation there would suffer a rather forlorn existence, given that their state convention not be in a position geographically to offer the kind of moral and spiritual support a church needed to survive and grow. But neither was any other state convention close enough to nurture the Manhattan Baptist Chapel. The new work needed to create its own fellowship of churches in the Northeast.

Fears that the Manhattan Church would be too isolated to function effectively were never realized. The church was simply too preoccupied with the challenge of its mission ever to feel alone! Within a short time, that passionate mission concern helped produce a family of churches in the Northeast.

The Northeastern Association

In February 1960, representatives from the Delaware Valley Baptist Church in Levittown, Pennsylvania, the Madison Baptist Church, and the Manhattan Baptist Church met with members of the Screven Memorial Baptist Church in Portsmouth, New Hampshire, to plan a new association. On April 29, 1960, the Northeastern District Association was constituted by messengers from five churches and six chapels. Officers of the association were: Paul James, moderator; Howard Hovde, vice-moderator; Sam Sorrell, clerk; and Norvell Jones, treasurer.[40] The geographical area of the association was a vast expanse of nine states from Pennsylvania to Maine. The new body immediately became by far the most populated associational territory in the Southern Baptist Convention.

The Home Mission Board appointed Elmer Sizemore, a native of Hell-for-Certain, Kentucky, as area missionary for the association. He served for a brief time in New York City assisting Paul James. In 1962 he went to New England to help develop new churches in that area. Ralph W. Neighbor Jr. also worked briefly as an area missionary in New Jersey before moving to Pennsylvania to cultivate new work.

The Northeastern Association, though expansive, engaged in a coordinated effort that involved all its churches. As in upstate New York, pastors and laypeople were willing to travel lengthy distances to share fellowship and ministry with one another. The association's agenda included a typical menu of activities and programs designed to provide a supportive network for the churches.

By 1962 the association had grown to nineteen churches and thirty-three missions. The three dozen faithful who comprised the Manhattan Chapel only five years before had, with their offspring, grown to number three thousand people "moving with determination to win lost souls to Christ and establish New Testament churches."[41] Such growth necessitated a parceling of the association into more functional geographic divisions.

Meeting at Wrightstown, New Jersey, messengers in October 1962 affirmed the dissolution of the Northeastern Association into three new bodies: the Delaware Valley Association, centered in Philadelphia; the New England Association; and the Metropolitan New York Association. Paul James expressed the hope that the same sentiment which had produced such gratifying results in the regional association would be found among the new associations. James wrote: "By the grace of God new and greater milestones will be reached in the days ahead if we jealously guard and zealously cultivate that which has brought our Southern Baptist Convention and our Northeastern Baptist Association to the advanced position of this present hour; namely, a sense of mission. Let us pray earnestly that none of us may lose this."[42] Messengers agreed that ongoing dialogue and fellowship be maintained among the associations to pave the way for the earliest possible formation of an area or state convention.

The Metropolitan New York Baptist Association

Of the nineteen churches which comprised the Northeastern Association in 1962, eight were located within the metropolitan New York area. Forty messengers from the Manhattan, Madison, Farmingdale, Ridgecrest, Suburban, Vassar Road, Bergen, and First Brooklyn (discussed in the next chapter) Churches convened while still at Wrightstown to constitute the Metropolitan New York Baptist Association. Paul James was elected moderator. In December 1963, he resigned his pastoral responsibilities to devote his full-time efforts to directing the ministry of the association. Peter Rhea Jones and James W. Cox, both visiting scholars at Princeton Theological Seminary, guided the Manhattan Church through an interim period until Maurice Fain arrived in 1965 as pastor.

Deeply held denominational loyalties were transferred to "Metro" as the association became the rallying point of home missions activity for the churches in New Jersey, New York City, and southwestern Connecticut. Paul James applied his skills in administration and public relations with the same enthusiasm and conviction he had brought to the Manhattan Baptist Church six years before. His message to Southern Baptists was that they were no longer represented in the metropolitan area by a few scattered churches and struggling chapels, but by an association—a missionary and

Pastors and leaders of the Metropolitan Association in 1962. Top row (left to right): Don Miller, DeLane Ryals, Herb Bidgood, Leobardo Estrada, David Morgan. Front row (left to right): Quinn Pugh, Robert Hildreth, Paul James, Gene Maston.

ministry infrastructure that signaled the denomination's permanent commitment to the region.

The Metro Association's visibility among Southern Baptists—enhanced by Paul James's service as first vice president of the SBC in 1963–1964—created opportunities for pastors, WMU leaders, and other laypeople to address conference gatherings and conventionwide meetings throughout the mid-1960s. Stories about the association's work were popular among convention publicists who highlighted the challenge and adventure of ministry in the nation's largest city. For much of 1965–1966, Kenneth Chafin of Southern Seminary, one of Southern Baptists' most respected leaders in evangelism, made the association his laboratory for studying urban evangelism.[43]

Student and youth ministry, church starting, and mission organizations were among the activities around which the churches of the Metro Association united. In May 1963, Gene Maston had the distinction of bringing the largest contingent to the Maryland Convention's annual student retreat. Ken Lyle was delighted in October 1964 to welcome 130 teenagers to the association's first youth retreat. By the mid-1960s, the association had in place a mission fund to provide substantial support to new chapels. And keeping the spirit and priority of missions at the forefront of associational life was a strong WMU organization guided by women like Eileen Morgan, Matrel McCarter, and Norma Pugh.

The Metropolitan New York Baptist Association represented the eastern or "Maryland" bloc of Southern Baptist life in New York, northern New Jersey, and Fairfield County, Connecticut. Much remains to be said, however, of churches in the region. Members of the Manhattan Church in the late 1950s, while possessing extraordinary missionary vision, could not then have comprehended the extent to which even the global parameters of the Great Commission were within their reach—just one borough away in Brooklyn.

CHAPTER SEVEN

Baptist Convention of New York

MISSION TO THE WORLD

Thus says the Lord God ... things shall not remain as they are." When David Morgan used this text from Ezekiel 21:26 for his sermon, he was encouraging messengers of the Northeastern Association to see a divine mandate in the proposed dissolution of their fellowship into three new groups. That October day in 1962, he spoke of the spiritual revolution Christ's coming had unleashed upon all the world. As pastor of New York Baptists' first "international" church—The First Baptist Church of Brooklyn—he was uniquely qualified to speak in such terms.

By the early 1960s, Southern Baptists were becoming increasingly aware that their churches could be found in all fifty states. Much fanfare greeted the announcement in 1963 that a new SBC church had been constituted in Vermont—the fiftieth state entered by the denomination. Terms like "southwide" and "southland," although still used by some even today, were no longer appropriate to describe the programs and emphases of the Southern Baptist Convention. Provincial pride was slowly giving way to a mission awareness for the whole nation—geographically, at least.

If Southern Baptists were content to be confined to their regional "Zion" prior to the breakthrough of an enlarged vision at midcentury, they were also intent upon remaining a "white" denomination. This intention derived both from a lack of vision for what Southern Baptists could become, especially in new work areas, but also from a prevailing racism epitomized by the dictum, "separate but equal."

When A. B. Cash broached the idea of a church in New York City, his thoughts and concerns were with the white population. He saw the metropolitan area as an immense mission field, in that it was served by only one hundred "white" Baptist churches—far less than in Chicago with half the population. He calculated that to replicate the same "density" of white churches in the Northeast that existed in parts of the South, Southern Baptists needed to start thirty thousand new congregations in the region— enough to realize the total goal established in the Thirty Thousand Movement![1] Cash's use of a southern, white context to discuss his vision for churches in the Northeast is revealing.

Paul James dreamed of a large family of churches to minister to the masses in the Northeast, but like Cash his vision initially did not include people of color. While he and the Manhattan Church were willing, even delighted, to welcome a Nigerian student for membership, neither James nor the church conceived of starting congregations that would reflect the ethnic and language diversity of the metropolitan area.

Neither Slave nor Free . . . But One in Christ

Word of economic opportunity brought Basil Hewitt and his family from the Panama Canal Zone to Brooklyn in 1959. He was part of a wave of migration in the 1950s that brought laborers to the United States from the Caribbean Islands and Central America.

Like many immigrants from the regions, Hewitt brought with him a deep religious faith that began in the home. Family devotions were an integral part of the religious culture of the Islands and parts of Central America. Following breakfast, devotions were a time of Scripture reading, recitation, and prayer around the meal table. In a Christian home, failing to observe this practice was unthinkable.

Shortly after his arrival in Brooklyn, Hewitt and friends he had known at the Bethany Baptist Church in the Canal Zone began gathering on Sunday afternoons to observe family devotions together. Although some families attended houses of worship in Brooklyn, none of these churches came even close to providing the kind of fellowship and nurture they were accustomed to back home. The afternoon devotions offered the spiritual refreshment and intimacy they longed for.[2]

By the winter of 1960, the group had outgrown Hewitt's house. David Morgan Jr., an immigrant of Nicaraguan and Jamaican ancestry, opened his Crown Street home for the fellowship, and initiated a Sunday morning worship service. His faith had been nurtured in the parsonage of David and Eileen Morgan, who at that time served the Bethany Church under the auspices of the Home Mission Board. Acquaintance with Southern Baptists in Panama led Hewitt and the younger Morgan to explore the possibility of their Brooklyn "mission" becoming affiliated with the SBC.

David Morgan Jr. felt a desire to relate to Southern Baptists despite a humiliating incident with a church in the United States. Blacks in Panama and the West Indies did not share the legacy of racial segregation that their brothers and sisters in America had endured, and thus were somewhat unfamiliar with traditional Jim Crow sanctions. While not oblivious to racial animosity in the United States, neither were they self-conscious about their own skin color.

During basic training at Fort Gordon, Georgia, David Morgan Jr. traveled early one Sunday morning to the train station in Augusta to meet a relative. The train's delay gave him an opportunity to worship in a down-town church. As he passed toward the colonnade of the old First Baptist Church, he no doubt noticed the historical marker reminding all that the Southern Baptist Convention had been founded there more than a hundred years before. The handsome, uniformed soldier made his way to the front pews in the center section of the sanctuary.

In a moment, David Morgan felt a hand on his shoulder. Behind him stood two deacons who wore concerned expressions. "While we welcome you in a Christian spirit," they said, "we do not allow colored people to sit in the front section." They were "sure" the young man "meant no harm or disrespect," coming as he surely did from some place unfamiliar with the social customs of the South. Morgan hurried through the back door and proceeded across the street to a lunch counter, where he was served without incident or delay.

Seven years had passed since this unforgettable incident. Now Morgan and his friends were ready to see what Southern Baptists were like in New York City, of all places. Through contacts with the Home Mission Board in the spring of 1960, Morgan, Hewitt, Harold Flowers, and several other members of the group arranged for a meeting with Paul James. The Manhattan pastor greeted them cordially as they shared with him home movies, tape recordings, and photographs of their fellowship gatherings. Their aim was to secure the endorsement of James, the sponsorship of the Manhattan Church, and the support of the Home Mission Board in reas-signing Pastor Morgan from the Canal Zone to Brooklyn.[3]

By midsummer they had accomplished their first two objectives. Just as the Manhattan Church had resisted "drawing circles" to prescribe the racial mix of their own congregation, so when the time came to embrace a mission that looked like few others in the Southern Baptist Convention, the church did not balk. Predominantly black congregations in the SBC could be counted on one hand in the late 1950s. The growing family of churches and mission chapels in the New York metro area was welcoming a member to the table no one had expected. Things were changing.

A Church Grows in Brooklyn

Once the Manhattan Church's sponsorship of the Brooklyn fellowship was established in the summer of 1960, the congregations invited Army chaplain Clayton Day, chair of the Manhattan Church's missions committee, to become part-time pastor of the new work. The Brooklyn congregation "went public" by relocating from members' homes to the Bedford Avenue YMCA. Although their meeting place was sometimes so cold that members worshiped in overcoats, the Y proved to be an adequate location for Bible study and worship for almost two years.

David and Eileen Morgan were intrigued with the possibility of ministering to a "United Nations" congregation in New York City. Before they committed themselves to the new calling, however, they had to know that Paul James was truly committed to a multicultural witness for Southern Baptists in the Northeast. Pastor Morgan arrived unannounced at the Manhattan Baptist Church on a Sunday morning in the summer of 1960. Having never met this distinguished-looking gentleman who spoke the King's English with such precision and vigor, James and the congregation had no idea who Morgan was.

James spoke that morning on the subject of spiritual sight. Using the gospel story of the man whose distorted sight made him see people "like trees walking," the pastor admonished congregants to see all people as Jesus saw them—as individuals created in the image of God. David Morgan was sure now of his calling to Brooklyn. Paul James was a man with whom he could work.[4]

In September word arrived from the Home Mission Board that David Morgan had been approved for reassignment to New York City. He assumed responsibility as pastor of the Brooklyn Chapel in January 1961, and in December of that year, the congregation was constituted as the First Baptist Church of Brooklyn. Among the charter members were many persons to whom Morgan had ministered in the Caribbean Islands and in Central America. Fermin Whittaker was a young "revolutionary" who once evaded police in Panama by hiding under his pastor's bed. Whittaker later became executive director of the California Southern Baptist Convention.[5]

David Morgan's first concern was to secure a permanent location for the Brooklyn Church. If the congregation was to "minister to the moral and spiritual needs of all people" as its charter stated, then a better, more spacious facility was needed. Morgan could not, for example, envision being able to touch the lives of U.N. diplomats with whom some of his parishioners were in contact. "You can't invite ambassadors to worship at the YMCA," he observed.[6] Neither did he anticipate being able to reach international students at such a locale. He knew, in fact, that only the "diehards" could be counted upon to crowd their way into cramped and inadequate quarters.

In October 1962, with assistance from the Home Mission Board, the First Baptist Church purchased a stately old church building in the Bushwick section of Brooklyn. Though somewhat in disrepair, the building which once housed a German Baptist congregation featured a four-hundred-seat sanctuary, considerable educational space, and an apartment for the pastor. Members of the Evergreen German Baptist Church, out of a desire to "pass the torch" to another Baptist witness in the transitional neighborhood, accepted the First Baptist Church's bid of one hundred thousand dollars— the lowest of several bids.

Pastor David Morgan directs the worship of the First Baptist Church of Brooklyn at the Bedford Avenue YMCA in 1961.

The banner draped across the front of the building heralded the "Grand Opening" of the First Baptist Church of Brooklyn at 455 Evergreen Avenue. Members representing sixteen nations gathered in January 1963 to share a service of thanksgiving for the new facility. Guests included Courts Redford, president of the Home Mission Board, Roy Gresham of the Baptist Convention of Maryland, and a sprinkling of United Nations personnel.

The joy of the service was dampened, however, by news that the Morgan family had been robbed at knifepoint by burglars in the early hours of the morning. Family members were bound and gagged while their apartment was ransacked. The bandits made off with Eileen Morgan's engagement ring, other jewelry, and $255 in cash. A rumor evidently had circulated at a neighborhood bar that the couple living in the apartment had purchased the church and were "loaded with money." Some of his family members required medical attention, but David Morgan was stoic and philosophical about the incident: "This dramatizes the need for a Christian witness," he said.[7]

The witness of the First Baptist Church of Brooklyn (renamed the Evergreen Baptist Church in the mid-1980s) was enhanced by the visibility and space the new building afforded. Under David Morgan's leadership the church grew rapidly, numbering almost five hundred members by the time of his retirement in 1969. The pastor's irresistible charm and wit, and his experience in dealing with all kinds of people in all kinds of situations, kept him in good stead as he guided a diverse congregation in which "an atmosphere of singleness of purpose was not always evident."[8]

Morgan's promotional skills also impacted the ministry of Southern Baptists' first "international" church in the Northeast. His tenure was punctuated by grand celebrations and observances, like an anniversary service in 1965 that featured Lord Hugh Caradon, British Ambassador to the United Nations, as the guest speaker.[9] David Morgan had many friends in high places and did not hesitate to call on them in the interest of advancing the ministry of the First Baptist Church.

The Good News *En Español*

Was the shape of the future for Southern Baptists in the Northeast a multicultural, multilingual family of churches? Visionaries pondered the possibilities.

While yet a mission, the Brooklyn congregation extended its witness to the Hudson Valley in June 1961. Summer missionary Fermin Whittaker went there to assist the Ridgecrest Church with a Spanish-speaking ministry to migrant workers in Kerhonkson. His efforts were typical of the Home Mission Board's language ministry work in rural areas of the South.

By this time, however, Paul James, David Morgan, and board leaders like Loyd Corder were coming to grips with the fact that a vast number of the area's permanent residents spoke Spanish. The potential for language ministry went far beyond providing for the spiritual needs of migrant workers. Large communities of Puerto Ricans in East Harlem and elsewhere, immigrants from Central and South America, and a growing number of Cuban refugees made the metropolitan area similar to parts of Texas and southern California where for decades the Home Mission Board had ministered to large Spanish-speaking populations.

Loyd Corder turned to Leobardo Estrada for help. One of the most gifted Hispanic Southern Baptist leaders of his time, Estrada was pastor of the First Spanish Baptist Church of Los Angeles, and weekly host of *La Hora Bautista*, the Spanish-language broadcast of the *Baptist Hour* heard throughout Latin America. Born in Culiacán, Mexico, he grew up in Corpus Christi, Texas, where his barrio adjoined the mean streets of *"Sal Si Puedes,"* roughly translated—"get out if you can!"[10]

So convinced was Corder of the potential for ministry among Hispanics in New York City that he asked Estrada himself to consider moving across the continent to direct the work in the Northeast. The pastor answered politely that he would think and pray about the matter, though he did not take the offer seriously. When Corder called a second time, Estrada began praying in earnest, but his prayer was, "Lord, help those people find someone."[11] They already had, and he knew it.

After much soul searching and assurances of the Home Mission Board's support, Leobardo Estrada agreed to leave his prominent Los Angeles pastorate to become the architect, engineer, and master builder of the language missions enterprise in the metropolitan New York City area. Like Paul James, he came to the Northeast with an auspicious title and job description, but at least the Manhattan pastor had thirty members to call a "flock" when he arrived. Estrada had only promises of cooperation from James, David Morgan, and the churches of the Northeastern Association.

"Lord, this work is too big, and I'm too small," Estrada prayed plaintively after unpacking his suitcases in a Manhattan YMCA in February 1962. The biting cold of the New York winter and the deep sense of loneliness he felt were almost more than he could bear. He had left behind his wife, Isabel, and their four children to complete the school year in California. Yet at the same time he felt confident in his calling.[12] Something new was on the horizon for Southern Baptists in the Northeast.

The challenge of the work in New York City was big—much bigger, actually, than the new director of language ministries even imagined. His assumption was that Manhattan was the extent of New York City. Only after beginning his work did he realize that four other boroughs needed his attention, not to mention areas in New Jersey and elsewhere beyond the city limits. Where would he begin? He determined to focus his efforts initially in the vicinity of the Manhattan Baptist Church on West Fifty-seventh Street. The congregation agreed to offer a Spanish-speaking Sunday School class with Estrada as the teacher.

Leobardo Estrada walked the midtown streets of Manhattan, distributing gospel tracts and promotional materials to anyone who looked Hispanic. When faced with inclement weather, he took his efforts downstairs to the subway stations. After making more than two hundred personal contacts over the course of a month, he was ready to launch his class on Sunday, March 11, 1962. Estrada stood at the entrance of the Manhattan Church, eager to greet a crowd of newcomers in his mother tongue.

Much to his chagrin, only four prospects arrived that morning. But Marcelena Scarpeta and Efraim Horta of Cuba and Guillermo and Aixa Basantes of Columbia liked what they saw, and promised to come back with friends the following week. "It is going to take time, work, and prayer to do this work," Estrada recorded in his report to the Home Mission Board—"We need to know that we are here to serve."

Heartened by the receptiveness of his first four prospects, Estrada continued his personal efforts with tracts and handbills, and took out ads in Spanish newspapers announcing the new class. Word began filtering back to places like Cuba and Columbia that Spanish work had begun in Manhattan. Each week the pastor received letters telling him of persons who recently had moved into the area from Latin American countries.[13]

Within three months the group had begun worship with an afternoon prayer meeting in the sanctuary of the Manhattan Baptist Church. During the English church's morning worship service, Estrada provided a translation over headphones for Spanish-speaking worshipers. The pastor also enlisted Manhattan Church members to teach basic English skills—a program that by the fall produced larger crowds than he ever could have imagined that Sunday in March, when the "first fruit" of his labor was only four persons in attendance. By year's end the Manhattan Church had organized a Spanish Sunday School department that soon became the Spanish chapel of the Manhattan Church.

José Ruiz, a Cuban, arrived as pastor of the growing mission in January 1964. Under his leadership the congregation was constituted with 107

Leobardo Estrada was featured on the cover of the Maryland Baptist *with baptismal candidate Xiomara Bacallao, the first convert won under his ministry in New York City.*

charter members in July 1964 as the *Primero Iglesia Bautista de Manhattan*.[14] Ruiz was succeeded in 1965 by Alfonso Flores, who also served a brief tenure. José Sanchez, who became pastor in 1967, guided the congregation to experience steady growth and in 1969 to purchase a church building at 178th and Wadsworth Avenue, not far from the George Washington Bridge.

In seven short years Estrada's efforts yielded an extraordinary harvest in Manhattan. Yet the First Spanish church was only part of a larger circle of churches and missions begun with his help during this period.

In Queens, Estrada worked with lay preacher Jaime Santamaria to establish a Spanish Sunday School department in what became the Highland Avenue Baptist Church. Santamaria, a medical researcher who fled Cuba in 1961, opened his home in Queens for Bible study and fellowship with Spanish-speaking members of the Highland Avenue Church.[15] The group became the nucleus of the Ebenezer Baptist Church, constituted in March 1969 with Eliseo Toirac as pastor.

In October 1963, Estrada assisted the Bergen Baptist Church in starting a Bible study fellowship among Cuban refugees in West New York, New Jersey. The Home Mission Board in June 1964 purchased a small building for the chapel, which was constituted the next year as the Nazareth Baptist Church.[16] Southern Baptist Convention President Wayne Dehoney was present for the dedication of the building. "There's something alive and vital here," he remarked as he reflected upon his experience in the metropolitan area. He hoped that the rest of the SBC could be galvanized by the kind of spirit he felt in the region.[17] José Ruiz was the congregation's first pastor; he was succeeded by Nicomedes Flores, who arrived in March 1968.

Estrada also helped Pastor José Juan Corti, a Venezuelan, gather a chapel in Paterson, New Jersey. Pastor Corti's effort, begun in 1963, was sponsored by the Suburban Baptist Church in Wayne. When that church left the Metropolitan Association in 1965, the Bergen Baptist Church assumed sponsorship of the chapel. In 1967 the congregation was constituted as the Central Spanish Baptist Church of Paterson.[18]

By the mid-1960s, ministry among Hispanics in the metropolitan area was gaining momentum. The First Baptist Church of Brooklyn sponsored a Spanish Sunday School department with Luis Segura as the lay leader. The Spanish Calvary Baptist Church was born of this effort in 1968. Eloy Cruz was pastor of the church from its inception until his retirement in 1989.

The Nazareth Baptist Church became a center of mission expansion in the densely populated urban areas of northeastern New Jersey, where a steady stream of refugees from Cuba resulted in a dramatic increase of the Hispanic population. In 1967 the church's outreach efforts to Passaic led to the establishment of the First Spanish Baptist Church. Heliodoro Fis was the congregation's first pastor. The Nazareth Church also planted Spanish churches in Hoboken (1968) and Hackensack (1969) which disbanded several years later.

Further to the south, the Nazareth Church in 1969 launched the Bethlehem Baptist Church in Elizabeth, New Jersey, with Rafael Urdaneta as pastor. The following year the congregation united with an American Baptist group from Newark to form the First Spanish Baptist Church of Elizabeth. Pentecostal or "charismatic" tendencies within the church resulted in a division of the congregation in the mid-1970s which ultimately produced the David Livingstone Baptist Church and its mission outreach, the Jerusalem Baptist Chapel.[19]

Leo Estrada's Sunday School "class" had grown remarkably. In the summer of 1964—only two years into his ministry in the Northeast— almost two hundred worshipers from eight points of Spanish work gathered at the First Baptist Church of Brooklyn to celebrate eleven baptisms. Wayne Dehoney, in his 1964 president's address to the annual session of the Southern Baptist Convention, acknowledged Estrada's accomplishments. "We must break out of the Bible-belt South!" he implored messengers. The Dallas gathering subsequently elected Estrada second vice-president of the convention.[20]

From Brooklyn to the Bronx

While Spanish work was growing at an almost feverish pace in the metro area, the First Baptist Church of Brooklyn kept pace with an active mission program of its own. The Brooklyn congregation reached out to other emerging communities of Central Americans and Caribbean Islanders in New York City.

Members of the First Baptist Church had friends and relatives in the Bronx who found it difficult to make a long journey to Brooklyn each Sunday. The church thus sponsored a community Bible study in the borough led by Lloyd Rose, who opened his home for the group. Within four years the fellowship was constituted as the Evangel Baptist Church, with Rose as pastor.[21]

In the mid-1970s, leadership problems and charismatic tendencies within the Evangel Church led some members to unite with the congregation's chapel in the northeast Bronx. This fellowship, under the direction of pastor Cleveland Henry, was constituted in 1982 as the Outreach Baptist Church. The Evangel Church dissolved its Southern Baptist ties shortly thereafter, and sold its building—a former synagogue purchased by the Home Mission Board.[22] Better results followed the board's investment in another Bronx synagogue on Honeywell Avenue.

Sam Simpson was among the first deacons ordained by the First Baptist Church of Brooklyn. The precocious young Jamaican had come to the States the year before for theological studies in Chicago. When he became discouraged about pursuing the ministry, due in part to the racism he encountered in America, he came to Brooklyn to live with his aunt. There he met David Morgan, who was to become his mentor.[23]

In 1963 Simpson knelt before his church family and a council of clergy from Baptist unions across the Caribbean to be ordained to the gospel ministry. While a student at Northeastern Bible College, he and his new bride Lola were commissioned by the First Baptist Church to begin a ministry in the Bronx. They began their work in the summer of 1964 in the home of Cecelia Robinson. The Simpsons met regularly with members of the Brooklyn Church and interested neighbors to pray for direction in the new venture.[24] Their answer was provided in part through the charm and intellect of a Mexican-born pastor who could speak a little Hebrew.

Synagogues were for sale in the transitional communities of the Bronx in the early 1960s. When Leobardo Estrada called on one rabbi to discuss a potential real estate deal, he greeted the congregational leader in a traditional Hebrew idiom. Surprised and puzzled, the rabbi responded similarly, asking to hear more of the strangely accented Hebrew. The two struck up a friendship and a favorable agreement for the First Baptist Church to secure the property with a grant from the Home Mission Board.

The following week the rabbi and language missions leader again exchanged greetings, but this time the mood was more somber. The rabbi explained that his congregation's by-laws unfortunately forbad him to sell the property to a religious organization. He could, however, circumvent the restriction by selling the building to Estrada personally. For a brief time, therefore, Estrada owned a dilapidated former synagogue in the Bronx![25]

In November 1964, the building was dedicated as the home of the Bronx Baptist Chapel, and of the Simpsons, who occupied the cramped living space above the corridor-like sanctuary. Core members Pat and Hervin Rattray, Hyacinth Francis, Joy Walker, and Cecelia Robinson helped put guests at ease who were taken aback by the depressed neighborhood and humble building. When newcomers entered the building, "they fell in love with the Word preached, the warmth of the fellowship, and the love of the people."[26] The Bronx Baptist Church was constituted in November 1966. Sam Simpson was later appointed by the Home Mission Board as pastor-director for the Bronx. In 1989 Carol S. Garrett produced a book chronicling Simpson's ministry—*Sam Simpson: Architect of Hope* (Birmingham: New Hope Press).

Under Pastor Simpson's leadership, the church grew rapidly as it addressed the spiritual, educational, and social needs of the community. By the end of the decade, the congregation had outgrown its Honeywell Avenue address, and relocated to a spacious sanctuary on East 187th Street. The Bronx church retained its original building as a mission point for an ongoing witness to the neighborhood. The Honeywell Avenue Baptist Chapel continues to resound with worship each Sunday.

. . . to Harlem

Once new work had been initiated in the Bronx, the First Baptist Church of Brooklyn turned its attention to the needs of its constituency in the Harlem section of Manhattan. In the fall of 1964, the church brought pastor David Jemmott from Panama to start a mission outreach in the community. The fellowship he gathered chose the Theresa Hotel at the corner of Seventh Avenue and 125th Street as its meeting place. This was the same hotel where Soviet chairman Nikita Khrushchev met with Fidel Castro in 1960, and where Malcolm X had his headquarters for a time.

Jemmott's ministry developed steadily among his fellow Panamanians and West Indian immigrants. With assistance from the Home Mission Board, the group was constituted as the Patmos Baptist Church in June 1968.[27]

Working in tandem with Jemmott to provide ministry in Harlem were members of the First Baptist Church: Roderick Loney and Rodolph Morgan. Loney, who earned a doctorate in education from Columbia

University, began his work in 1966, developing a literacy program with mobile "reading units." In 1968 he was appointed by the Home Mission Board to continue his literacy efforts and to develop a counseling program as director of the Harlem Educational Services Mission.[28]

Rodolph Morgan was a bivocational pastor who divided his time working for the National Council of Churches and assisting the First Baptist Church and the Metropolitan Association in mission outreach. He was founding pastor of the Atonement Baptist Church (1970), a congregation on the west side of Brooklyn that was developed under the sponsorship of the Patmos Church. Like its parent congregation, the Atonement Church was heavily involved in community ministries.

. . . and to the Haitian Community

When Francois Duvalier declared himself president of Haiti for life in 1964, many Haitians lost hope of ever experiencing relief from the dictator's oppressive and corrupt regime, or of escaping their grinding poverty. An exodus from this poorest of nations in the Western Hemisphere began in the mid-1960s, bringing a large community of Haitians to the metropolitan New York area.

Among the refugees was Pierre Ludovic St. Phard, a pastor who in 1947 had helped organize the first Baptist seminary in Haiti. St. Phard became a well-known and outspoken Christian leader whose views put him at odds with political authorities. Forced out of his homeland in the early 1960s, he and his wife Emma moved to Brooklyn where they met David Morgan, whom Pierre had known while studying in Jamaica.[29]

St. Phard noticed an ad in a local newspaper describing Leobardo Estrada's desire to start Baptist churches among various language groups. The Haitian leader contacted Estrada, who suggested that he share his burden for a French-speaking ministry with David Morgan. The First Baptist Church already had a small contingent of Haitians who expressed interest in initiating such a new work. Estrada encouraged St. Phard to invite friends to his own two-bedroom apartment to discuss the idea. He did, and fifty-seven showed up for the first meeting in February 1965![30]

Given this overwhelming response, the First Baptist Church immediately established the St. Phard residence as a mission point for Sunday afternoon worship and fellowship. Within months the group began meeting at the Hanson Place YMCA in Brooklyn, with a full program of Bible study and worship in French. In June 1966 the *Église Baptiste Française* (French-speaking Baptist Church) of Brooklyn was constituted with almost seventy members.[31] Pierre and Emma St. Phard were appointed that year as missionaries by the Home Mission Board, which also helped the congregation secure two synagogues for church buildings in 1968 and 1978.

The St. Phards were assisted in their ministry by a house guest, Jean-Baptiste Thomas, who had come to the States for his education at the City University of New York. The young man intended to return to Haiti after completing his degree to pursue a teaching job as a supplement to his income as a pastor. While in Brooklyn, he learned from his mentor, Pastor St. Phard, who sent him to Asbury Park, New Jersey, to launch the French-speaking church's first chapel in 1966. Later in the decade, Thomas was assigned to assist a fellowship of Haitians in Manhattan who wished to start a church.[32]

Jean-Baptiste Thomas became pastor of the French-speaking Baptist Church of Brooklyn after Pierre St. Phard's retirement in 1969. By then, several hundred Haitians were gathering each Sunday for worship in Brooklyn. The foundation was laid for the church to become a sponsor of new Haitian congregations across the metropolitan area and beyond.

Ministry among Eastern Europeans

John Kasa, bivocational pastor of the First Polish Baptist Church of Brooklyn, also heard of Leobardo Estrada's work. The first Baptist ministry among Polish immigrants in New York City was initiated in 1908 by the New York Baptist City Mission Society. In 1932 the ministry was constituted as a church. Never before in its history had the tiny church had a pastor to devote his full-time efforts to ministry. Kasa, who had been pastor of the church part-time for seven years, had his hopes dashed for seeing that pattern change when the society announced in 1962 that it was terminating support for bilingual churches.

Kasa contacted Estrada to explore the possibilities of becoming a part of Southern Baptists' growing family of churches in the Northeast. Fortunately for Kasa, the Home Mission Board's northeastern representative for language missions was Elias Golonka, a Polish-American. Estrada had no difficulty convincing him to get the board involved in ministry to the large Slavic population in the metropolitan area.

John Kasa was appointed by the board as a pastoral missionary, allowing him to devote full-time effort to the church. Additionally, the board loaned the church seventy-five hundred dollars which, along with gifts from other Slavic churches, enabled the church to purchase its first building in fifty years. In December 1963, the First Polish Baptist Church of Brooklyn became the first church in the Metropolitan New York Association not originally organized as a Southern Baptist church, and the first Polish church ever affiliated with the Southern Baptist Convention.[33]

Multicultural Urban Ministry in Queens and Brooklyn

By the late 1960s, the Metropolitan Association had begun incorporating into its strategy for church extension a strong emphasis upon "multiple" ministries (after-school care, literacy work, youth programs, etc). The Harlem Educational Services Mission was an excellent example of this new priority. This broader purpose developed as a natural outgrowth of churches penetrating some of the most destitute urban areas of the nation. Pastor Lloyd Burrus, who led the African-American Zion Temple Baptist Church in Brooklyn to unite with the association in 1968, became a powerful and articulate advocate for increased social ministry among the churches.[34] In his thinking the programs were far more than just "spin-off" ministries, as Paul James sometimes called them.

James questioned what he perceived as the Home Mission Board's shifting emphasis toward social ministry, feeling that funds used in such projects could better be spent in developing self-supporting churches to strengthen the financial base of the association. The church-centered missions program that had served the metro area so well for a decade did not, in his opinion, need to be abandoned for this new approach. The associational leader preferred a "both-and" approach to church planting and social action, but felt that the latter should always be a secondary concern. The Highland Avenue Baptist Church in Queens epitomized for him what a Southern Baptist church in the Northeast should be.[35]

Begun in May 1963 as a chapel of the Manhattan Baptist Church, the Highland Avenue congregation was a unique blend of cultures and nationalities. German-born Siegfried Enge was the church's first pastor. James Wright became pastor of the Highland Avenue Church in January 1967, following his resignation from the Emmanuel Baptist Church in Riverhead, Long Island. Describing his ministry as "theologically conservative, but sociologically and ecclesiologically liberal," Wright said his goal was to reach "as many different kinds of people in the area by following the pattern of Jesus in caring for their needs, both physical and spiritual."[36] He immediately embarked on a dedicated effort to discover those needs in the multi-cultural apartment "cities" not far from the church.

Among other ministries, Wright led the church to develop a nursery school, a job placement and apartment locator service, passport and visa assistance for immigrants, and a youth hostel. He received generous assistance from the Home Mission Board for these projects, each of which was intended to attract core groups for Bible studies and chapels. With Spanish, Portuguese, Korean, Chinese, and Japanese families in his church, he sought to gain entré into each of these language groups with new work. Wright's creative, multifaceted approach to ministry led to a cover story about his work in the June 1968 issue of *Home Missions.*

The Highland Avenue Church was successful in initiating chapels in a variety of locations among different language and culture groups. In Richmond Hill, the church established a Portuguese chapel in 1969 under the direction of pastor André Besler. In the community of St. Albans, the church began an American and Caribbean black congregation in the home of Alwyn and Miriam Dennis which was constituted in 1970 as the Bethel Baptist Church. Rodwell Morgan was the congregation's first pastor. He was followed by Alwyn Dennis who served the congregation as pastor from 1975 until his death in 1993, when he was succeeded by his widow, Miriam Dennis.

In Corona, the Highland Avenue Church launched a Spanish chapel with Heriberto Gross as pastor. The congregation later relocated to Elmhurst, and was constituted as the *Getsemane* Baptist Church in 1972 with Roberto Arrubla as pastor. Orlando Castrillon has been pastor of the church since 1975.

LeFrak City, a housing complex in Corona composed of twenty high-rise apartment buildings, was also a mission field for the Highland Avenue Church. In 1967 Donald Rhymes organized a Bible study fellowship and ministry program there called Trinity Chapel. With pastor Avery Sayer's leadership, the LeFrak City work was constituted in 1984 as the United Trinity Baptist Church. At the time of its constitution, the church had five deacons—each from a different country.

The Highland Avenue congregation also reached out to Brooklyn in 1967 to create another diverse, ministry-centered church. Located in a decaying inner-city district of the borough, the church's mission occupied the once-stately Twelfth Street Reformed Church building, complete with a four-hundred-seat auditorium and a gymnasium. The Home Mission Board purchased the building as a house of worship for the new Park Slope Baptist Church (constituted in 1968), and as a weekday ministry center. Larry Patterson came in 1969 as pastor of the congregation and director of the center.[37]

. . . No Respecter of Persons

David Morgan's words from Ezekiel—"things shall not remain as they are"—were more prophetic than he realized in October 1962. Morgan and others like him helped unleash upon the metropolitan New York area the "revolution" which he said Christ had begun for the whole world. Could an association overcome racial and ethnic barriers to form a multicultural, multilingual family of churches?

Many white Baptists were used to dealing with their black or Hispanic neighbors in kindly and affectionate ways, but also with a subtle paternalism that assumed the other's inferiority of worth or potential. References about "our black churches" or "our language ministry" betrayed a naive exclusiveness that disturbed some non-whites. Status-quo Southern Baptists had difficulty with progressive black leaders who wished to loosen the Home Mission Board's purse strings for social ministries. And what place would Hispanic churches have in an English-speaking association? Would they follow a pattern typical of the Southwest in forming a separate Hispanic association?

The churches of the Metropolitan New York Baptist Association resolved that they would be one family—even though the idea would take some getting used to, and divine wisdom to implement. Pentecost became a compelling metaphor for the association, and soon for the larger family of New York Baptists.

CHAPTER EIGHT

A NEW CONVENTION "BORN TO SERVE"

A"Who's Who" of pioneer missions in the Northeast gathered at the Manhattan Baptist Church in August 1960 to celebrate the "northern expansion" of Southern Baptists. The historic meeting, dubbed the "Northeastern Regional Fellowship," brought together for the first time pastor-directors, mission pastors, and laypeople representing scattered churches and chapels in a nine-state territory. Also at the meeting were A. B. Cash of the Home Mission Board; state convention leaders Ray Roberts of Ohio and Roy Gresham of Maryland; and, representing the Southern Baptist Executive Committee, Albert McClellan, who gave the keynote address.

If Southern Baptists were eager to find new people with whom to share their witness, those seated in the Manhattan Church were sure they had found them in the Northeast. The pastors and laypeople who shared testimonies spoke of their sense of discovery and wonder at ministering in the most densely populated quadrant of the nation. Their sentiment was aptly reflected in the theme of the gathering: "People, people, people—millions of them."

Albert McClellan was so moved by what he heard that he likened the mission reports to "pages from the Book of Acts." The denominational leader set aside his prepared address to speak from the overflow of his emotions. He commended his listeners for their resolute sense of mission, noting that the missionary imperative, more than any other single factor, held the Baptist family together. He cautioned laypeople not to become dispirited in humble beginnings and setbacks with new churches, but to realize that "God means for churches to begin and flourish as little things for a time." Finally, he declared, "We must never let die an aggressive, hopeful, dynamic, glorious evangelism because when we do we will pass away."[1]

The initial gathering of Northeastern Regional Fellowship concluded much as it had begun—without a formal structure, elected officers, or a sharply focused agenda. A. B. Cash's primary purpose in calling the meeting was to provide inspiration and fellowship for those on the frontier of mission advance. But he also hoped to instill among the churches a broader sense of kinship and regional identity. Southern Baptists were entering new territory, not as a few isolated congregations, but as a denominational presence with long-term objectives. The shape this presence would take remained to be seen. Although "messengers" said they wanted to meet the following year, the group did not reconvene until almost three years later. Interest in broader inter-church relationships took a backseat to the priority of establishing regional associations.

The First Southern Baptist Church of Syracuse hosted the second gathering of the Northeastern Fellowship in May 1963. Inspiration was again high on the agenda, but the tenor of this meeting was more businesslike, as leaders began considering potential denominational relationships.

A. B. Cash and Arthur Rutledge, president of the Home Mission Board, led a symposium—"Trends Toward Regional Goals"—in which they discussed the board's suggested guidelines for forming state conventions. What at the time were stated as suggestions soon became ironclad requirements for the board's support of new state bodies. The Northeast as a whole, or any section thereof, needed either seventy fully constituted churches with ten thousand members or fifty churches with 12,500 members to receive support from the Home Mission Board as a "state" convention. Moreover, the churches were required to support the Southern Baptist Convention's Cooperative Program with gifts averaging not less than 10 percent of their undesignated receipts.

Fellowship leaders were eager to begin the process of forming a new state convention. The noteworthy example of mission work in Ohio, made possible in part by the timely organization of a state convention, suggested the kind of impact a similar denominational structure could have in the Northeast. The leaders were confident that if the growth of new churches continued at a steady pace, the Home Mission Board's requirements could easily be met in a few years for the Northeast as a whole.

But was a "Northeast Baptist Convention" desirable, given the particularities of the regions it would encompass? Was it feasible, given the vast geographic expanse of the territory? Was it prudent, given that projected growth in a short time might allow for the development of more than one convention in the region? These were the thorny questions that as yet were unanswered. Roger Knapton, the newly elected moderator of the fellowship, appointed J. T. Davis, Walter Heilig, and Don Miller to consider these matters over the next year with representatives from Pennsylvania, South Jersey, and New England.[2]

What Kind of Convention?

The Haines Road Baptist Church in Levittown, Pennsylvania, was the site of the May 1964 meeting of the Northeastern Regional Fellowship. No longer did the meeting have the informal air of a fellowship gathering—the time had come to begin the difficult process of mapping out a denominational configuration for the Northeast.

Pastor Joe Waltz of Pittsburgh reported that the special study committee had concluded that at least three separate conventions were needed for the Northeast. The committee based its recommendation primarily upon a consideration of the distances involved with a regional convention, and a concern that the outlay for a new convention would be too costly, given that within a few years other state conventions would likely be parceled from the larger body.

Messengers from the metropolitan New York area, who had lost their representative on the committee during the year with Don Miller's departure, questioned the wisdom of the report. In their minds, the benefits of a regional convention far outweighed the detriments. They argued that much of the work in the Northeast had developed as a unit. Convention status would likely be reached within two years, thus enhancing the promotion of pioneer missions for the whole region. Financially, the churches were strong enough to sustain a new convention, and in time would be able to support the formation of smaller, regional conventions. A convention for the entire Northeast was desirable, feasible, and prudent—and the time to act was now.[3]

The session turned stormy with their protests, so much that prayer was needed to ease tensions. Quinn Pugh, pastor of the Bergen Church in northern New Jersey, helped avoid an impasse by moving that the committee's recommendation be tabled and that the program be altered to allow for group meetings before a final vote was cast on the matter.

In the end, the Pennsylvania/South Jersey proponents of smaller, regional conventions carried the day. New England churches, represented by Elmer Sizemore, were largely noncommittal, offering only a vague resolution to work with the Maryland Convention and the Home Mission Board in determining what was best for their region. The New York/

New Jersey contingent acceded to the idea of separate conventions, but left open the door for churches in New England or anywhere else in the Northeast to affiliate with their group. Their report was given by John Tollison: "Resolved, that the Metropolitan and Central Baptist Associations take immediate steps to consult their constituent churches with regard to the formation of either a regional convention, or a state convention which would welcome all churches that would wish to seek membership in the new convention."[4]

By this point, the process of creating new conventions in the Northeast had become largely a project of the Baptist Convention of Maryland, with which a majority of churches in the region were affiliated. Only churches in western Pennsylvania and western New York maintained ties with the Ohio Convention. Joe Waltz was ready to rally the churches of the Pittsburgh Association to affiliate with the proposed Pennsylvania/South Jersey Convention, but as yet, the churches of the Frontier Association had not embraced the idea of affiliating with a new convention. The New York/New Jersey Fellowship extended to them an invitation to be a part of the new convention.

By the fall of 1964, the Frontier Association was on record supporting the effort. The association's action formally united the Ohio and Maryland pioneer mission "blocs," giving the New York/New Jersey Fellowship a total of twenty-eight churches, twenty missions, and more than five thousand members.

Representatives from churches in New York, New Jersey, and southwestern Connecticut assembled at Endicott, New York, in September 1964 to begin mapping out a strategy for a new convention. The fellowship elected Ira Adams, a layman from the Bergen Church in New Jersey, to head the steering committee.

No longer obliged to the sentiments of leaders from Pennsylvania and South Jersey, representatives debated the advisability of inviting all New England churches into the fellowship. They considered that by enlisting the sixteen congregations with twenty-five hundred members from the region, a new convention could be organized as early as January 1967. Yet the New England churches seemed to lack cohesiveness, strong leadership, and decisiveness on the convention issue. These factors, some argued, could later hinder the process at a more critical juncture. Those favoring a regional body, however, felt that the promise of a new convention within two or three years would rally the New England churches just as it had captured the interest of New York and New Jersey churches.[5] The fellowship postponed resolving the question until some of the New England churches could be contacted.

In October 1965, the New York/New Jersey Fellowship reclaimed the name, the "Northeastern Fellowship," due to the interest New England churches expressed in forming a new convention. The action was taken at the Rome, New York, meeting despite the lack of any New England representative. Even with the addition of churches from the region, however, the steering committee recommended moving the target date for the new convention back to January 1968. The fellowship chose Paul Becker, pastor of the Southport Church in Elmira, New York, as chairman, and Curtis Porter, pastor of the Amherst Baptist Church in Tonawanda, New York, as secretary.[6]

By the fall of 1966, messengers to the annual meeting of the Northeastern Fellowship were growing increasingly frustrated with their slow progress toward achieving convention status. The goal of having a state convention in operation by January 1968 was by then seemingly out of reach with only forty-nine churches and 8,233 members to report. But the problem was more than just statistics. Even with growth leveling off at a modest rate, the requisite numbers for a new convention were expected to fall in place within three or four years. More than anything else at this point, the fellowship felt it needed a capable "point man" who could both inspire confidence and build a consensus, chart a practical, achievable plan for the future, and attend to the details of such. Most importantly, the churches needed someone who could devote his full-time effort to organizing a new convention.

Paul James was especially concerned about this matter. He sent a letter in February 1966 to steering committee members asking what could be done to turn good ideas into action. Paul Becker shared his sentiment. The Southern Tier pastor noted the difficulty of bringing together four diverse associations into one cooperating unit, but also observed that a "business as usual" attitude seemed to prevail within the fellowship despite the rapidly approaching target date for beginning convention operations.[7]

At the September 1966 steering committee meeting, Paul James suggested that the Home Mission Board appoint an experienced field-worker who could devote his total effort to launching the convention. Arthur Walker concurred with the idea, reminding the group that the Ohio Convention was begun in this way with Ray Roberts's leadership. Wendell Belew, who in 1966 succeeded A. B. Cash as the board's director of pioneer missions, was sympathetic toward James's suggestion, but doubted that the administration would be willing to fund what he called a "public relations" position. The board's priority was to support mission pastors, and funds were said to be tight. The Metro Association leader reminded Belew that the Home Mission Board, not the fellowship, had originally promoted the idea of forming a new convention as soon as possible. Quinn Pugh remarked, perhaps "we have the car moving too fast," to which Paul James quipped: "I don't know if we have it going!"[8]

The evident lack of organizational progress and the unresolved issue of leadership left leaders with feelings of consternation. One clear item of consensus did, however, emerge from the meeting. The committee agreed that while greater regional self-consciousness, a field-worker, and better communication between churches were needed, in the final analysis, more churches and more people were needed to facilitate the convention effort. On a motion from John Hughston of New England, the committee eliminated altogether a target date for the new convention and accepted an invitation to hold the next fellowship meeting in Boston.

The 1966 meeting of the Northeastern Regional Fellowship at Tonawanda was largely a ceremonial and inspirational event, except for a business session in which many of the issues the steering committee had wrestled with were again raised, this time by pastor David Morgan of the First Baptist Church of Brooklyn, who subsequently was chosen as chairman of the fellowship for the coming year. Wendell Belew assured the gathering that even though the Home Mission Board was lukewarm toward the idea of a regional coordinator for the Northeast, he would use his influence as chair of a new interagency "Northeast Emphasis Committee" to pursue the fellowship's concerns.

Roy Gresham sensed the group's frustration. He used his time on the program to remind messengers why a new convention was needed for the Northeast:

1. A good state convention and state missions program create a healthy, vigorous atmosphere for carrying out the Great Commission.

2. It would put a responsible promotional force closer to the people.

3. It would give the people mission projects closer to home.

4. It would keep sister churches in closer touch with each other in work that is important.

5. It would make a workable group, the state convention, responsible for expansion—more churches—more converts—more tithers and more missionary support.

6. It would afford greater opportunities for responsible leadership and fellowship.

Not wishing to leave the impression of a growing adversarial relationship between the fellowship and the Home Mission Board, Paul James recommended that the group express its appreciation to the Northeast Emphasis Committee and to Wendell Belew for their "outstanding help." The fellowship expressed its confidence in Belew and pledged the churches' continuing cooperation with the board in all phases of planning for a new convention.[9] If an olive branch needed to be extended, it had been. But with it came higher expectations of the Home Mission Board in the coming year.

A Pivotal Year for Convention Planning

Questions critical to the formation of the new convention were settled in 1967. First, the Home Mission Board continued to resist the idea of placing a coordinator in the Northeast to spearhead organizational efforts. This responsibility would continue to rest upon the steering committee. The board did, however, offer promises of increased funding for church planting.

Wendell Belew's insistence that "there are more open doors in the Northeast for the witness of Southern Baptists than anywhere else in America" was apparently heeded by the board, which launched "Northeast Thrust"—a campaign to focus the denomination's attention and resources upon the region. The Northeast was also beneficiary to a large number of Project 500 sites—strategic new church start locations targeted for special funding through the board's 1968 Annie Armstrong Offering. More sites were proposed in New York than in any other state.[10]

While not all, or, even in a few cases, any of the funds eventually materialized, the impetus given by the program resulted in a renewed aggressiveness for church planting. By the fall of 1967, sixteen new churches and missions had been added to the previous year's total for the Northeastern Fellowship. Membership stood at 10,554—an increase of 2,321 in a year's time. With a total of fifty-six churches and fifty-one chapels, the fellowship was fast approaching the requisite 70/10,000 mark needed for achieving convention status. But also by this time the question of geographical configuration was being mulled over in a way that threatened to delay for some time the realization of convention status in the region.

Despite the initial interest churches in New England expressed in being part of a convention that encompassed the entire Northeast, that interest seldom was demonstrated by attendance at annual fellowship gatherings.

Part of the problem, of course, was the distance involved in reaching the meetings which were always held somewhere in New York. Yet there was also something unnatural about the supposed affinity represented in a northeastern convention. Few people were as regionally self-conscious as New Englanders, and for Southern Baptists to succeed in reaching them, this regional identity needed to be valued and capitalized upon. By the late 1960s, the New England churches were beginning to outgrow their sense of organizational unity with the churches of the Mid-Atlantic region.

Churches in New York and New Jersey were similarly influenced by regional identity, especially those in the metropolitan New York City area. The Metro Association displayed something of an independent—some would even say, "maverick"—spirit from its founding in 1962. In July 1967, for example, the association's executive board endorsed a mission support process that encouraged churches to channel their Cooperative Program gifts through the association rather than the Baptist Convention of Maryland. The association was then to retain half the contributions, and forward the other half to the Maryland Convention.[11]

That same summer associational leaders proposed a bold new initiative for forming a state convention. Their idea was to fashion an "intermediate" convention from the forty-six churches and missions of the association. They envisioned a "Baptist General Association of New York" which would encompass the metropolitan area, subdivided into three smaller associations. Nowhere in their proposal was there any mention of the New England, Frontier, and Central Associations. The proposal did, however, extend an open invitation to any other association that might wish to join their fellowship.[12] The leaders' hope was that the Frontier and Central Associations would join with the three associations of the metropolitan area to form the new "general" association, and that the New England churches would be encouraged by the action to pursue their own destiny.

Roy Gresham responded swiftly to the Metropolitan Association's initiatives. "I am disturbed to learn that you are even suggesting the thought that money retained by the local association be considered Cooperative Program," wrote the Maryland Convention executive to Paul James. Gresham felt that the association's proposed method of handling funds ultimately would hinder, rather than advance, the New York work. Referring to a prior conversation with the director of the Metropolitan Association about "going ahead and making plans for a state convention," Gresham implored James to allow time for "all concerned to sit down together and be agreed on plans."[13]

The New York mission leader answered by first explaining the practical advantages of the new method of giving which he called "simply a suggestion to the churches." He noted that if the churches adhered to the recommended contribution of 15 percent of undesignated gifts channeled through the association, the 7.5 percent allotment sent to the Maryland Convention would be an increase over what the traditional Cooperative Program method was then eliciting from fourteen of the association's twenty-four churches. He wondered if Cooperative Program giving could be increased any other way, given the churches' growing sense of financial responsibility for the association. James nevertheless promised to share Gresham's reservations about the funding method.

Finally, James assured the state executive that he would be included in discussions about the New York work, but he also implied that the association would not stand by idly waiting for others to act on its behalf. "After these ten difficult beginning years," explained James, "we feel that progressive new approaches to the opportunities we face are indicated."[14]

The association's suggestion for channeling Cooperative Program funds was abandoned not long after the above exchange, but not before a number of churches were in the habit of dividing contributions equally between the association and the Cooperative Program—a practice still followed by some churches in the Metropolitan Association. Associational leaders also became more explicit in their desire to work with the Central and Frontier Associations in organizing a New York/New Jersey-based convention. Just days before the Northeastern Regional Fellowship was to convene in Boston, the association went on record expressing its intention to organize a smaller regional convention with its upstate partners.[15] The die was thus cast for a redefined denominational configuration for Southern Baptists in the Northeast.

On September 22, 1967, the steering committee of the Northeastern Fellowship endorsed with little debate a proposal that called for discontinuing the meetings of the fellowship in favor of smaller, regional gatherings. The committee felt that "localizing" the mission work in the Northeast was "natural and healthy, and indeed, imperative" for the fullest possible development of Southern Baptist work in the region.[16]

The two hundred messengers who gathered the next day in Boston for what would be the final meeting of the fellowship agreed. They amicably adopted the recommendation of the committee, acknowledging "God's wonderful blessings" in adding a substantial number of new churches and members over the previous year.[17] The prospect for two new conventions rather than one had never seemed brighter.

The only issue remaining to be resolved at this point between the New York/New Jersey and New England Fellowships was the precise boundary that would separate their future conventions. Would the Champlain Valley

Church in Plattsburg, New York, continue to affiliate with the New England work as it had done since shortly after its founding in 1960? Would the Greenwich and Wilton, Connecticut, Churches maintain their ties to the metro New York area?

With encouragement from the Home Mission Board, the Champlain Valley congregation elected to join other northern New York churches in forming the Adirondack Association in 1967. Like congregations in New Jersey, the Hudson Valley, and Long Island, the Greenwich and Wilton Churches were intimately related to the mission program of the metropolitan region. The political boundary that separated them from New York State thus was of little consequence in determining their affiliation. Wendell Belew concurred with the churches' decision to affiliate with the New York and New Jersey work, but the Home Mission Board leader insisted upon imposing the Saugatuck River as an arbitrary boundary to prevent future border disputes between state conventions.[18]

Prior to their departure from Boston, messengers from churches in the Central, Frontier, and Metropolitan Associations formed a loosely organized "Association of Baptists in New York/New Jersey" with David Morgan as chairman. J. T. Davis was elected vice-chairman and program committee leader, while Curtis Porter remained secretary-treasurer. The new steering committee consisted of associational directors and moderators: John Tollison and Bob Jacks (Central); Charles Magruder and Dan Connally (Frontier); Paul James and Ken Lyle (Metropolitan); and members-at-large: Clifford Matthews (Central); Jim Bullis (Frontier); and Marvin Haire (Metropolitan). Representatives from the Adirondack Association, scheduled to be constituted in October, were named before the end of the year, as were additional members at large: Leroy Stewart, Austin Matthews, Roger Knapton, and David Hall.

Groundwork for a New Convention

Buoyed with optimism and a clearer sense of direction, the steering committee launched almost immediately into the business of organizing a new state convention. The committee named budget and finance and constitution committees in December 1967.

The budget and finance committee's first task was to petition the Maryland and Ohio Conventions to begin escrowing a portion of the New York/New Jersey churches' Cooperative Program gifts as seed money for the new convention. The Maryland body complied with the request, but not until the beginning of 1969. In the spring of 1968 the churches of the

Frontier Association negotiated an arrangement with the Ohio Convention to divide their gifts 60/40 percent between that convention and the New York/New Jersey "association." These gifts, added to modest contributions from the Adirondack, Central, and Metropolitan Associations, funded steering committee operations for 1968, and provided an eleven-hundred-dollar contribution to SBC causes worldwide though the Cooperative Program (20 percent of an anticipated income of $5,450).

The constitution committee began its work in February 1968. Using the constitution of the West Virginia Fellowship of Southern Baptists as a guide, the committee worked to forge a document and create an administrative structure that would serve the immediate needs of an interim organization, as well as the permanent needs of the new convention. Among the committee's more difficult tasks was that of recommending a name for the new convention.

Any title bearing the name "New Jersey" needed to be qualified, given that churches in the southern part of the state were affiliated with Penn/South Jersey Fellowship. A "New York/New Jersey" designation ignored churches in Fairfield County, Connecticut. The committee settled upon the name "New York Baptist Fellowship" for its clarity and inclusiveness of the majority of churches in the region. Given that churches in northern New Jersey and southwestern Connecticut had from their inception been directly identified with the metropolitan New York area, "New York" could be understood as encompassing them. The name was also easily adaptable for later identifying the new convention in a manner characteristic of several other state bodies across the SBC. The "New York Baptist Convention" would take its place alongside the Alaska Baptist Convention, the Kentucky Baptist Convention, etc.[19] Grammatical purists later prevailed in convincing messengers to rearrange the title to "The Baptist Convention of New York."

Except the Lord Build the House . . .

The Baptist Fellowship of New York was formally organized at the Lincoln Avenue Baptist Church in Endicott, New York, on March 29, 1968. Messengers from the Adirondacks to central New Jersey, from Buffalo to Long Island, responded to a "vital call" to join hands in making the new convention a reality. "When the evening comes to a close," declared David Morgan, "all of us will feel we have been a part in making history . . . but we must remember the scripture's word of caution, 'Except the Lord build the house, they labor in vain that build it.'" Roy Gresham echoed the fellowship leader's sentiments: "As you move ahead in an organizational structure," he counseled, "remember that the plan and purpose is of Christ."[20]

Messengers approved recommendations from the budget/finance and constitution committees, and endorsed January 1, 1970, as the date for initiating convention operations after a fall constituting session. David Morgan was reelected leader of the Baptist Fellowship of New York with a new title: "president." J. T. Davis was similarly re-elected as first vice-president, and Quinn Pugh was elected second vice-president. Curtis Porter continued to serve as recording secretary.

The fellowship's constitution called for the formation of an interim executive board which would hold office until the fall of 1969. Each association was allotted two seats on the board, with additional representation of up to ten seats based upon church membership. Roger Knapton was elected as chairman of the board.

Formalizing the bond that united the churches of the Frontier, Adirondack, Central, and Metropolitan New York Associations was of historical significance. But the messengers also perceived that much "history" remained to be written if the schedule for constituting the new convention was to be kept. The fellowship, numbering only forty-eight churches comprised of approximately eight thousand members, was far short of the necessary 70/10,000 or 50/12,500 statistical combination needed for organizing a new convention. The real work of building the convention was not so much in holding committee meetings and attending rallies as in nurturing existing chapels into churches and launching additional new work.

By September 1968, when the Baptist Fellowship of New York convened for its fall meeting, encouraging numerical growth had occurred. Charles Magruder reported to messengers assembled at the First Baptist Church of Brooklyn that the Frontier Association had welcomed two new churches and four chapels in the previous year. Although Eldon Jones had been on the field less than a month as director of the Central and Adirondack Associations, as well as the new Southern Tier Association, he also spoke of significant interest and movement in church starting in the areas he served. Paul James told the gathering that the previous year had been the most encouraging of his eleven-year tenure in New York City. Ten new churches and fourteen chapels had been organized since the previous September, and prospects for continued growth were strong in the coming year.[21]

The fellowship had grown organizationally as well since its last meeting. Having consulted with the Ohio and Maryland state offices and with national SBC leaders, the board adopted a streamlined organizational scheme that divided the work of the convention into three divisions: administration, education, and missions.[22]

An enlarged sense of regional identity was becoming apparent in the fellowship. In the spring of 1968, the executive board began publishing the *New York Baptist* under the editorship of Curtis Porter. Begun originally to promote special areawide meetings of the fellowship, the paper quickly became an important communications link between churches and associations.

The ministry of Woman's Missionary Union produced a network of associational women's groups that helped create a broader denominational consciousness. Bernice Elliott, WMU representative to pioneer areas, assisted associational WMU directors like Maurice Sullivan and Mildred Boisture in laying plans for a conventionwide organization to be launched at the constituting session of the Baptist Convention of New York.[23]

Kenneth King, pastor of the Terrill Road Church in Scotch Plains, New Jersey, worked with Mary Knapton of the Lincoln Avenue Church in Endicott, New York, to facilitate a state missions emphasis for September 1968. Receipts from this first "conventionwide" offering for New York Baptists were designated for offsetting expenses of the fellowship and for providing space, equipment, and supplies for future operations of the convention.[24]

Momentum appeared to be building for a final surge of growth over the next twelve months that would produce the requisite numbers for convention status. The two most important matters remaining to be addressed were the location of the convention's administrative offices and who would serve as the first executive director of the Baptist Convention of New York.

Paul James was, in many people's minds, a man of unusual grace and ability who could cement relationships between Baptists whose heritage and affinity were with the Ohio tradition and those who were tethered to a theology and practice associated with Maryland Baptists. In many ways the regional differences within the fellowship were as pronounced as political rivalries between New York City/John Lindsay Independents and upstate/Nelson Rockefeller Republicans. Yet by this time, Baptists in both regions were coming to feel a brother-and-sister-in-arms kinship inspired by the challenge of a broad mission field. Many thought the kind of statesman-like leadership James had given the northeastern seaboard work commended him for the task of leading the Baptist Convention of New York.

The move to draft Paul James for conventionwide leadership began in September 1968 when Jerrell Buchanan nominated the Metro Association leader to succeed David Morgan as president of the Baptist Fellowship of New York. Two messengers from the Frontier Association, Stanley Bullis and Jim Bullis, nominated Roger Knapton and Quinn Pugh, respectively, for the post, both of whom asked that their names be withdrawn. Even so, James was reluctant to accept the nomination, citing the demands of the position and his heavy administrative load as an associational director. After numerous assurances of support, he consented to the wishes of the body and was elected by a unanimous vote.

At the conclusion of the session, the new president sought to allay the fears of any who might question his commitment to all the churches. James reminded the messengers that he had been born in the Adirondacks, spent many years in central New York, and buried his parents in western New York. He felt an obligation to all New York Baptists.[25]

James's commitment and the commitment of downstate leaders to the larger convention territory were tested early when the study group charged with recommending a location for convention offices selected Syracuse. In the mid-1960s, when thought was being given to forming a northeastern convention, many regarded Albany as the site of choice for establishing central offices. Downstate churches outnumbered upstate congregations by more than a two-to-one margin. For many Metropolitan Association leaders, Albany was already a "compromise" choice.

The argument for a location determined by a preponderance of churches was a two-edged sword. Indeed, the southernmost part of New York/ New Jersey was home to the largest number of churches, which suggested that the upstate work was most in need of being strengthened. Just as Columbus had become a center of growth for Southern Baptists in Ohio, despite an early preponderance of churches in the Cincinnati area, so the Syracuse area and other northern locations might develop similarly. Brief consideration was given to the Binghamton area—the geographic center of the convention territory—but the committee quickly recognized the city's limited accessibility to air transportation. Syracuse was a "central" upstate metropolitan area, conveniently located on the New York Thruway, and well-serviced by a modern airport.[26] Despite some misgivings about the choice, James and executive board members from the Metro Association signed off on Syracuse as an accommodation to the concerns of upstate brothers and sisters. In the 1970s, the issue of site location again surfaced, but no serious consideration was given to relocating convention offices. All things considered, Syracuse was still the optimal location.[27]

The Choice of New Leadership

More than perhaps anyone else, Fred Boehmer was convinced that Paul James was the man both to lead the fellowship and to serve as the new convention's executive director. The pastor of the Greenwich Baptist Church admitted to James after the September 1968 meeting that it had taken "some politicking" to get him elected, but in this case the "end justified the means." Boehmer saw the fellowship as sectionally divided and badly lacking in proper procedure. "If any man can bring unity out of chaos and unite our forces," he confided to James, "it is you."[28] As a member of the administrative committee of the executive board the next year, Fred Boehmer became the primary advocate for inviting Paul James to be the convention's chief administrator.

Not everyone on the committee was inclined to give serious thought to calling James, despite the wide respect he commanded as a leader. Some members expressed up front in the search process their desire to see a new face in leadership—someone who was familiar with pioneer mission work, but who had not been involved in the formative stages of the convention. This would help ensure a balanced interest in the whole region. Others, upon hearing James mentioned as a possible candidate for the position, privately questioned the wisdom of calling a man so near retirement age.[29]

The most compelling reason, however, for not wishing to consider James may have been the fact that he was already the "executive director" of the Metropolitan New York Association—something of a "convention" within itself. His friendships, his roots, and his heart were in New York City, giving upstate leaders pause to wonder whether James could provide balanced leadership for the whole convention.

At the beginning of 1969, the consensus of the committee, which included Paul James, was to seek someone from outside the region for the position. Such "outsiders" as Ray Roberts of Ohio and Roy Gresham of Maryland were discussed, as were candidates like Wendell Belew who were advanced by the Home Mission Board leadership. All either declined or otherwise proved not to be right for the job. Having cooperated patiently in the search process, Boehmer finally broke his silence and stated what he considered to be obvious: "There's a man in our midst eminently qualified for the job—Paul James!" The Connecticut pastor argued that the right "familiar face" could be trusted to provide evenhanded leadership for the convention. Moreover, he pointed out, James had extensive experience with the Home Mission Board which would serve him well as the executive of a convention heavily dependent upon national denominational support.[30]

Boehmer's eloquent paean to James's character and administrative savvy left the New York City leader red faced and at a loss for good reasons why he should not be considered. After James dismissed himself from the meeting, the committee began mulling over the possibility of his leadership. Boehmer's logic was hard to resist. This much was certain: if James were chosen, the convention could expect enthusiastic support from the Metro Association which accounted for a large majority of the churches. No consensus was reached that afternoon, but by the time the committee reconvened on March 18, a decision had been reached. James was the unanimous choice to serve as the first executive director of the Baptist Convention of New York.

James's decision to accept the call did not come easily. His initial impulse was to decline the offer, cutting as it did "right down to the roots" of his and Mrs. James's planning for the future. With a comfortable retirement in sight, he was inclined to turn down the opportunity. Yet, after he and Ava spent several days in prayer and consulted with close friends about the matter, they both became convinced of God's calling. "Out of hard struggle has come joy in anticipating a great new adventure," wrote James, "so we move together from the known to the unknown, confident of Him who has been our help and is now our hope."[31]

". . . For Such a Time as This"

In July 1969, Paul and Ava James moved to Syracuse to begin setting up convention operations and laying plans for the constituting session, scheduled for September 25–26. Working with the executive board, James made arrangements in August to lease office space in the Powelson Building, 400 Montgomery Street. Convention offices remained at this site until March 1974, when they were relocated to more spacious quarters at 500 South Salina Street.

The board also worked with the new executive director in securing the convention's first staff member, John M. Tubbs. Having been employed by the Baptist Convention of Maryland for almost ten years, Tubbs was no stranger to the New York work. His assignment as director of the education division encompassed a broad range of responsibilities, including Sunday School, Training Union, church music, summer missionaries, church architecture, and supervision of state student work. Tubbs remained on the staff of the Baptist Convention of New York until June 1979.[32]

With Paul James attending to the daily details of administration, the Baptist Convention of New York appeared to be on schedule for becoming a reality in September 1969. But while the fellowship was advancing on a steady path of organizational development, growth in the number of new churches had faltered. From January to June 1969, only four new churches had been added to the fellowship, for a total of sixty fully constituted congregations—ten short of the necessary number with less than three months to go.

In response to this pressing need, James issued a plea to all mission chapels and sponsoring churches to consider expediting the nurturing process of new units. Curtis Porter employed a curious biblical analogy in a *New York Baptist* editorial to stress the urgency of the situation: "In yesterday years Abraham looked for ten righteous souls in Sodom. Today a diligent search is on for ten rugged and ready chapels who are led of God to constitute into New Testament churches: these alone under God can prove the salvation of modern Sodom. . . . It is time for us to move forward!"[33]

Several churches did move forward—with precious little time to spare. On the weekend prior to the organizational session of the convention, the Calvary (Matawan, New Jersey), Twin County, Somerset Hills, Hope, Rockland, Floyd, and West Main Churches were constituted. On the day before messengers assembled in Syracuse for the historic meeting, the First Spanish Baptist Church of Hackensack became the seventieth church to be constituted within the convention territory. After several years of praying, planning, and wrangling over the convention issue, the time had come to turn dreams into a reality.

On September 25, 1969, messengers from those seventy churches met at the Central Baptist Church in Syracuse. It was poetic justice that Hartman Sullivan, pastor of the LaSalle Baptist Church in Niagara Falls, had the privilege of calling them to order for the constituting session, and offering the motion that brought the Baptist Convention of New York into being. The BCNY story had begun fifteen years before with the founding of the LaSalle Church. Sullivan had become president of the fellowship upon the resignation of Paul James to become executive director.

State executives Ray Roberts and Roy Gresham came to bring greetings. Roberts encouraged messengers to maintain Baptist distinctives and

On hand for the 1969 constituting session of the Baptist Convention of New York were (left to right) Ray Roberts, executive of the Ohio Convention, Arthur Rutledge, president of the Home Mission Board, and Roy Gresham, executive of the Maryland Convention. Paul James stands to the right.

priorities. Gresham offered no charge, but an observation: "The eyes of all Southern Baptists are focused here tonight. We have been rescued from provincialism by the pioneer areas and this has kept the cutting edge sharper for the SBC."[34]

The constituting session was blessed with an unusual array of gifted speakers. Professor William Pinson of Southwestern Seminary led Bible study segments, while Cal Guy, also of Southwestern Seminary, led mission studies. In his convention address, Owen Cooper, a layperson from Mississippi, challenged pastors to elevate the role of the laity in missions (Cooper was elected president of the Southern Baptist Convention in 1973). Arthur Rutledge, president of the Home Mission Board, preached the concluding sermon. He noted the significance of Southern Baptists formally entering the Northeast with their thirty-first state convention almost 125 years after the founding of the SBC.[35]

Messengers paid special tribute to leaders who had helped shape the beginnings of the New York work. Telegrams were dispatched to A. B. Cash, Courts Redford, Zig Boroughs, Paul Becker, and David Morgan. Arthur Walker, who pioneered work in western New York from 1958 to 1961, recognized numerous others present who had planted churches across the convention territory.

An energetic and amiable leader like Ken Lyle, pastor of the Central Nassau Church in Westbury, Long Island, seemed to embody the spirit of the new convention. By acclamation, messengers elected him as the first president of the Baptist Convention of New York. The body also elected J. T. Davis first vice-president; Gene Fant second vice-president; Curtis Porter recording secretary; and Richard Roberts assistant recording secretary.

Fred Boehmer moved the adoption of the BCNY's first budget which reflected generous support from the Baptist Sunday School Board and Home Mission Board. The $422,060 budget was the largest ever for a new state convention. The document called for the churches and chapels of the new convention to contribute one hundred thousand dollars in Cooperative Program gifts, of which 15 percent would be forwarded to the SBC Executive Committee in Nashville for worldwide causes. This amount was to be increased by 1 percent each year over the next five years.

The sense of wonder and historical significance messengers felt was summed up in the text Paul James chose for his sermon—"Who knows whether you have not come to the kingdom for such a time as this?" (Esther 4:14). After assuring the crowd of more than three hundred of the rich Providence of the moment, he quoted the Scottish thinker Thomas Carlyle: "Our main business is not to see what lies dimly in the distance, but to do what clearly lies at hand." "This, God helping us, we will do," he declared.[36] The session concluded with messengers joining hands and singing the "Doxology."

CHAPTER NINE

Baptist Convention of New York

GETTING STARTED, 1970-1979

I n his 1970 president's address, Ken Lyle reflected upon the sense of wonder he had felt upon becoming a Christian. "I stood in awe of God's grace," he reminisced. "I was amazed that Christ loved me so." Lyle observed that a similar sense of euphoria had for the past year pervaded the churches and associations of the Baptist Convention of New York. "Having survived the labor pains of tedious preparation, our convention was born. . . . Those early moments were exciting . . . tense . . . inspiring!" But now the baby was home, and the time to grow with health, with soundness, and with strength had come. Even so, Lyle counseled, a sense of the "wonder of it all" needed to be maintained at this new stage of development. He hoped that an unconquerable optimism and zeal would mark the formative years of the new convention.[1]

Paul James approached his task in the same spirit. He urged New York Baptists to understand that while their convention was a humble denominational structure, it still could be big—big in spirit, in praying, in vision, in planning, and in carrying out its goals. The churches' prior relationships with the Ohio and Maryland Conventions meant they were somewhat familiar with Baptist polity, but the leader took nothing for granted. Throughout his tenure he imparted to the churches the rudiments of cooperative, Southern Baptist denominationalism within their state convention.

James also worked diligently on the national scene to help Southern Baptists grasp the critical importance of their mission work in the Northeast. One of the frustrations of his ministry was the length of time it took to "sell a new idea" to the denomination. By the time the BCNY had been founded, however, the national convention was paying closer attention to the Northeast, at least with their missions education programs. The theme for the Home Mission Board's annual study in 1970 was "Mission to the Northeast." Word was getting out.

By the fall of 1970, the benefits of the new convention were already being felt in the churches. With Syracuse as a center for strategic planning, program promotion, and the disbursement of mission funds, a more equitable distribution of human and financial resources was possible. Decisions about mission priorities, funding, and leadership were made by local or regional colleagues who better understood the setting and needs of New York area churches.

A Strategic Plan for the New Convention

For as long as most leaders could remember, the defining vision for Southern Baptist work in the Northeast had been the organization of a state convention. What came next? In 1971 the BCNY executive board named a Long-range Action Committee to study the needs of the convention territory and to offer recommendations for future priorities in ministry and mission. The committee brought its detailed report to the convention's annual session in October 1973.

The document began with a statement that could have been lifted from a textbook on Baptist polity. Again, nothing was taken for granted; Paul James and company spelled out the essence of a state convention: "We conceive of our primary mission as that of bringing men to God through Jesus Christ. We understand this to be the purposes of the churches which have created the state convention as an extension of their ministries, so it becomes the overriding purpose of the state convention. . . . The state convention exists to serve the churches. Its programs and services are designed to help the churches in accomplishing their mission which is sharing Christ with the whole world and developing mature believers."

The strategic plan offered by the committee was noteworthy more for its optimism than for its creativity, although some new ideas for starting and equipping churches were advanced. Their proposal was a blueprint for helping the convention come of age. Given that the convention numbered 140 churches and chapels with 13,000 members (1972), the committee saw no reason why these figures could not be increased to 250 congregations with 25,000 members by the end of the decade. Constituting eight new churches and starting ten new mission chapels each year would yield these numbers and allow the Baptist Convention of New York to gain representation on SBC boards and agencies as early as 1980.

Similarly, challenging incremental goals for growth were suggested for Sunday School enrollment, stewardship development, and budget planning. Recommendations for new staff included establishing positions for student work and music, youth, children's ministry, church extension and social ministry, evangelism and stewardship, and WMU work.[2] Clearly, the churches had their work cut out for them.

Early Growth in Giving

How would the churches respond to the financial needs of the new convention? Would previous levels of Cooperative Program giving to the Maryland and Ohio Conventions sustain the ministry of the Baptist Convention of New York in 1970? The budget and finance committee pondered these questions long and hard in laying plans for the new convention.

The churches responded with gifts of $93,334 in 1970 and $94,417 in 1971. While these figures were gratifying enough, they did not meet budget expectations, nor were they sufficient to fund the needs of an expanding program and staff. Fred Boehmer, chairman of the executive board, acknowledged in a March 1970 *New York Baptist* editorial that tremendous strides had been made with the new convention, but added that if the BCNY was to become a "reality of fact," the churches needed to give more.[3] Real growth toward something more than an organization on paper required an expanded financial base.

By 1972 the idea of generously supporting the state convention was apparently catching on. Even though only four new churches were added to the convention that year, Cooperative Program gifts totaled $134,335—a dramatic increase of more than 40 percent. By the mid-1970s, New York Baptists were contributing almost $200,000 toward a total budget of more than $750,000. Such steady growth in giving, coupled with ever-increasing support from national denominational boards and agencies, helped the convention quickly enlarge its program staff. Increased funding also provided for an able support staff that included Betty Glass, administrative assistant to James; Genny Henderson, office secretary in the missions division until her retirement in 1994; and Rosemary LeFevre, who joined the convention staff in 1975 as secretary to the executive director.

The Missions Division

The Baptist Convention of New York benefited enormously from a cooperative agreement with the Home Mission Board that matched every six dollars the BCNY budgeted for mission expenditures with ninety-four dollars in HMB funds. Budget priorities and spending levels were jointly established between the convention and the board.

One of the first administrative priorities for the new convention was to organize a missions division. Jon F. Meek Jr., pastor of the Calvary Baptist Church in Aberdeen, New Jersey, assumed responsibilities as director of the missions division in January 1971. Although Meek's primary assignment was to carry the banner for starting new churches, his administrative tasks were quite demanding. Much of the work the Home Mission Board had done in the region prior to the establishment of a state office was transferred to his care.

The division director had administrative oversight for pastor-directors, pastoral missionaries, Christian social ministries and weekday ministries workers, US-2 workers, and student summer missionaries. Church pastoral aid—salary assistance provided for pastors of new churches—was also distributed through his office. Meek's other responsibilities included the promotion of Brotherhood (Baptist Men and Royal Ambassadors), Woman's Missionary Union, stewardship, and Annuity Board interests. Jon Meek remained as director of the missions division until his resignation in March 1980.

The ambitious program assignment of the missions division was not undertaken by the director alone. Coming also to Syracuse in January 1971 as the associate director of the division was Leobardo Estrada, whose language missions assignment with the Metropolitan Association was enlarged by the Home Mission Board to include the entire state convention territory.[4] Estrada struggled to maintain close ties with the large number of non-English language congregations in the New York City area, while seeking to cultivate new work in other metropolitan areas. Estrada remained with the convention until 1973, when he accepted an assignment with the Baptist General Convention of Texas. He was succeeded by James Benson (1974–1977) and Manuel Alonso (1978–1989), whose offices were located in the New York City area.

Volunteers Mildred Boisture and Helen Fling, who had served nationally as president of WMU, carried out administrative responsibilities for Woman's Missionary Union in the early years of the convention. For most of the 1970s, these women alternated tenures as president of the statewide organization. They provided valuable leadership.

In 1972 the convention welcomed Edwina Robinson as acting staff director of Woman's Missionary Union. The retired WMU executive for the Mississippi Baptist Convention was sponsored by the Home Mission Board. From 1972 to 1975, she traveled the state convention territory six weeks in the fall and six weeks in the spring to help establish and strengthen the BCNY's program of Woman's Missionary Union.[5]

"Surely such good news calls for thanksgiving," announced the *New York Baptist* in the fall of 1976. The good news was that after seven years the Baptist Convention of New York had a state WMU director. Gloria Grogan left her position as a ministry consultant with the national WMU office in Birmingham to assume responsibilities with the BCNY in October 1976. In addition to her work with Woman's Missionary Union, Grogan was also assigned as a consultant to assist in the convention's growing programs of Christian social ministry.[6]

The missions division completed the decade with a well-rounded staff and program to meet the needs of the churches and associations. By 1979 the division's total budget had reached almost $950,000.

Complementing the ministry of the missions division in the early 1970s were personnel assigned to the BCNY territory who worked under the supervision of the Home Mission Board. Glenn Igleheart was director of Interfaith Witness for the Northeast, and Rodney Webb was the board's regional representative for deaf ministry. Both men lived in the New York City metro area and worked closely with BCNY churches. George Sheridan assumed the Interfaith Witness duties in 1976.

In 1974 the Home Mission Board appointed Elias Golonka to launch an outreach to foreign diplomats and other short-term internationals in New York City. Golonka's efforts resulted in the founding of Christian Ministries to the United Nations Community.[7] Ted Mall succeeded Golonka as director of the program in October 1983.

The Education Division

One of John Tubbs's first priorities as director of the education division was to recruit a cadre of volunteers to lead local educational training events. The Sunday School Board was generous in making its own personnel available for annual conventionwide clinics and seminars, but Tubbs recognized the need of developing a pool of trained educational leaders within the BCNY to provide for the ongoing needs of the churches with Sunday School, Church Training, and Vacation Bible School. He organized advanced leadership conferences in New York, New Jersey, and

Connecticut, and arranged for volunteers to receive specialized training at the Ridgecrest Conference Center in North Carolina.

The early 1970s was an auspicious time for Christian education among Southern Baptists. In 1970 the Sunday School Board introduced a revamped curriculum and program structure for Sunday School that necessitated extensive training for teachers. The first event ever sponsored by the education division was a "Shaping the '70s" conference held at the Central Baptist Church in Syracuse. Participants were instructed not only in utilizing the board's new materials, but also in techniques for communicating with a generation of bell-bottomed, polyester-clad baby boomers who were swelling enrollments in youth programs and college campuses. The interest young people showed in the "Jesus Movement," Christian "coffee houses," and in youth music programs that featured lively "rock-tatas" as an alternative to traditional hymnody demanded a more creative effort to meet their needs.

John Tubbs also assembled a team of dedicated youth workers and teenagers who organized the BCNY's first youth convention. Almost 250 young people gathered in Syracuse for the event in May 1970.[8] In subsequent years the convention proved to be a much-anticipated rallying point of fellowship for youth and an event that undergirded local programs through a sharing of ideas and leadership training.

Campus ministry was a major concern of the education division. Ray Gilliland continued the ministry he had begun in January 1969 to campuses in the metropolitan New York City area. Originally supervised through the Maryland Convention's student department, the Kansas native's work came under the direction of the education division in January 1970.

Gilliland's ministry extended to more than a dozen campuses through his coordination of volunteer efforts. George Glenn, for example, a professor at Rutgers University, helped organize a program at that school with the help of graduate student Nancy Bair. Graduate students or their spouses, local pastors, and faculty members provided ministry in a similar way at Columbia University, New York University, and Queens College. Gilliland was also successful in cultivating the involvement of international students in friendship programs and other ministries supported by the Metropolitan New York Association.[9] He remained as campus minister in New York until he accepted a social ministry position with the Metro Association in 1975, from which he retired in 1987.

In January 1971, Alton Harpe began his work as campus minister for the United States Military Academy at West Point. The former Florida State and Miami University BSU director was joined by his wife Fairy, who served as something of a surrogate mother to countless cadets, and as a

WMU leader for the state convention.[10] Alton Harpe later became founding pastor of the West Point Baptist Church—a congregation formed in 1986 from his ministry to cadets and officers on post.

The education division welcomed a valuable new member to its Syracuse staff in March 1975, when William R. Dunning assumed responsibilities for music and student ministry. Previously, Dunning had been an associational director and BSU leader in Tennessee. He expanded the BCNY's music program beyond annual associational leadership conferences to include sessions in music planning and direction at all major conventionwide events.[11] Much of Dunning's time, however, was spent supervising the convention's growing program of campus ministry. In 1980 he became director of the education division, and remained with the BCNY until April 1985 when he accepted a pastorate in Delaware.

Deal Hudson, one of Ray Gilliland's many volunteer leaders, and a handful Southern Baptist students like Stephen Hollaway, Michael Arges, Bob Boisture, and Charles Scalise helped revive a program of campus ministry at Princeton University in the 1970s. Gilliland enlisted the help of Hudson, a student at Princeton Theological Seminary, to organize the small fellowship during the 1971–1972 academic year. Hollaway and Arges, who later enrolled in Princeton Seminary, sought to maintain the group in the mid-1970s. In September 1977, the Home Mission Board reassigned campus minister John Walsh from the Boston area to the Princeton University campus.[12] The Missouri native established the Baptist chaplaincy at Princeton, which he directed until his resignation in 1986 to accept a similar position at Middlebury College.

Quentin Lockwood Jr. (Chip) became campus minister for New York City in October 1976. He previously had been director of the Baptist Student Union at Virginia Commonwealth University. During his tenure, the New York City position became more focused upon Columbia University, which provided office space. In 1981 Lockwood became an associate in the education division, with responsibilities for supervising programs of campus ministry, discipleship training, church media, and church recreation.

All of the BCNY's fully funded campus ministers were located in the Metro Association area, but more than just that region was served by the convention's program of campus ministry. Volunteers, US-2 workers, semester missionaries, and local pastors ably carried out student work in a variety of other areas across the convention.

Pastor Gene Fant, for example, initiated a program at the State University of New York at Fredonia. Fred Wilson, a professor at the Rochester Institute of Technology, formed a student group that was led in subsequent years by US-2 personnel like June Campbell. Leroy Stewart, pastor of the Emmanuel Baptist Church in Potsdam, began a campus ministry program for the Adirondack Association in the early 1970s that also was perpetuated by US-2 workers. In 1979 the association welcomed David Book in a multiple role as campus minister, church planter, and resort missionary for the 1980 Winter Olympic Games at Lake Placid.

New Executive Leadership

"A solid foundation by the grace of God has been laid for future expansion," observed Paul James in a February 1974 letter to the executive board. ". . . Mrs. James and I have found deep joy in serving Christ during these formative years of our state convention, but now time dictates that I should relinquish my responsibilities to other hands."[13] With these words the first executive secretary of the Baptist Convention of New York, and the "founding father" of Southern Baptist work along the eastern seaboard, tendered his resignation, effective March 1, 1975.

By the time James reached his retirement date, the executive board had found a successor. Jack P. Lowndes, pastor of the Memorial Baptist Church in Arlington, Virginia, was named executive director at a called meeting of the board on January 6, 1975. The Georgia native had just completed two terms as president of the board of directors for the Home Mission Board.

In his first editorial, Lowndes identified New York as the "greatest mission field in the world." He commended New York Baptists for their openness to diversity; their strength in "crossing the barriers of culture

This picture was taken the day Jack Lowndes was called as executive director of the BCNY. Flanking him on the back row are (left) Fred Boehmer, pastor of the Greenwich Baptist Church, and (right) Charles Jolly, pastor of the Madison Baptist Church. Front row (left to right) are Paul and Ava James, Doris Lowndes, and Dorothy Jolly.

with the Gospel." The new administrative leader spoke of guiding the convention as it "crystallized" and matured with a full program of ministry and mission. Finally, he described his management style as laissez-faire, but centered in well-defined organizational objectives and expectations.[14]

Lowndes inherited a challenging game plan for growth, drawn up by his predecessor and the long-range action committee three years before. In it, objectives were clear and expectations were high. The new leader proved to be a quick study in becoming acquainted with the character and needs of the convention. He subscribed to the ambitious plan and guided the process of updating it in 1976.

Seeing the immensity of mission opportunity in New York, New Jersey, and southwestern Connecticut, Lowndes felt that resources beyond what the churches and national denominational agencies provided were needed to advance the BCNY's plan for growth. He turned to friends in his home state for help. In the fall of 1977, the Georgia Baptist Convention entered into a "sister" state relationship with the Baptist Convention of New York. Searcy S. Garrison, executive director of the Georgia body, was impressed by Lowndes's Macedonian call for help. "Dr. Lowndes is a native Georgian," he explained to his fellow Baptists, "a former Georgia pastor who has found needs and opportunities beyond description in New York."[15] Garrison envisioned potential financial support for the New York Convention, but he also hoped the relationship would provide Georgia Baptists with opportunities for hands-on involvement in home missions.

Voluntarism was a popular theme among Southern Baptists in the late 1970s. Acting on a suggestion from President Jimmy Carter, SBC agency leaders formed the "Mission Service Corps" to strengthen the short-term volunteer phase of Bold Mission Thrust, an aggressive conventionwide plan to cover the globe with a gospel witness. The plan called for enlisting five thousand new volunteers to serve alongside career missionaries in home and foreign fields.[16] Jack Lowndes, who helped design the program, saw the MSC as "help on the way!"

In October 1978, the Home Mission Board appointed the BCNY's first Mission Service Corps volunteers. The board commissioned Eulas and Bernice Carroll for ministry to the Adirondack Association; Steve and Sally Cosgrove to Syracuse for church planting and student work; Jimmy and Donna Crawford to Canton for church planting and student work; and Edwin and Mildred Hewlett to Rochester for a church planting assignment.[17]

Cooperative Program gifts from the churches continued to rise steadily in the latter half of the 1970s, as did support from the Sunday School Board and the Home Mission Board. Between 1975 and 1979, contributions from

BCNY churches increased from $190,238 to $319,230. Executive board members were wide-eyed with vision and expectation in June 1976 when they proposed the convention's first budget totaling more than one million dollars.[18]

The board set ambitious budget goals each year that stretched to the limit the churches' ability, or willingness, to support the convention. Double-digit inflation in the national economy necessitated significant budget increases just to maintain personnel and programs at previous levels of support. Gifts increased annually but seldom kept pace with budgeted spending levels which were not always carefully controlled. The late 1970s was a time of unprecedented organizational growth for the BCNY, but it was also a time when budgets and deficits were frequent front-page items for the New York Baptist, and often the subject of Jack Lowndes's editorials.

The Evangelism Division

Until 1976 responsibility for the convention's program of evangelism rested with the executive director. Each year the BCNY hosted a well-attended evangelism conference that featured gifted speakers from a broad spectrum of Southern Baptist life and beyond. Not even the distraction of occasional snow storms that blanketed the midwinter event diminished the spirit of revival that usually prevailed in the sessions.

In addition to this annual event, the convention sponsored numerous lay evangelism clinics in the early 1970s, often led by Don Miller, pastor of the North Shore Church on Long Island. Beyond this, there was little BCNY programming for evangelism events. Churches held revival meetings, trained laypeople in personal witnessing, and emphasized evangelism within the Sunday School—all of which contributed to an annual increase in the number of baptisms reported for the convention.

Daniel R. Sanchez brought to the Baptist Convention of New York a broad-based, holistic approach to evangelism. The former associate in the language missions division of the Home Mission Board arrived on the field as the first director of the evangelism division in December 1976. A Latino with missionary experience in Panama, Sanchez was well equipped to meet the diverse needs of a multicultural setting.

One of Sanchez's first priorities was leadership development. He helped arrange for associational directors, pastors, and lay leaders to attend national training events in specialized areas of evangelism. The division director was also successful in bringing some national and regional evangelism training events to the BCNY territory. The ministry of the evangelism division was broadened under his leadership to include multifaceted emphases in youth evangelism, apartment complex evangelism, urban evangelism, and rural evangelism.

The BCNY sponsored "crusade" evangelism events in communities like Harlem, where ground was broken for a Southern Baptist witness a decade before with an interracial revival sponsored by the Metro Association.[19] The evangelism division helped organize a crusade among Haitians in 1978 that attracted a crowd estimated at three thousand—the largest evangelistic gathering in the history of the BCNY at the time. Rome, Corning, and the North Country of New York State were other areas touched in the late 1970s by the crusade ministry of the BCNY.[20]

The annual evangelism conference continued to be a spiritual rallying point for New York Baptists and a time when special SBC evangelistic programs were launched, like the "Living Proof" campaign for simultaneous revivals. In 1979, almost four hundred gathered in Syracuse to hear J. Edwin Orr speak of spiritual awakenings. R. Quinn Pugh provided a series of his trademark dramatic monologues for the meeting.

In 1978 the evangelism division was expanded to include an associate's position for urban evangelism. The Home Mission Board and the Baptist Convention of New York appointed Bob and Nancy Saul that year to serve as urban evangelism missionaries. Although they lived in the New York City area, the couple was assigned to undertake projects in all urban areas of the convention territory. The Sauls resigned in 1980, but remained in New York City to help start a new work, the City Church.

Daniel Sanchez became director of the missions division in July 1981, leaving the evangelism division to the oversight of Jack Lowndes. In June 1983, Sanchez resigned to join the faculty at Southwestern Baptist Theological Seminary.

Annual Sessions of the Convention

Ken Lyle's new responsibilities as director of missions for the Metropolitan New York Association led him in 1970 to withdraw his name from consideration for reelection as president of the convention. Messengers elected Gene Fant, pastor of the West Main Church in Fredonia, New York. Following his one-year tenure, the convention turned to a layman, Homer C. Schumacher (Bud), for its next president. A member of the Calvary Church, Aberdeen, New Jersey, the IBM executive presided with distinction for two terms.

At mid-decade the convention chose Fred Boehmer as president. The seasoned pastor and convention leader also held office for two terms. Throughout the remainder of the 1970s, messengers expressed their confidence in pastors for leadership of the convention, electing the following: C. Nelson Tilton, Rochester Baptist Church (1976); Charles Jolly, Madison Baptist Church (1977); Ron Madison, Terrill Road Baptist Church (1978); and Wallace A. C. Williams, Wilton Baptist Church (1979).

In the early years of the convention, the executive board was an almost exclusive preserve of Anglo males. The lone exception was Noel Henry Scott, who succeeded David Morgan as pastor of the First Baptist Church of Brooklyn. Helen Fling's arrival mitigated the gender barrier somewhat. The former national WMU leader was elected to the board in 1973. The convention elected two other women that year as well: Elsie Leamer and Marilyn Malone. For the remainder of the decade, no more than two women ever served on the board simultaneously.

The racial/ethnic limitations of the board did not yield easily either. In 1973 messengers nodded approval to the following resolution: "Because we believe in the equality of persons in God's eyes, and because we desire that the gifts of all God's children in the BCNY be utilized, we therefore resolve to be more sensitive to the need to broaden representation on our programs, committees, boards and offices to include the complete spectrum of our constituency." The next year, when neither board representation nor involvement in other areas of convention leadership appeared to be distributed on an equitable basis, messengers reiterated the resolution.[21] Thereafter, the board typically included several Hispanics and/or African-Americans.

New York Baptists were not shy in expressing their sentiments about a remarkably broad range of social, moral, and political issues in the 1970s. The convention adopted resolutions on topics ranging from voting responsibility to transcendental meditation; from the ABC television sitcom, "Soap," to the New York City financial crisis.

In 1971 messengers registered their displeasure with the threat of state-sponsored prayer embodied in House Joint Resolution #191, allowing for "nondenominational" prayer in public schools. Three years after the historic *Roe v. Wade* decision in the Supreme Court, the convention issued a strong statement condemning abortion "for selfish, nontherapeutic reasons." Messengers affirmed the "biblical sacredness and dignity of all human life," and rejected the use of abortion except in cases of rape, incest, or endangerment to the life of the mother.[22]

Not all resolutions were aimed at the government, society, or popular culture. In 1977 and 1978 the convention adopted resolutions reaffirming the priority of prayer in the churches (particularly on Wednesday evenings), and the importance of supporting the Foreign Mission Board's efforts to raise funds for world hunger. After celebrating the convention's tenth anniversary in 1979, messengers had the issue of stewardship on their minds. The budget shortfall at that time and the challenge of ministry in the 1980s compelled them to adopt a resolution asking the churches to make even further financial sacrifices for the BCNY.

Coming to "Belong"

The "new" did not wear off the Baptist Convention of New York for several years. Annual sessions during Paul James's administration were times of celebration; occasions both to do business and to share glad reunions; and settings in which to remember and marvel at the progress Southern Baptists had made in the Northeast.

The latter half of the 1970s was a time of turning toward maturity and the harsh realities of budget pressures. With Jack Lowndes's leadership, the convention became focused upon, if not preoccupied with, organizational growth. Such growth often turned out to be more expensive than the churches were willing to afford. Yet BCNY congregations had high expectations for the young convention. Their mandate for expanding staff and programs was delivered each year by messengers who enthusiastically endorsed long-range plans and approved larger budgets. Excitement about ministry fed convention growth.

The Baptist Convention of New York indeed grew significantly in the 1970s. The number of churches more than doubled, increasing from 74 to 157. Total membership rose from 10,413 to 18,581. While these figures did not come close to achieving the ambitious goals set earlier in the decade, they represented real growth—growth into the fabric of the region. The immeasurable "statistic" was the degree to which New York Baptists were coming to be firmly established in a region they heretofore had viewed primarily as "pioneer." After almost a quarter century since the founding of their first church in Niagara Falls, Southern Baptists were beginning to be at home in the Northeast. The gospel recording artist, Ken Medema, a member of the First Baptist Church of Montclair, New Jersey, was often featured on the program of annual convention sessions in the 1970s. He expressed the feelings of New York Baptists with a song he composed especially for the tenth anniversary session in 1979—"We Belong":

We belong in the farming country,
on the rich and fertile land,
Where the earth is close and fragrant,
and the soil is in our hand

(Refrain)
In the name of the one who cared enough,
to face his cross alone,
In the power of the one who rose
to give us hope when hope was gone,
We will live the love of the one who came
to set the pris'ners free.
He is Lord, and His servants we shall be.

We belong in the cold North Country,
where the snow-capped mountains shine,
to extend to the cold and lonely,
the warmth of love divine.

We belong in suburban neighborhoods,
where the lawns are rich and green,
and the rich, who are poor, try frantic'ly
to escape their life's routine.

We belong in the streets where the skyscrapers loom,
and it's hard to breathe the air,
and they'll ask in a hundred languages,
"does anybody care?"

We belong in the darkened corners,
where the children cry for bread,
and they're tired of worn out promises,
and hope is all but dead.

For we are poor and the blind and lame whose
lives have been made new,
and the one who has given life to us,
has work for us to do.

CHAPTER TEN

GROWTH IN ASSOCIATIONS AND CHURCHES, 1970-1979

The Baptist Convention of New York matured and grew stronger in the 1970s as the churches continued to reach out to new communities with mission chapels and ministry programs. Growth was slow early in the decade, but by the late 1970s the convention was adding new and "adopted" congregations regularly to its fellowship. Associations formed in the years immediately prior to the convention's founding welcomed new leadership and adopted strategies for church extension that bore fruit within a few years. Older associations representing the major regional blocs which formed the convention maintained their momentum with new church starts and enhanced programs of ministry.

The Greater Rochester Association

A month after the Baptist Convention of New York was constituted, the Greater Rochester Baptist Association was organized from three churches and two missions that originally had been part of the Frontier Association. The amicable separation of the Bayview (renamed Jackson Road), Pinnacle Road, and Rochester Churches received the whole-hearted endorsement of the Frontier Association. In 1973 the Geneva Southern Baptist Church transferred its affiliation from the Southern Tier Association to the Greater Rochester Association.

The Rochester Baptist Church, under the leadership of pastor/director Nelson Tilton, continued in its role as a "mother" of churches in the Rochester area. In 1972 the church launched a Spanish-speaking congregation that was constituted in 1977 as the First Spanish Baptist Church of Rochester. Two years later the Rochester Church reached out to establish a congregation in the community of Pittsford. The church also extended its witness in 1976 to North Greece, where several of its families resided. That fellowship became the Community Baptist Church in 1978.

Mission Service Corps volunteers Edwin and Mildred Hewlett arrived in Rochester in 1978 to begin their ministry. The following year, the couple initiated the Brighton/Pittsford Chapel in their daughter's home. Sponsored by the Pinnacle Road Church, the chapel grew quickly and was constituted in 1980 as the Metropolitan Baptist Church. The congregation later changed its name to the Browncroft Baptist Church.

Ellis B. Turner, a former mission worker in Florida, came in July 1971 to serve as director of missions for the Frontier Association, but with added responsibilities in the Rochester area. With his leadership and broad-based support from the churches, the Greater Rochester Association rallied to have a collective impact on its region through Woman's Missionary Union, children's camp, special recreational events, mission studies, and Christian education programs. In the fall of 1979, the association called Norman Beckham as its first director of missions.[1]

At mid-decade the association was characterized by growth and vitality, with bright prospects for the future. By the end of the 1970s, however, a far different atmosphere prevailed.

Represented within the Greater Rochester Association were viewpoints that spanned a broad evangelical spectrum. Jim Tomlinson, who succeeded Royce Denton in 1977 as pastor of the Jackson Road Church, became increasingly uncomfortable with the diversity of thought and practice he observed within the association. The Criswell Bible Institute graduate was especially troubled by the action of the Rochester Church in ordaining women deacons, and by the indifference other churches seemed to have for what he saw as liberalism. Tomlinson found support in fellow CBI alumnus David Shirkey, pastor of the Community Church in North Greece, and among a few other leaders, but he was unable to influence the association to take action against the church.

Frustrated, Tomlinson led the Jackson Road Church to withdraw from the association and to drop its affiliation with the Southern Baptist Convention. The action and agitation that preceded it had a ripple effect that polarized the association, and indirectly damaged the North Greece Church, which disbanded in 1983.[2] These losses, added with the dissolution of the

Pittsford Church, left the association weakened but determined to press ahead with hope.

The Adirondack Association

Nowhere in the Baptist Convention of New York were the churches more indigenous, more rooted in the local culture, than those which comprised the Adirondack Association in the 1970s. And nowhere do the churches appear to have been more mission minded or more determined in their efforts to start new works than those in the North Country. A revival meeting in a synagogue, a mobile chapel, bus ministries, laypersons purchasing buildings for new churches, chapels reclaiming abandoned old church buildings for worship—the churches of the Adirondack Association spared no ingenuity or creativity in getting the job done. The First Christian Church of Brushton, led by pastor Norman Bell, was the center of missions activity for the association, but by the end of the decade a majority of the churches were sponsoring mission chapels.

After seven years of sharing an area missionary with the Central and Southern Tier Associations, and having no administrative leader from 1973 to 1975, the Adirondack Association called Norman Bell as its own director of missions in January 1976. Bell was a natural choice, embodying as he did the spirit of the association. John Simmons became pastor of the Brushton Church.

Church starts did not come easily in the area; in many cases, they came in "fits and starts," as Norman Bell put it. He likened the spasmodic beginnings of some churches to a person learning to drive with a standard transmission.[3] Many of the churches developed in the 1970s had disjointed histories as Bible study fellowships and chapels dating back to the early 1960s. A high turnover in pastoral leadership often created this difficulty, as did internal conflicts in churches which led to the abandonment or temporary suspension of new works.

The Sharron Woods Baptist Church reestablished a Southern Baptist witness in the Plattsburgh area after the Champlain Valley Church, begun in 1959 by Zig Boroughs, declared bankruptcy and lost its building in 1972. The few remaining members reorganized themselves and with help from the Home Mission Board and other large churches in the South, were able to constitute as a church and dedicate a new worship facility in 1974. Remarkably, the Sharron Woods Church was also lost to Southern Baptists less than ten years later.[4]

The Emmanuel Baptist Church of Potsdam and the Alexandria Bay Baptist Church were "mother" congregations to several new churches in the western half of the Adirondack Association. After seeing its Richville Chapel constituted as the Richville Baptist Church in 1969, the Emmanuel Church directed its attention toward launching new work in the Ogdensburg and Canton areas. The church established its Ogdensburg Chapel upon groundwork laid by the First Christian Church of Brushton in the early 1970s. In 1977 both churches celebrated the birth of the Grace Baptist Church in Ogdensburg. Roger Best was pastor of the church from its inception as a chapel until his retirement in 1995. Preparation for a new work at Canton was begun in the summer of 1977 by First Christian member Bruce Aubrey and two summer student missionaries who conducted surveys in the community. Mission Service Corps volunteers Jimmy and Donna Crawford and Jim and Peggy Ethetton helped launch the chapel in July 1978. The congregation was constituted as the Calvary Baptist Church in January 1983.

The Indian River Baptist Church of Philadelphia, New York (1977), was begun in the home of Richard and Mona Graves in Theresa. Members of the Alexandria Bay Church, the Graves family was joined in its church-starting effort by mission pastor Steve Dinzler, who utilized the Adirondack Association's mobile chapel for an additional worship service in the nearby community of Philadelphia. For a short time, Dinzler maintained chapel fellowships in both Theresa and Philadelphia. The groups merged in the late 1970s to form the Indian River Church. Richard Graves later became pastor of the church.[5]

In the mid-1970s, pastor John Follett led the Alexandria Bay Church to initiate yet another mission, this one in the village of Gouverneur. With substantial financial support and visiting work crews from churches in the South, the congregation constructed its own facility before the end of the decade. Pastor Jimmy Merck guided the mission in its formative stages. The congregation was constituted as the West Side Baptist Church in 1983 with Tom Sochia as pastor.

The Richville Church reached out to the communities of Pyrites and North Russell in 1977 with a mission under the leadership of Maurice and Florence Lindsay—a couple instrumental in starting both the Emmanuel (Potsdam) and Richville Churches. A lay pastor, Lindsay led the Richville Church to rent a vacant, dilapidated church building in North Russell for the chapel. The "work of faith and labor of love" by the Lindsays and fellow church members in renovating the building was rewarded with the birth of a new church in the community, the Baptist Church of the Good Shepherd, constituted in 1982.[6]

Throughout the 1970s, the First Christian Church of Brushton sponsored a large family of mission congregations. The church nurtured a mission in the Brasher Falls area that was constituted in 1974 as the Victory Baptist Church. Harold Lefler was the congregation's first pastor. In October 1976, the Brushton Church's mission begun four years earlier at Lawrenceville was constituted as the Lawrenceville Baptist Church. Two pastors who later served Adirondack Association churches, Jim Meola (Richville) and Tom Sochia (West Side), were members of the Lawrenceville Church. The Shiloh Baptist Church of Malone (1980) was begun as a Bible study in the home of First Christian Church member David Aubrey in April 1976.

In 1975 two deacons of the Brushton Church, Ralph Russell and John Edwards, purchased and remodeled an apartment house to provide worship space and a parsonage for a new mission in Bangor. Russell and Edwards were "landlords" for the fellowship until 1977, when the congregation purchased the building and was constituted as the Bangor Baptist Church.[7]

Harold Clark, also a member of the Brushton Church, helped reestablish a chapel at Saranac Lake in 1977. Launched originally in 1967, the chapel suffered from inconsistent leadership until Clark's arrival. He led the congregation to erect a new building with the help of work teams from Georgia and South Carolina. The chapel remains a mission of the First Christian Church of Brushton.

In an effort to begin planting churches near the southern end of Lake Champlain, the Adirondack Association undertook a cooperative extension project in Whitehall beginning in 1979. Pastor Larry Pridmore organized the chapel, which was constituted in 1985 as the Grace Baptist Church.

By the end of the 1970s, the number of churches in the Adirondack Association had multiplied almost threefold, with additional chapels developing in Watertown, Tupper Lake, and Schuyler Falls. Growth had not come easily, but it surely had come.

The Southern Tier Association

The image of an automobile lurching forward erratically and screeching to a halt is apropos as well for describing mission expansion among the churches of the Southern Tier Association in the 1970s. But unlike the Adirondack Association, which experienced a significant net gain in churches over the decade, the Southern Tier Association suffered disappointing results.

Before the Ackley Avenue Chapel in Johnson City disbanded in 1971, pastor Waylen Bray started a new work in Ithaca under the sponsorship of the Lincoln Avenue Church in Endicott. The group called Glenn Huisinga as pastor, and in 1973 merged with a chapel in the community of Caroline. The Ithaca/Caroline Chapel appeared to be well on its way to constituting as a church until Huisinga resigned in August 1975. Without pastoral leadership, the work floundered and disbanded a short time later.[8]

The Southern Tier Association welcomed its first director of missions—A. Wilson Parker—in September 1976. Parker's ministry seemed to breathe fresh life into the association's church planting efforts, but the leader remained in the association only eighteen months.

In the mid-1970s, the Lincoln Avenue Church revived a chapel at Apalachin which had faltered earlier in the decade, and launched a new work in the community of Owego. The Apalachin congregation was constituted in 1978 as the Fellowship Baptist Church, but by 1980 it had disbanded. The Owego Chapel fared better under the close supervision of Wilson Parker, who assisted the congregation from its inception in August 1977 to January 1978 when the congregation called its first pastor, Harold Lefler. The Owego Southern Baptist Church was constituted in 1979.

In 1977 the Southport Church in Elmira extended an outreach westward to Corning and eastward to Waverly. The Corning Chapel developed rapidly, calling a pastor, David Lay, in July. By the end of the year, the congregation was constituted as the Corning Baptist Church; but by the mid-1980s, this church had also failed. The Faith Baptist Chapel of Waverly, organized with the leadership of pastor George Elam, continues as a mission of the Southport Church.

Despite efforts to start new works in a variety of communities, the churches of the Southern Tier Association reported a net gain of only one church in the 1970s. By the end of the decade, however, things were looking brighter for the association. In late 1979, John Simmons, pastor of the First Christian Church of Brushton, agreed to come as director of missions. New work was again underway in Ithaca, and plans were being made for chapels in Binghamton, Norwich, and Watkins Glen.

The Central Association

Organized in 1961, the Central Association was an close-knit family of churches by the time the Baptist Convention of New York was organized. Woman's Missionary Union, training opportunities in Sunday School and evangelism, youth ministry, summer camp—the association excelled in providing churches with a well-rounded program of fellowship and ministry. A strong spirit of cooperation prevailed within the association.

When, for example, bus ministry was seen as the wave of the future for church growth, several churches participated in a plan to acquire busses from school district salvage yards. Seven churches pressed the vehicles into service in 1972.

The temptation was strong for churches to rest "at ease in Zion" within a secure circle of cooperating sister churches, but associational leaders like J. T. Davis and Clifford Matthews recognized the immensity of the mission task for central New York. The geographic region served by the association was deemed so large, in fact, that the mission committee in 1971 divided itself to handle responsibilities in east and west zones of the association.

The Central Baptist Church of Syracuse continued its tradition of church planting into the 1970s. The church established a new work at Elbridge that constituted in 1974 as the Temple Baptist Church, with James Knapton as pastor. In June 1971, the Central Church initiated a fellowship in the home of Bob and Betty Taylor that within one year had become the Bellewood Chapel. The chapel was guided by interim pastoral leadership until January 1973 when the congregation called Charles Sharp as its first full-time pastor. With his leadership and the work of laypersons like the Taylors, the chapel was ready by its second anniversary as a mission to constitute as the Bellewood Baptist Church.[9]

Charles Sharp utilized his musical talents in forming a Central Association youth choir that toured parts of the Northeast in the mid-1970s. His career as a home missionary later took him to Colorado, where he was executive director of the Colorado Baptist General Convention from 1984 to 1992.

Like the Central Church, the Grace Baptist Church of Rome persisted in its steady pattern of mission outreach. In August 1972, the church launched the Beacon Light Chapel in the Verona area, after a summer of Vacation Bible Schools and a tent revival in the community. The Beacon Light Baptist Church was constituted in March 1974 under the leadership of pastor Frank Adams.[10]

In 1970, after eleven years of ministry at the Grace Baptist Church in Rome, J. T. Davis became pastor/director of the Trinity Baptist Church in Schenectady. Clifford Matthews resigned as pastor of the Clinton Road Church in 1973 to join the staff at the Trinity Church as mission outreach coordinator. The BCNY had high hopes for developing a cluster of churches in the Capital District and committed significant resources to the work through the convention's annual state missions offering. After J. T. Davis accepted the call in March 1974 to become the director of missions for the Central Association, Matthews became pastor of the Trinity Church.

The J. T. and Bertie Mae Davis family—Davis was pastor of the Grace Baptist Church in Rome and the Trinity Baptist Church, Schenectady, before becoming director of missions for the Central Association in 1970.

Davis and Matthews helped lay the groundwork for chapels that began taking shape in the mid-1970s in the village of Ballston Lake and in Albany. Sponsored by the Trinity Church, the congregations matured rapidly and were able to acquire property with assistance from the Home Mission Board and large churches in the South. The Albany Chapel, which called pastor Dean Allen in 1976, purchased the old First Baptist Church building in downtown Albany for its home. In 1979 the congregation was constituted as the Albany Baptist Church. The Ballston Lake fellowship welcomed its first full-time pastor, George McDearmon, in 1977, and was constituted the same year as the Ballston Lake Baptist Church. Within two years the church had begun cultivating missions of its own in Glens Falls and Saratoga Springs.

After almost ten years with only one church in the Capital District, New York Baptists felt they were gaining a foothold in the area. Disturbing developments in the next few years, however, jarred this confidence.

The Ballston Lake, Albany, and Adirondack (former Glens Falls Chapel) Churches were all lost from the BCNY fellowship in the mid-1980s. Pastors Dean Allen, George McDearmon, and Robert Lynn became involved in the "Reformed Baptist movement," a hyper-Calvinistic theological perspective that led them to diminish the value of associationalism, mission outreach, and evangelism as typically taught by Southern Baptists.[11] The churches rejected the very process of interchurch cooperation that had helped develop their congregations and provide compensation for their pastors.

Waylen Bray's earlier disappointing experience in the Southern Tier Association left him with the haunting feeling that his efforts there had done more harm than good for the Southern Baptist name. Still convinced of his calling to New York, he returned to the state in 1975 to create what he called "Tri-County Baptist Ministries"—an effort to start new churches in Otsego, Delaware, and Schoharie Counties. Bray aligned his missionary work closely with the program of the Central Association and the Baptist Convention of New York.[12] Through his efforts, the Maryland Baptist Church (1977); the Stamford Baptist Church (1979); and, later, the Jefferson Baptist Church (1988) were organized.

By the end of the 1970s, the churches of the Central Association were concentrated roughly in three areas along the New York State Thruway: greater Syracuse, Utica, and the Capital District. The prospect of new associations to be parceled from the larger association was a lively topic of discussion within the congregations of each area. With a chapel begun near Syracuse University, with others started in Ilion, Cortland, Oswego, and Fayetteville, the churches of the Central Association were living up to their theme for 1979: "Bold missions while it is yet day."

The Frontier Association

Western New York—the cradle of Southern Baptist work in the state—continued to be a fertile mission field into the 1970s. The Frontier Association, which in 1958 stretched across an enormous part of the state, by 1970 had been whittled down to a far more manageable eight-county region.

For most of the decade, Ellis Turner guided the association as director of missions. Clifford Matthews assumed that task in 1978. Prior to coming to New York in the late 1960s as pastor of the Clinton Road Baptist Church, Matthews and his wife Peggy requested that the Home Mission Board send them someplace "so hard that if someone is saved, we'll know God did it."[13] Their experiences in central New York, in the Capital District, and in the Frontier Association made the couple confident the board had honored their wishes.

The Frontier Association benefited from the able leadership of Turner and Matthews and pastors like Jim Bullis, Byron Lutz, and Curtis Porter. The stable, foundational strength of the association, however, was its high level of lay involvement in ministry. Dale and Jean Meredith, who arrived in the Buffalo area in 1973, epitomized the eager, cooperative spirit of many laypeople in the association. "God called us here," they observed. ". . . We live in the most beautiful part of America. Fall is magnificent, summer is cool, and the snow is beautiful. And God has blessed us with much to do to serve him. What more can you ask?"[14] The same missionary spirit marked a growing number of lay leaders indigenous to the region.

A strong sense of community was also apparent among the churches of the Frontier Association. Disputes over issues such as alien immersion were pressed in ways that sometimes seemed to threatened the harmony of the association; yet a spirit of mutual dependency, a unity of mission, and a bond of fellowship among the churches mitigated against division over controversial matters of doctrine or church practice.[15]

The historic LaSalle Baptist Church was among several congregations of the Frontier Association launching missions that constituted as churches in the early 1970s. Its new work, the Friendship Baptist Church in Niagara Falls (later, North Tonawanda), was constituted in 1971. John and Martha Mathison, among the early Alabamians who formed the LaSalle Church in the 1950s, organized the Faith Baptist Church in Niagara Falls in 1976. The church was received into the Frontier Association in 1984. Church planter Paul Bard led in the development of the Grossman Avenue Baptist Church in Olean, which was admitted to the association by petition in 1972.[16] The First Baptist Church of Silver Creek was organized in 1973 after five years as a mission of the West Main Church in Fredonia. At this time the West Main Church also began cultivating a Spanish chapel—*Mision Bautista Hispaña*—in Dunkirk.

In the summer of 1970, the North Tonawanda Church sponsored a Vacation Bible School in Lancaster that led to the formation of the Veteran's Park Baptist Church. Jim Bullis resigned as pastor of the North Tonawanda Church to shepherd the eight adults and fifty-two children who comprised the congregation. Remarkably, the church was constituted in July 1970 and soon was able to purchase property in the Depew area.

More than anything else, the Veteran's Park Church was known in the 1970s for its weekday children's programs and massive Vacation Bible Schools held in local parks. Jim Bullis and his wife Mary led multiple programs with the assistance of student summer missionaries. In some cases the VBS programs laid the groundwork for new churches. The Sullivan Road Baptist Church, constituted in 1979 with the leadership of pastor Gil Samuelson, had its beginnings in a VBS effort, as did a later church start in Clarence. Mary Bullis chronicled her and her husband's missionizing adventures with "sno-cone" evangelism, i.e., Vacation Bible School, in a 1982 Broadman Press publication, *Mary, Come Home!*

The Veteran's Park Church was also responsible for initiating a chapel in Cheektowaga that became the French Road Baptist Church in 1978. Curtis Monday was the congregation's first pastor. He guided the congregation through a difficult period in the late 1970s when their building was destroyed by fire.

Byron Lutz continued to lead a program of weekday ministries at the Fillmore Avenue Baptist Church—the only Frontier Association church within the city limits of Buffalo. Seeking new ways to minister to troubled, inner-city youth, he established a rural retreat center: "Camp Iron Bell."

The camp was made possible with generous support from the Home Mission Board and the federal government. Student missionaries toiled four summers to prepare the property. Lutz reported numerous "miracles" of changed lives at the camp.[17]

Among the students who labored to prepare Camp Iron Bell were Jerry and Janice Jones. The couple moved to Ellington in 1978 to be caretakers of the camp. Finding no Southern Baptist church there, they determined to start one under the sponsorship of the Fillmore Avenue Church. In July 1979, they launched the chapel in the Ellington Odd Fellows Lodge. More than a decade later, the congregation moved into a renovated barn where Jones and volunteer work groups turned cattle stalls into Sunday School classrooms and an upstairs dance floor into a sanctuary. The Baptist Church of Ellington was constituted in 1991 with Jerry Jones as pastor.[18]

The Metropolitan New York Association

In 1970 the Metropolitan Association elected Ken Lyle to succeed Paul James as director of missions. Lyle's love for youth work, his concern for racial reconciliation, and his heart for ministry impacted significantly on the character of the association. He directed the association until his resignation in 1978 to become pastor of the Tabernacle Baptist Church in Atlanta. In March 1979, R. Quinn Pugh, former pastor of the Bergen Baptist Church (1962–1972), became director of missions. He returned to the metropolitan area after a tenure in Bel Air, Maryland, as pastor of the Calvary Baptist Church.

Lyle attempted to harness the energies of the association's teenagers through the "Youth Corps," a ministry and service organization for high schoolers. Members of the Youth Corps shared their faith, were catalysts for their local youth groups, and undertook projects from painting buildings to holding youth rallies. With the help of volunteers like Nancy Ryals, Reyes Rodriguez, and Malachi Roundtree, Lyle was able to develop an effective youth ministry that spanned the diversity of the association. In 1974 more than six hundred teenagers and youth leaders attended winter retreats.[19]

In the early 1970s, the Metropolitan Association became involved in efforts to improve race relations and impoverished neighborhoods in New York City. The "Central Harlem Association of Neighborhood Churches Endeavor," or C.H.A.N.C.E., was an organization of churches which banded together in 1970 for ministry and mission outreach. The Metro Association shared in programs with the organization, providing seminary extension classes, children's and youth programs, and other ministries aimed at ameliorating conditions in one of the nation's poorest ghettoes.

As a result of its involvement with C.H.A.N.C.E., the association received several Harlem and Bronx area churches for membership. Most of the congregations maintained a dual-alignment with the National Baptist Convention and the SBC. Pastor Jasper Simmons led the Greater File Chapel Baptist Church to become the first C.H.A.N.C.E. church to affiliate with the association. When the Christ Temple Baptist Church was admitted to the association in 1972, the event made history for Southern Baptists. The church's pastor, Drucillar Fordham, became the first woman pastor of a Southern Baptist Church.[20] Other churches admitted during this period included the Good Shepherd Baptist Church in the Bronx, Bertram Price, pastor; Greater Universal Baptist Church, Robert Woolbright, pastor; Greater Victory Baptist Church, Grady Donald, pastor; Mount Hope Missionary Baptist Church; Mount Zion Baptist Church of Christ, Robert Bullock, pastor; and the Walker Missionary Baptist Church, W. William Tolton, pastor. During this time the Unity Freedom Baptist Church in Newark, Isaac Martin, pastor, also united with the association.

Professor Cal Guy of Southwestern Seminary helped begin another social ministry in 1970 while serving as interim director of missions for the association. Led by pastors and laypersons, T.O.N.E., or "Total Operations for Neighborhood Environment," was a non-profit corporation formed to "provide resources and training to effect an urban environment which fostered hope and pride rather than despair." The bold initiative was led primarily by corporate leaders like Joe H. Hunt, J. D. Callender, and Bob Bell. Wes Bratcher arrived in January 1972 to become the full-time director of the organization. Although not "officially" affiliated with the Metro Association, T.O.N.E. was vitally related to the association's ministry. Difficulties with the New York City housing authority limited T.O.N.E.'s effectiveness, but some projects proved successful, like the renovation of an apartment building that housed the Atonement Baptist Church, where the organization's secretary, Rodolph Morgan, was pastor.[21]

The rapid growth of the Metro Association necessitated additional staff in the mid-1970s. DeLane M. Ryals, pastor of the West Monmouth Baptist Church, became director of church extension in January 1974. M. Ray Gilliland, who since 1969 had directed the BCNY's program of campus ministry in New York City, became the association's director of Christian social ministries in October 1975.

One of the most significant events of the 1970s for the association was the purchase of its six-story office building at 236 West Seventy-second Street. The facility provided adequate office space, a chapel, space for ministry programs, a fully equipped kitchen and dining area, and rooms to be converted into apartments. The association purchased the Upper West

Side building from the American Board of Missions to the Jews at a remarkably discounted price of $350,000. Generous support from the Home Mission Board, Metropolitan Baptist Ministries (a nonprofit corporation formed to raise capital for the association), and the churches of the Metro Association made the acquisition possible.[22]

The churches of the Metropolitan New York Association celebrated their diversity throughout the 1970s, adding churches representing new language groups to what some called a "beautiful weave of humanity." Chinese, Korean, Portuguese, Romanian, and Arabic churches were woven into the tapestry of the association during these years.

In 1972 pastor H. C. Au-Yeung, a graduate of New Orleans Baptist Theological Seminary, led the Trust in God Baptist Church in lower Manhattan to affiliate with Southern Baptists. Founded in 1888, the historic congregation was deeply rooted in the culture of New York City's Chinatown. In the mid-1970s, the church established an English-speaking Chinese congregation under the direction of Ken Tom. The mission program of the association led to the development of a Chinese congregation in the Bay Ridge section of Brooklyn. In 1975 the Raritan Valley Baptist Church "adopted" the fledgling mission guided by Mark and Florence Hui. The congregation was constituted nine years later as the Brooklyn Chinese Baptist Church.

The Korean Baptist Church of New York, gathered initially in the home of James and Martha Chun in 1974 and led by Army Chaplain Robert Maples, was admitted to the association in 1976. H. M. Kim was the congregation's first pastor. Michael Chiew, who later was employed by the Baptist

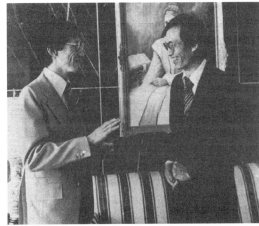

Peter Kung (left), the Home Mission Board's national consultant for Chinese church growth, discussed mission strategy with Mark Hui, pastor of the Brooklyn Chinese Baptist Church.

Convention of New York as a church planter, was one of the congregation's first deacons.

The First Portuguese-speaking Church of New York was begun in 1976 as a chapel of the Highland Avenue Church in Jamaica, Queens. The church was constituted and admitted to the Metropolitan Association in 1983, with Humberto Fernandez as organizing pastor.

Pastor Cornel Pascu led in organizing the First Romanian Baptist Church of Ridgewood, New York, in 1972. The congregation was later sponsored by the First Polish Baptist Church of Brooklyn, and became a part of the association in 1979 under the leadership of pastor Aureliam Popesku.

Mission pastors William Khalil, George Wassily, and Sabry Elraheb began ministry among peoples of Middle Eastern descent in the 1970s. Khalil organized the First Arabic Baptist Church of Jersey City in 1975. The congregation became a part of the association in 1980 and later relocated to Aberdeen, New Jersey, to share facilities with the Calvary Baptist Church. Wassily laid the groundwork for what became the First Arabic Baptist Church of Yonkers. His efforts there were sponsored by the East Brunswick Church. Elraheb's first assignment upon his arrival from Egypt was to serve as pastor of an Arabic mission in Queens.

Churches from existing language groups continued to expand their ministry across the metropolitan area. The Resurrection Baptist Church in Bergenfield, New Jersey, a suburban Spanish-speaking congregation, was organized in 1976 with the leadership of pastor George Comesanas. Later, the church purchased a building in Dumont, New Jersey. The Emmanuel Spanish Baptist Church of Union City was also gathered in 1976. Led by pastor Juan Couso, the church was admitted to the Metro Association the following year. The Calvary Baptist Church in Medford sponsored and hosted a Spanish congregation that became the William Carey Baptist Church in 1980. Jesus Martinez was the organizing pastor. In 1977 the now defunct Woodside Spanish Baptist Church launched what became the First Spanish Baptist Church of Rockaway. Also in 1977, the Canaan Baptist Church in Corona joined the association by petition. Founding pastor Ernesto Chaparro led the church later to sponsor a Brazilian chapel in Queens and a church in Ecuador. He became a leader not only among the Hispanic fellowship of churches in the Metropolitan Association, but also in the wider context of the Baptist Convention of New York.

The French-speaking Baptist Church of Brooklyn, led by pastor Jean Baptiste Thomas, helped create in the mid-1970s a network of Haitian chapels across the metropolitan area. In a massive service at the Brooklyn church, five new Haitian churches were born. Scattered from Connecticut to the Jersey shore were the French-speaking Baptist Church of Stamford, Connecticut, Emmanuel St. Juste, pastor; Bethany Baptist Church, Jamaica, New York, Pierre Leonidas, pastor; French-speaking Baptist Church of Far Rockaway, New York, Ismael Pierre, pastor; First French-speaking Church of Asbury Park, New Jersey, Guy Jean Florival, pastor; and the French Haitian Baptist Church of Manhattan, Karnest Joseph, pastor. Two additional Haitian congregations in Brooklyn—the Ebenezer French Baptist Church and the Good Shepherd Baptist Church—were added to the association in 1971 and 1977.

Several American and Caribbean black congregations became a part of the Metro Association's family of churches in the 1970s. The Wake Eden Community Baptist Church in the northeast Bronx was a joint project of the Bronx Baptist Church and the Greenwich Baptist Church. Pastor Sam Simpson of the Bronx Church launched the chapel in 1972. With support from laypeople like Bob Bell in the Greenwich Church, the Wake Eden Church became a reality, constituting in 1979. The Wake Eden Academy, a weekday ministry of the church, was established in 1976 under the direction of Maisie Bruce.[23]

The Genesis Baptist Church in Newark, led by Horace P. Sharper, joined the association by petition in 1972. Pastor Sharper ministered extensively in the Georgia-King Village housing complex. Elder James Paige led the Evangelical Reform Baptist Church of Newark to unite with the association in 1975. The church sponsored energetic street rallies that featured services of anointing and healing. The First Baptist Church of Montclair began a new work in the mid-1970s in East Orange—the First Baptist Chapel. Arnold Fox, a bivocational pastor, was also volunteer Baptist chaplain at the East Orange General Hospital. The Greater New Jerusalem Baptist Church of Morristown, Howard Anderson, pastor, joined the association in 1973.

The Fellowship Baptist Church in Irvington, New Jersey, became a part of the Metropolitan Association by petition in 1977. Founded in 1961 by pastor Herbert Graves as a National Baptist Convention congregation, the Fellowship Church became a center for seminary extension classes in the Newark area. In central New Jersey the Raritan Valley Church worked with pastor Fred Jackson and a core group of laypeople like Ernesto and Doris Robinson in launching a new work in the late 1970s that was constituted within a few years as the Somerset Baptist Church.

Two predominantly African-American churches on Staten Island affiliated with the Metropolitan Association in the mid-1970s. The Greater New Hope Baptist Church and the Fellowship Baptist Church were led, respectively, by pastors Robert Moody and Arthur Phillips.

Church extension among predominantly Anglo congregations also produced significant growth in the association. On Long Island, the Calvary Baptist Church in Medford sponsored a congregation in Shirley that in 1973 became the Trinity Baptist Church. James Wingate was the organizing pastor. The North Shore Baptist Church in Kings Park sponsored the Washington Avenue Baptist Church in Brentwood. The church was constituted in 1978 under the direction of its first pastor, Robert Sommer.

The Southside Baptist Church in Kingston, New York, was a sponsoring church to two new congregations in the Hudson Valley. In 1975 the church launched a Bible study fellowship that led the next year to the formation of the New Hope Baptist Church in Kingston. Don Crum was the church's first pastor. Harry and Betty Watson, who figured prominently in the earliest Southern Baptist work in the Hudson Valley, started the New Salem Baptist Church in Monticello in 1977 with the sponsorship of the Southside Church. The church was constituted in 1982 with Harry Watson as pastor.

The Wilton Baptist Church also assisted in starting a new work in this northernmost territory of the association. In 1978 the church assumed sponsorship of a Bible study fellowship in Stormville, New York, that was generated by a Praxis team.[24] The group formed the nucleus of what became the Dutchess Valley Baptist Church in 1994.

A Praxis team in 1975 generated the initial interest that led to the formation of the Lakeland Baptist Church in Franklin, New Jersey. Sponsored by the Madison Church and assisted by the Hope Church in Flanders, the church was constituted in 1991 with Larry Wood as pastor. In March 1975, the Madison Church also became the sponsor of a new fellowship organized in the Bridgewater, New Jersey, home of Jim and Ann Benton. The congregation shortly thereafter moved to the Bridgewater 4-H Club Center, and in January 1976 called their first pastor, Reid Doster. The Bridgewater Baptist Church was constituted in February 1977.[25]

In northern New Jersey, the Living Gospel Baptist Church was organized in 1973 from a merger of the Rutherford Baptist Church (ABC) and the Living Gospel Chapel, under the sponsorship of the Bergen Baptist Church (now Christ Community Church in Waldwick). The Living Gospel Chapel emerged amidst the "Jesus People" movement on the campuses of Fairleigh Dickinson University and Montclair State University. Elias Gomes was the founding pastor of the church. George Gera, the first indigenous New York Baptist appointed as a missionary by the Foreign Mission Board, was a member of the Living Gospel Church.

In the southernmost territory of the Metro Association—Monmouth County—the Calvary Baptist Church in Aberdeen, New Jersey, began a chapel in the community of Colts Neck in 1973. Cosponsored by the

Monmouth and West Monmouth Churches, the chapel was constituted in 1976 as the Colts Neck Baptist Church. John Lindsey was the church's first pastor.

By the mid-1970s, the Manhattan Baptist Church was worshiping in a small chapel facility at the associational office building. Since its founding in 1958, the church had continually given itself away by spinning off new churches. This factor, coupled with numerous leadership difficulties and the development of a new midtown congregation, diminished the church's numerical strength. By 1980 the church that had given birth to all Southern Baptist work along the northeastern seaboard had become dormant.

The Metro Baptist Church was a successor to the Manhattan Church. Begun in 1974 as a mission of the Greenwich Church, the new work attracted a diverse constituency and had a decidedly urban focus of ministry. John Halbrook, former pastor of the Manhattan Church, was the congregation's first pastor. The Metro Church was constituted in 1982 under the direction of pastor W. Eugene Bolin. Bolin also led the congregation to purchase a church building on West Fortieth Street in the heart of what once was known as "Hell's Kitchen." In the mid-1980s, the church became sponsor of the Metro Brazilian Baptist Mission, Paulo Capelozza, pastor, and the Metro Baptist Mission (Spanish), under the direction of Walter Montalvo.

The Metro Association's program of social ministry led to the formation of another Manhattan congregation. In the summer of 1974, Ray Gilliland, Bruce Schoonmaker, and others established a ministry center on the Lower East Side of Manhattan known as "Graffiti." Sponsored by the Greenwich Church and later by the Metro Church, the ministry by 1982 had developed into a small congregation guided by pastor/director Bill Berry. After more than twenty years as a mission, the Graffiti/East Seventh Chapel was constituted as the East Seventh Baptist Church, under the direction of Taylor and Susan Field.

Evangelist Billy Graham, whose 1957 Madison Square Garden crusade provided some of the impetus for Southern Baptist work in the Northeast, predicted that Paul James would live to see one hundred churches planted in the New York City metro area.[26] In a little more than twenty years after that prophetic statement, with James very much alive in retirement, the Metropolitan New York Baptist Association numbered more than one hundred churches and chapels, ministering to the diverse population of the region. Not even the most visionary of leaders could possibly have imagined such an abundant harvest.

CHAPTER ELEVEN

Baptist Convention of New York

COMING OF AGE, 1980-1989

Ken Medema's lyrical refrain, "We belong . . ." expressed more than just a desire to "fit in" on the part of Southern Baptists in the Northeast. The song reflected a growing reality. Southern Baptists were no longer newcomers to New York, New Jersey, and Connecticut, nor were they so sparse in number as to be inconsequential to the religious life of the region. The churches were becoming increasingly indigenous and representative of the ethnic pluralism of the region.

After a decade of steady organizational development and growth in new churches, the Baptist Convention of New York was coming of age with a more regionalized configuration of associations, firmer institutional moorings, and a broader-based program of ministry.

Poised for Growth—New Associational Alignments and Leadership

By the early 1980s, the BCNY was beginning to dot the landscape with a wider distribution of churches, especially in upstate New York. The creation of new associations followed this development.

The Central Association—once a vast territory stretching east to west from Syracuse to Albany, south to Binghamton, and north to the Canadian border—divided itself to facilitate further growth in two areas of the Baptist Convention of New York. Having developed the Adirondack and Southern Tier Associations in the late 1960s, the association spun off the

164

Greater Syracuse and Hudson Associations in 1980. In June 1982, J. T. Davis retired as director of missions for the Central Association. That fall, the churches afforded their former leader a rare honor in renaming the association the Davis Baptist Association. D. Wayne Dyer became director of missions in April 1983.

The Greater Syracuse Baptist Association was organized in September 1980 at the Northside Baptist Church in Liverpool. Larry Coleman, pastor of the Bellewood Church in North Syracuse, was elected moderator.[1] Darwin Bacon, pastor of the Farmingdale Baptist Church on Long Island, became the association's first director of missions in 1982. He was followed by Michael Anderson (1985–1993).

To the east, the churches in the area of the Capital District joined with congregations scattered along the upper Hudson Valley to form the Hudson Baptist Association. The association was organized in October 1980 at the Ballston Lake Baptist Church, with the pastor of that church, George McDearmon, elected as moderator. The Whitehall Chapel, developed through the mission program of the Adirondack Association, joined the Hudson Association in 1982.

The churches of the North Country created a new association from the western zone of the Adirondack Association in September 1982. The organization of the Thousand Islands Baptist Association was part of a long-range plan developed for the region in the 1970s. James Perry, who replaced Norman Bell as director of missions for the Adirondack Association after the latter's medical retirement in 1982, served double duty as leader for both associations. Roger Best, pastor of the Grace Baptist Church in Ogdensburg, was the new association's first moderator.

The churches on Long Island were intimately related to the history of the Metropolitan New York Association. By the late 1970s, however, some pastors and lay leaders on the island had come to feel that their area was being neglected; that the Metro Association was focused more upon reaching the city than the suburbs. A Long Island pastors' fellowship led in the formation of the Long Island Baptist Association in December 1981. Robert Brooks, pastor of the Grace Baptist Church in Lake Grove, was the first moderator.[2] Joseph Causey was the association's first director of missions (1984–1985). David Leary arrived in 1989 and held the position until 1994.

Serving the Churches in the Early 1980s

By 1980 the Baptist Convention of New York had developed a well-rounded, versatile program of support for the churches. Divisions adapted and expanded to address the specialized needs of the convention and to make the programs and mission support of the Southern Baptist Convention accessible to the churches.

In January 1980, the BCNY opened a Baptist Book Store at the Central Church in Syracuse, with Doris Lowndes as manager. The contract outlet store was intended to provide New York Baptists with a convenient means of securing religious books, SBC program support materials, and church supplies. Profits from sales were to accrue to the state convention. After losses in three of the first four years of operation, the convention began utilizing Mission Service Corps volunteers as managers. Valera Cranford was the first MSC store manager (1984–1985).

Under Bill Dunning's direction, the education division continued to emphasize its basic program assignment: the Bible teaching ministry of the churches. Workshops and training institutes were held across the convention territory, including "Getting Ready" Sunday School clinics in Syracuse and Madison. These events were the precursor to a BCNY Sunday School "convention"—a comprehensive training event launched in September 1983 that provided instruction in teaching methods, administration, growth, and outreach.

In conjunction with the Sunday School Board's efforts in the early 1980s to pump new life into Church Training, the education division promoted an array of new materials for the traditional Sunday evening program. It also introduced "MasterLife"—an intensive discipleship training tool designed for church leaders.

The education division initiated a program of family ministry in 1980. That year the BCNY began a series of marriage enrichment retreats for couples who wished to improve their own marriages and to be trained as leaders for enrichment events across the convention territory.

By 1980 about one-fourth of the 285 universities and colleges within the BCNY territory were being touched in some way by Baptist campus ministry. Dunning continued to utilize a large corps of volunteers to complement the work of full-time, US-2, and Mission Service Corps campus ministers.

Daniel Sanchez became director of the missions division in August 1981 after five years of leadership in the evangelism division. Sanchez's promotion of the language mission program led to the establishment of a Spanish "Center for Theological Studies in New York City" and to the development of Brazilian, East Indian, Korean, and Laotian work in Rochester and Syracuse.

The 1980 federal census revealed that the largest concentration of African-Americans in the United States lived in the territory of the Baptist

Convention of New York. In 1981 the missions division developed a program of black church relations to help BCNY churches establish cooperative relationships with National Baptist Convention churches, and to assist predominantly African-American BCNY churches in mission outreach. The Fillmore Avenue Baptist Church in Buffalo and the Central Baptist Church in Syracuse, which by the early 1980s were becoming predominantly black congregations, joined the African-American churches of the Metropolitan Association in working to strengthen the convention's program of ministry for black churches. Leroy Gainey, pastor of the Central Church, was an early advocate of a stronger program for the convention.[3]

The missions division's program of seminary extension became an important avenue for ministry to black and Hispanic communities in the early 1980s. Under the direction of language associate Manuel Alonso, multiple centers for theological training were opened in local churches. Classes in the metropolitan New York City area were offered in Spanish and French.

Following Gloria Grogan's departure for a position in Washington, D.C., the missions division in May 1982 welcomed Nona Bickerstaff as director of Christian social ministry/Woman's Missionary Union. The former missionary and North Carolina WMU staff member began her tenure working closely with Barbara Nesmith, who as president of the state WMU (1978–1983) did much to advance the BCNY's ministry to women.

Jack Parrott became director of the evangelism division in September 1982, after having served in a similar position on the Maryland state staff. The Michigan native inherited a broad-ranging program centered in evangelism development in local churches, mass evangelism, and personal evangelism. His first assignments included preparing churches for simultaneous evangelism events during the Northeast Evangelism Thrust campaign (April 1984), and hosting the convention's first seminar for Continuing Witness Training—an intensive personal evangelism program developed by the Home Mission Board. George Russ, pastor of the Emmanuel Baptist Church in Riverhead, Long Island, joined the BCNY staff in August 1983 as urban evangelism consultant.

Administrative Tensions

Executive Director Jack Lowndes inherited a young, high-spirited, and optimistic convention in 1975. Given the remarkable growth that had occurred since the founding of their first churches in Niagara Falls and New York City less than a generation before, New York Baptists pondered almost unlimited possibilities for their convention in the years ahead.

Could a state office building; a fully-developed, specialized staff—even a "Northeastern Baptist Theological Seminary"—be long in coming? Many thought not.

Lowndes attempted to guide the BCNY to fulfill its highest expectations. From 1975 to 1980, he oversaw a period of growth in the convention where the number of churches increased by 50 percent and the budget doubled. By the early 1980s, growth had leveled off, but budgetary pressures had not. In 1980 and 1981, the executive board revised budgets downward at midyear when projected offering goals were not met. The convention experienced cash deficits, which were financed in part through monies diverted from gifts designated for SBC purposes.[4] A laxity in accounting procedures and reporting made the financial status of the convention difficult to analyze. As one leader complained, "The bottom line never really was the bottom line."

The state office also experienced a rapid turnover of staff during this time. Abrupt resignations of division directors and associates in 1979, 1980, and 1981 necessitated a reshuffling of staff assignments. Such changes brought frustrations to some of the staff and created an uneasiness within the convention. The sensitive nature of personnel matters necessitated a confidentiality that left many wondering what really was happening in Syracuse. Office morale waned, and by early 1982, members of the staff and the board had begun questioning Lowndes's management style, bookkeeping, and office procedures.

In December 1982, Jack Lowndes resigned as executive director of the Baptist Convention of New York. In accepting his resignation, the board granted him severance benefits for a time to reevaluate his ministry. Wallace Williams, pastor of the Madison Baptist Church and chairman of the executive board, cited "differences in management" in the decision to accept Lowndes's resignation.

Jack Lowndes left with his vision for New York Baptists unfulfilled, but with a sense of accomplishment for what had transpired in his eight years with the BCNY. "I wish God's blessings on this convention as the churches work to meet the great challenge in the Northeast," he wrote. "It is a good time for me to serve my Saviour in another environment." Three months later the executive board adopted a resolution of their appreciation for Lowndes, assuring the former leader of their "sincere interest, love, and prayers for [his] years of service ahead."[5]

In January 1983, Roy Gresham became "acting" executive director. The recently retired executive of the Maryland Convention was uniquely qualified for the position, given his long history with New York Baptists. He worked closely with the board in restructuring business, financial, and personnel policies, and in hiring an accountant, David Losito, to oversee convention finances. Gresham's backlog of statesmanlike missionary leadership made him a stabilizing influence—a "Barnabas," as some called him—during this difficult time of transition.[6]

New Executive Leadership

Administrative acumen ranked high on the list of qualities desired in a new leader, but more than anything else at the time, the Baptist Convention of New York needed a pastor. In R. Quinn Pugh, director of missions for the Metropolitan New York Association, the convention found what it was looking for.

An experienced home missionary, Pugh was involved as pastor of the Bergen Baptist Church in the formation of the Metropolitan New York Association and the Baptist Convention of New York. He was a leader within each organization—admired for his cooperative attitude, his desire for inclusiveness, but most of all for his affable, embracing spirit. His wife, Norma, recognized these qualities in him. When asked about her husband's capabilities, she was quick to note, "His greatest strength is in relating to people. He sees potential in others. He accepts persons as they are."[7]

The search committee, chaired by Roger Knapton, was confident that at a time when healing was needed in the convention, and when a growing controversy threatened to divide the larger Southern Baptist family, Pugh could pull together divergent elements within the BCNY. "With every assurance of God's help and the full confidence of His leadership," Pugh wrote to Knapton in October 1983, "I accept the call to serve. . . ."

In laying out his vision for the Baptist Convention of New York, Pugh highlighted the need to inculcate among the churches a stronger sense of ownership for the convention. He pledged that the activities, committees, and program assignments of the BCNY would reflect the broad scope of churches. Of note was his reluctance to utilize standard SBC terminology in describing non-Anglo churches as "ethnic" churches. His experience in the Metro Association taught him that "we are all ethnics working in partnership, one with another."[8] Pugh assumed responsibilities with the BCNY in February 1984 after recovering from coronary bypass surgery.

Pursuing the Vision

One of Quinn Pugh's first administrative actions was to urge the convention to bestow upon Paul James the title "Executive Director Emeritus," and to name the annual state missions offering in honor of the

Quinn and Norma Pugh, pictured with Paul James at the 1994 annual session.

Jameses. At the fifteenth annual session of the convention in November 1984, BCNY president Wesley Ellis and executive board chairman Waylen Bray joined in offering recommendations to honor Paul and Ava James for their missionary service. Messengers enthusiastically endorsed the honorary title for James and created the "Paul and Ava James Offering for BCNY Missions." Paraphrasing a line from Nehemiah 2:8 that she often cited to describe her own propitious missionary career, Ava noted: "The good hand of God had been upon the fellowship of the convention."[9]

In March 1984, Pugh led the executive board to launch a comprehensive, in-depth planning process. He envisioned a long-range plan that would bring a sense of renewal and fresh vitality to the convention. Dale Meredith, a member of the First Baptist Church of Grand Island, Frontier Association, was chosen to lead the steering committee. Other team leaders were Jack Mercer, pastor of the Bergen Baptist Church; Eugene Henderson, pastor of the Ithaca Baptist Church and campus minister at Cornell University; C. L. Chappell, layperson from the Trinity Baptist Church, Schenectady; and Mary Knapton, layperson from the Lincoln Avenue Church, Endicott. Carlisle Driggers led a team of consultants from the Home Mission Board and the Sunday School Board in assisting the committee.

BCNY: VISION 2000—a blueprint for convention growth and development in the final years of the twentieth century—was the culmination of a year-long process of steering group meetings and overnight planning retreats that involved more than a hundred people. Executive board members, associational leaders, and the BCNY staff were involved in forging the document which was presented at the 1985 annual session in Rochester.

Each division of the BCNY provided an audiovisual presentation of its VISION 2000 goals and strategy plans. Some of the particularities of the long-range plan evoked spirited discussion, but the document as a whole received a ringing endorsement from messengers. VISION 2000, while replete with detailed strategy and action plans, revolved around a single controlling idea for the convention. The purpose of the Baptist Convention of New York, as stated in the plan, was to "assist the cooperating churches in fulfilling the Great Commission (Matt. 28:19–20) and the Great Command (Matt. 22:37–40) by eliciting, combining, and channeling resources." Pugh initiated his monthly column in the *New York Baptist*, "Pursuing the vision," with an even plainer statement about what VISION 2000 represented: "[It] means pursuing the vision of thousands coming to know the Lord; the vision of dozens of new churches from the St. Lawrence to the Shore of Jersey, from the western frontier to the waters of the Atlantic; the vision of growing, serving, ministering disciples in every congregation; the vision of churches joyfully cooperating through the Baptist Convention of New York and with all Southern Baptists, as they carry the Good News of our Lord Jesus to the ends of the earth."[10]

New York Baptists financed their vision in the mid-1980s with generous giving. In 1985 Cooperative Program gifts increased by 20 percent over the previous year to $457,099. Support from the Home Mission Board and Baptist Sunday School Board in 1985 resulted in a total budget of more than two million dollars. For the first time in anyone's memory the convention slightly exceeded its budget goal in 1987. By the end of the decade receipts had risen to $552,631—representing an average annual increase of 9 percent since 1984. Such steady growth was encouraging for the convention, even if spending levels usually exceeded support and revenue. By 1989 the convention had accumulated a cash fund deficit of $72,755. The hope of even greater financial growth in the years ahead, however, made the deficit a problem for another day.

The Center for Missions and Ministry

Another priority Quinn Pugh addressed early in his tenure was that of securing a permanent facility for convention offices. With the lease on space at 500 Salina Street expiring at the end of 1985, the time was right to take action.

After a year of investigating commercial real estate options in the Syracuse area, Pugh discovered a seven-thousand-square-foot office building for sale just off the New York State Thruway in East Syracuse. The former New England Life building was well-suited to provide office space, conference rooms, a chapel, and space for the Baptist Book Store. At a cost of $410,000, the building appeared to be an answer to prayer for New York Baptists.

Messengers received the details of the proposed purchase at a rare special-called meeting of the convention during the March 1986 evangelism conference in Liverpool, New York. In order to stay within the annual budget allocation of $33,000 for office space, the BCNY needed: 1) to provide a $50,000 down payment at the time of the closing; 2) to pay off within one year a $150,000 note held by the owner; and 3) to take out a $210,000 mortgage for the remaining balance.

The convention enthusiastically accepted the proposal and authorized a capital campaign to raise funds for the down payment and the one-year note. Jon Meek, who returned in 1982 as pastor of the Calvary Church, Aberdeen, was asked to lead the effort to raise fifty thousand dollars by the May 15 closing date. Larry Brown, a layman from the Madison Church, was put in charge of the campaign to secure funds for paying off the note.[11] Adding closing costs, moving, and start-up expenses, $79,500 was needed for Phase I of the capital plan; interest and taxes raised the Phase II total to $176,000.

Jon Meek's job was made easy by the Georgia Baptist Convention with which the BCNY extended its "sister" convention relationship in 1985. In May 1986, Georgia Baptists provided a generous gift of fifty thousand dollars toward the purchase of the building. With gifts from other friends of the convention and the cooperating churches, the BCNY had $103,000 in hand for the building by the end of May. In June the purchase was finalized.

The following month work teams from Georgia and South Carolina helped prepare the building for occupancy. J. W. Edwards of Frost Industries in Ellijay, Georgia, donated new carpet which was installed by volunteers from that state. A group of carpenters from the First Baptist Church of Lancaster, South Carolina, remodeled offices and built new cabinets throughout the building. Volunteers from BCNY churches and staff cleaned, painted, and provided finishing work. Larry Badon, pastor of the Emmanuel Baptist Church in Cortland, oversaw the retrofitting of the

The Baptist Convention of New York Center for Missions and Ministry, 6538 Collamer Road in East Syracuse.

building for the convention's use. A team from the Rochester Association supplied some of the muscle and a van for the move on July 21, 1986.[12]

The Baptist Convention of New York dedicated its Center for Missions and Ministry on March 19, 1987. A crowd of 150 assembled at the 6538 Collamer Road location in East Syracuse for a service of thanksgiving and praise. Quinn Pugh summed up the significance of the moment with words he quoted from a pastor attending the ceremony: "This [building] is a symbol that we are here to stay until Jesus returns," he declared. "We have planted our roots here to do the work God has called us to do."[13]

An additional gift of twenty-five thousand dollars from Georgia Baptists, contributions from the churches, and a loan of more than twenty thousand dollars from a friend of the convention enabled the BCNY in June 1987 to pay off the $176,000 note held by the owner. The hope of paying back the personal loan and retiring the remaining mortgage of $210,000 within five years proved to be overly optimistic. Designated capital contributions tapered off in the late 1980s as the initial enthusiasm over the project waned. The building was scheduled to be paid for in 1997. (The debt on the building was retired earlier than anticipated—in May 1996.)

The Baptist Convention of New York Foundation

Almost lost amid the excitement over the new building was the development of a foundation to handle gifts, bequests, grants, and other investments for New York Baptists desiring to place these in trust for causes related to the convention. The effort grew directly out of the administrative objectives of BCNY: VISION 2000.

In March 1986, the BCNY executive board endorsed Mission Service Corps volunteers Glen and Edna Marshall as special assistants to the executive director. The Georgia couple was assigned administrative duties and asked to serve as a liaison with the Georgia Baptist Convention, but their primary responsibility was to help in developing a foundation. Mr. Marshall, a retired bank president, consulted with a task group led by Roger Knapton to secure the appropriate instruments for chartering a foundation.

The Baptist Convention of New York Foundation was chartered in February 1987. The first gift arrived from William L. Sanders of Atlanta in the amount of ten thousand dollars as a scholarship endowment fund. Sanders expressed gratitude to his former pastor, Quinn Pugh, by naming the scholarships in his honor. Pugh called the BCNY Foundation a "major step into the missionary future of New York Baptists," and the fulfillment of a long-held dream.[14]

The Northeastern Baptist School of Ministry

In 1983 the Baptist Convention of New York formed a partnership with the Metropolitan Association and Southeastern Baptist Theological Seminary in opening a New York City center for seminary studies. The "studies" program, in contrast to seminary extension, was designed for college graduates who wished to pursue a theological degree through the "lead" seminary of the program. When trustee actions at Southeastern Seminary resulted in the school being placed on academic probation in December 1991, the New York City center turned to Southern Seminary as its lead school, following a one-year hiatus in the program.

The seminary studies program was developed in response to a mandate by the Southern Baptist Convention to make theological training available in newer convention areas. But while the New York City center provided an excellent, contextualized opportunity for seminary training, its appeal was limited by its minimal course offerings (one or two per semester) and its on-site requirements for graduation. Students were not able to complete their degree programs in a timely fashion, nor without spending a year of study on a Southern Baptist seminary campus.

In November 1984, the Baptist Convention of New York joined with the New England, Pennsylvania/South Jersey, Maryland/Delaware, and Washington, D.C., Conventions in forming a task team to determine how the SBC mandate could be met more adequately. Initial BCNY representatives on the Northeast Task Team on Theological Education (NETTE) were Quinn Pugh, Bill Dunning, Wallace Williams, Sam Simpson, Conrad

Navarro, and Joyce Munro. The acronym for the task team was changed to "NeBEC" in the early 1990s to indicate "Northeast Baptist Educational Consortium."

After almost three years of extensive planning in conjunction with the SBC Seminary Presidents' Council and the Home Mission Board, the task team called its first full-time coordinator: Doran McCarty, professor of ministry at Golden Gate Baptist Theological Seminary. McCarty assumed the post in January 1988 and arrived at his office in the Metro New York Association building that spring. He was joined there in September by administrative assistant Becky Slade, a US-2 missionary.

By the end of 1987, the task team had also arrived at a name and an innovative format for the new school. The "Northeastern Baptist School of Ministry" was designed to be a multisite program, featuring contextualized training initially in Boston and Pittsburgh, and later in other areas. The school would have no permanent building but would utilize space from associational and state convention offices. Its "classrooms" would be churches and other ministry locations where students could receive close supervision from mentors.[15]

In August 1989, the Northeastern Baptist School of Ministry launched its master of arts degree program with courses offered in the Boston area. Later, NEBSM expanded its curriculum to include a master of divinity degree program and a program of continuing education. The school is now represented in seminary studies centers across the territory of the four state conventions (the Washington, D.C., Convention withdrew from the program).

Numerous BCNY staff members, associational leaders, and pastors have been adjunct faculty members and mentors in the program. Among these are: Robert Kim, DeLane Ryals, David Buck, Taylor Field, Steve Hollaway, Michael Pak, and Jeffrey Zurheide. Maurice Fain, retired pastor of the Rockland Baptist Church, joined the NEBSM staff in August 1989 as a Mission Service Corps volunteer "Associate Director." Andrew Lee, former English-speaking pastor of the Trust in God Chinese Baptist Church, became director of the Northeastern Baptist School of Ministry in August 1993.

Serving the Churches, 1984–1989

In November 1984, Glenn Igleheart joined the BCNY staff as director of the missions division, succeeding Daniel Sanchez. No stranger to New York Baptists, Igleheart lived in New Jersey from 1968 to 1975 while working with the Home Mission Board department of Interfaith Witness. It was through his encouragement as a supply preacher for the Cedar Grove (New Jersey) Chapel that Ken Medema, a member of the congregation, became involved in the ministry of the BCNY. Prior to joining the convention staff, Igleheart was director of the department of Interfaith Witness for the Home Mission Board.[16]

The missions division continued to expand its ministry in the late 1980s, engaging in creative efforts to meet the broad range of needs in the convention territory. The VISION 2000 mandate for the division was to discover new areas of need, develop appropriate ministries, and start new churches.

Cooperating with George Sheridan, the Home Mission Board's regional representative for Interfaith Witness, the division sponsored training events to help New York Baptists relate positively to the religious pluralism of the region. In April 1987, the division sponsored the convention's first major Brotherhood event—a Baptist Men's retreat in Mt. Bethel, Pennsylvania. Paul Schlett, a layman from the Hope Baptist Church, was elected the following year as the first state Brotherhood president. In the area of special mission ministries, the division held the BCNY's first "Campers on Mission" rally in October 1988. Claude McGavic, pastor of the Geneva Southern Baptist Church, coordinated the event at Sampson State Park in Seneca County, New York. In 1989 Bob Freeman and Linda Hokit were appointed by the Home Mission Board to guide the convention's efforts in resort ministries. Their responsibility was to discover ways for churches and associations to reach out with ministry in recreational settings and through cultural and sporting events held in the convention territory. Freeman was also part-time campus minister at the University of Buffalo.

In addition to these newer areas of ministry, the missions division continued to oversee an extensive program of church extension and language missions. Language leader Manuel Alonso was assisted by Michael Chiew, Asian church growth consultant, and Romeo Manansala, Filipino church growth consultant.

Directed by Nona Bickerstaff, the BCNY's program of Christian social ministry encompassed multiple sites in New York City, as well as ministries in the Buffalo and Rochester areas. Bickerstaff resigned in October 1987 to become director of the Metropolitan New York Association's social ministry program. Other CSM missionaries serving in the Metropolitan Association area included: E. Maisie Bruce at the Wake Eden Community Center; Taylor and Susan Field at the Graffiti Baptist Ministry; Avery and Myra Sayer at Lefrak City, Queens; and Michael and Glendora Williams at the Harlem Ministry Center. In western New York, Tom and June Cairns directed CSM efforts for the Greater Rochester Association from 1981 to 1988. Barbara Wallace became director of the program in 1989. Mark and Lisa Cain coordinated the Frontier Association's program of Christian social ministry from 1984 to 1990.

In February 1989, Elizabeth Pearson (Liz) became BCNY director of Woman's Missionary Union and church and community ministries (as the CSM program was renamed). She previously was employed by the Georgia Baptist Convention.[17] Fairy Harpe, who was state WMU president from 1988 to 1992, was primarily responsible for recruiting Pearson. Together with leaders like Arlene Collins and Monnie Anderson, they guided BCNY's program of Woman's Missionary Union in observing its twentieth anniversary and in launching a "Second Century" of service (the national WMU organization observed its centennial in 1988).

Daniel Paixao became director of the convention's education division in October 1985. A native of Brazil, he brought with him experience in Spanish and Portuguese-speaking churches in South America and in the United States.[18] Paixao sought to lead BCNY churches to embrace the Sunday School Board's "10/90 Challenge"—a campaign to increase Sunday School enrollment across the Southern Baptist Convention to 10 million by 1990. He emphasized associational Sunday School growth efforts that netted gratifying results, and promoted multilingual educational conferences and seminars to meet the needs of a broad spectrum of BCNY churches in a single setting.

With the leadership of Michael Chance, director of educational development for the Metro New York Association, the division sponsored Southern Baptists' first Chinese MasterLife workshop in September 1989. That event marked the beginning of Chance's close-knit involvement with the convention's Chinese congregations. Chance also cultivated the involvement of Metro Association churches in programs of continuing education sponsored by the education division. Diploma programs through seminary extension and Southern Seminary's Boyce Bible School flourished especially among Hispanic, Haitian, and African-American churches. A Korean program was begun in the early 1990s.

The education division continued its sponsorship of well-attended youth conventions which featured contemporary Christian music, speakers' tournaments, and Bible drills. Conventionwide education conferences were held each fall throughout the late 1980s, but with diminishing effectiveness. Encouragement from education leaders like Steve Blake of the Hudson Association, Michael Chance, and Katie Hill of the Madison Baptist Church led to a revamped format of regional conferences. In 1988 the division launched a single adult ministry, hosting a June retreat at Camp Taconic, New York.

David Buck, pastor of the Terrill Road Baptist Church, recognizes campus ministers at a 1988 executive board session. From left to right are: Nana DeBerry, Syracuse University; Ginger Ward, University of Buffalo; Steve Hollaway, Columbia University; Terry Minchow-Proffitt, Princeton University; and Alton Harpe, West Point.

Teacher training, discipleship development, family ministry, church music, and continuing theological education—the education division addressed each of these programs in some way.

The BCNY's program of campus ministry was realigned in 1985 from the education division to the newly established office of communications and campus ministry under the direction of Quentin Lockwood Jr. The program benefited from several new staff members. From 1985 to 1988, Stephen Hollaway was campus minister at Columbia University. He was succeeded by J. Scott Hudgins, who held the position from 1989 to 1991. Assistance from US-2 missionaries Sarah Hamm and Ron Jones led to the reemergence of a strong international student program at Columbia. Terry Minchow-Proffitt directed the Baptist chaplaincy program at Princeton University from 1987 to 1989. During this time he helped organize a fellowship and dialogue group at Princeton Theological Seminary for the growing number of Southern Baptist students attending the school. Many other campuses across the convention territory were reached in some way by volunteers from local churches, US-2 and semester missionaries, and Mission Service Corps volunteers.

In addition to supervising campus ministers, Lockwood was assigned to edit and produce the *New York Baptist*; direct the convention's programs related to the Southern Baptist Radio and Television Commission; coordinate an annual "Centrifuge" youth camp at Cazenovia College in New York; and sponsor a building tour each year with specialists from the church architecture department of the Sunday School Board leading on-site consultations with churches.[19]

The creative and energetic efforts of Jack Parrott and George Russ advanced the ministry of the evangelism division in significant ways. Together they promoted a series of regional evangelistic campaigns between 1985 and 1987 that involved more than 150 BCNY churches. "The Offer Still Stands" and "Good News America" efforts contributed to record baptism totals for the convention in the late 1980s. In 1988 and 1989, the evangelism division helped churches prepare for a series of Billy Graham crusade meetings in Buffalo, Rochester, and Syracuse.

New York Baptists were also involved in "partnership evangelism" projects cosponsored by the evangelism division and the Southern Baptist Foreign Mission Board. Spanish-speaking pastors and laypeople primarily from the Metropolitan New York Association traveled to Honduras in the summer of 1985 for a two-week evangelistic campaign that yielded almost a thousand professions of faith. In 1987 volunteers from across the convention participated in a partnership venture with Baptists in England.[20] Through his experiences in Honduras, George Russ realized the value of a bilingual ministry. He learned Spanish, and began a fruitful teaching and preaching ministry among the BCNY's Spanish-speaking congregations.

The state evangelism conference continued to be the centerpiece of the division's strategy for evangelism development, but other events like annual urban forums and specialized workshops helped equip the churches. In 1984 the division inaugurated the "Finney Institute"—an annual training event in evangelism named for Charles Grandison Finney, the so-called father of modern revivalism who experienced his conversion and call to ministry in the village of Adams, New York. Some of the SBC's most respected voices in evangelism, church growth, and spiritual renewal headlined programs and training events sponsored by the evangelism division in the 1980s.

Church administration was another assignment for the evangelism division. Regional preaching seminars, deacon ministry workshops, "Shared Ministry" conferences, and emphases related to the "Year of the Laity" (1989) addressed this program responsibility. Jack Parrott coordinated the BCNY's evangelism efforts until his resignation in February 1988 to accept a position with the Florida Baptist Convention.

New York Baptists and the Southern Baptist Convention

The opening volleys of what came to be called "The Controversy" among Southern Baptists were fired in June 1979 when Adrian Rogers, pastor of the Bellevue Baptist Church in Memphis, Tennessee, was elected

president of the Southern Baptist Convention. The conservatives who organized to help elect Rogers were committed to a ten-year plan to reclaim the
heart and soul of the denomination from what they perceived as growing
liberal tendencies in leadership and in the seminaries. Moderates dismissed
these concerns as a cloak for a fundamentalist coup d'état to redefine the
Southern Baptist Convention according to a right-wing social and political
agenda. By the early 1980s, battle lines were clearly drawn. Whatever the
real issues, Southern Baptists were at war for control of their convention.

Associations and state conventions became "precinct" battlegrounds
where the issues debated at the national level trickled down to polarize
Baptists over local concerns. Given the diversity within the Baptist
Convention of New York, the potential for damaging fallout from the
controversy was apparent.

And just how diverse were New York Baptists? After new SBC president Bailey Smith declared in August 1980 that "God Almighty doesn't
hear the prayer of a Jew," many Baptists in the metropolitan New York area
were mortified. How would their Jewish neighbors regard their witness
and credibility? Within two years, however, the Frontier Association
featured the gifted evangelist in its summer "Starlight Crusade."

Following the particularly acrimonious Kansas City session of the
convention in 1984, the June/July *New York Baptist* recorded these
responses from messengers:

> This year's SBC was one of the best I can remember in recent years! There
> was a sense of urgency to deal with critical issues which had been missing.
>
> Curtis Porter, Amherst Baptist Church

> I cannot remember a convention more clearly divided between two
> "camps." . . . Especially troublesome were the moves to reduce debate, the
> abuse of parliamentary machinery to obscure issues, and the uncoopera-
> tive, isolationist spirit. . . .
>
> Larry Bethune, Westchester Baptist Church

> Without any reservation this was the best Southern Baptist Convention I
> have ever attended. . . . I returned with a desire to lead my church in an
> even greater commitment to the Southern Baptist Convention and its
> ministries and programs.
>
> Lloyd Farmer, Emmanuel Baptist Church, Potsdam

> An undercurrent of shrillness, separatism and unwillingness to listen to
> and reason with one another was evident. . . .
>
> Jamie and Joyce Munro, Bridgewater Baptist Church

The pronounced differences among New York Baptists regarding the SBC controversy were visible primarily in editorials, but occasionally opinions were ventilated in floor debates during annual sessions. Motions in 1987 and 1989 by DeLane Ryals and Somerset Hills pastor Charles Long for the BCNY to express its support for the Baptist Joint Committee on Public Affairs provoked considerable debate, but passed by a comfortable margin. Other politically and theologically charged issues embodied in resolutions touched off spirited discussion at annual sessions throughout the 1980s.

To be sure, the controversy gave messengers much to talk about. It prompted breakfast table and corridor strategy sessions for electing candidates or advancing views favorable to conservative and moderate persuasions, and it produced a few "torchbearers" from both sides of the denominational "aisle" who occasionally brought into painfully sharp relief the ideological differences between New York Baptists. But in the end, the controversy did not rupture the fellowship of the Baptist Convention of New York.

Although moderate sentiment ran deep in some parts of the convention—especially in the disproportionately large Metropolitan New York Association—the BCNY did not adopt an openly defiant stance towards trends in the Southern Baptist Convention. Only a handful of BCNY churches ultimately chose to affiliate with new moderate organizations like the Cooperative Baptist Fellowship, which was organized in 1991.

Some conservatives decried the fact that the BCNY had not, in their words, chosen to "flow with the mainstream" of the national body. No "takeover" bid, however, was ever mounted. Such an attempt would have hopelessly polarized the convention and likely proven counterproductive.

Geographical, political, and theological balance was also reflected in the choices New York Baptists made for leadership. Convention presidents in the 1980s represented a healthy cross section of the BCNY, a lack of lay leadership notwithstanding.

Wallace Williams, pastor of the Wilton Baptist Church, completed his second term as president in 1980. Curtis Porter, a longtime convention leader from western New York, was elected in 1981. Messengers chose the pastor of the Amherst Baptist Church for a second term in 1982. Wesley Ellis, pastor of the Vassar Road Baptist Church, Metropolitan Association, was president 1983–1984. Former Mission Service Corps volunteer J. Edwin Hewlett, pastor of the Browncroft Baptist Church, Greater Rochester Association, served two terms, 1985–1986. The election of Sam Simpson, pastor of the Bronx and Wake Eden Churches, Metropolitan Association, broke new ground for the BCNY. Elected for two terms (1987–1988), Simpson, an African-American, was the first non-Anglo chosen as convention president. Roger Knapton, who in the late 1980s approached his thirtieth year of ministry in the convention as pastor of the Lincoln Avenue Church, Southern Tier Association, was president for two terms, 1989–1990.

Less balance was reflected in the choices the Southern Baptist committee on nominations made in 1988 for New York Baptists' first representatives on national boards and agencies. Upon reaching the twenty-thousand-member mark, the BCNY was granted seats on four boards and committees. The first representatives from the convention territory—all recognized fundamental-conservatives—were Roger Knapton, Foreign Mission Board; Jon Meek, Home Mission Board; Ondra Black, Baptist Sunday School Board; and David Button, SBC Executive Committee.

Having surpassed twenty-five thousand members in 1989, the BCNY was allotted seats on a broader range of SBC boards and agencies. June Andrews and Allen Baldwin were on the 1990 SBC committee to nominate members of boards and agencies which selected the following BCNY church members to serve on national boards and agencies—Norma Pugh, Historical Commission; Luis Nieto, Annuity Board; Larry Brown, Southwestern Baptist Theological Seminary; Ron Norman, New Orleans Baptist Theological Seminary; Bruce Aubrey, Golden Gate Theological Seminary; Alan Todd, Brotherhood Commission; Sherri Cerny, Christian Life Commission; Romy Manansala, Stewardship Commission; and Robert Brooks, Radio and Television Commission.

One important reason that the Baptist Convention of New York was able to remain not just intact but unified during the SBC storm was the leadership of Quinn Pugh. His inclusive spirit, his missional focus, but most of all, his respect for the cherished Baptist principle of the autonomy of local churches and associations served the convention well. After the 1984 Kansas City session, when many feared Southern Baptists were at the brink of a devastating schism, he offered these thoughts about where New York Baptists stood: "While others may have the luxury of being absorbed in the petty politics of the presidential election and the protective posturing for doctrinal purity, every day New York Baptists face too many lost people to be loved for Christ's sake to get bogged down in the bitter contests of denominational rivalry. After Kansas City, the challenge is the greater for renewed commitment to missions and evangelism."[21]

CHAPTER TWELVE

GROWTH IN ASSOCIATIONS AND CHURCHES, 1980-1989

In less than a generation, the once expansive Central Baptist Association had given itself away to form four new associations. Such self-sacrifice spoke volumes about the churches' genuine commitment to mission expansion, but the process of carving out new boundaries also left the Central Association weakened. In the fall of 1980, fourteen of twenty-one churches bade farewell to their "mother" association to form new groupings. Although gratified by the results of growth, associational leaders felt a sense of loss—an organizational "grief" not unlike that which many congregations experienced when giving away families to new missions.

J. T. Davis stepped forward in October 1981 to speak a challenging and encouraging word to the churches of the Central Association. The veteran home missionary observed that while New York Baptists had made great strides with their missionary program, much remained to be accomplished in the decades ahead. The work of the Central Association was far from complete—"We have hardly scratched the surface," he pointed out to those gathered for the annual associational meeting. Davis exhorted them to seize the moment in launching a new day for mission advance. In his thinking the association was not suffering from any malaise that some new chapels could not cure.[1]

In many ways Davis represented the "old guard" among New York Baptists. The leaders who in the late 1950s pioneered Southern Baptists' expansion into the Northeast were by the early 1980s a rapidly diminishing group. Much had changed in the intervening years, but planting new churches remained the most viable strategy for mission growth and evangelism. Davis reminded pastors that their primary goal was not to grow a big church but to reach people—and starting new churches was the most effective means of doing that. Davis spoke a word that a new generation of pastors and lay leaders in the BCNY needed to hear. The 1980s was not a time to pull up and consolidate gains but to press on.

The Davis Association

Under the direction of D. Wayne Dyer, the Davis Association maintained a balanced program of ministry and fellowship, and experienced growth through new church extension and by welcoming unaffiliated churches into the SBC fold.

The First Baptist Church of Frankfort, which joined the association in 1981 as a dually aligned ABC/SBC congregation, became actively involved in associational life with the leadership of pastor John Barnett, a Southern Baptist. The Inlet Community Church, an independent congregation, united with the Davis Association in June 1983 through the influence of Roger Best, pastor of the Grace Church, Ogdensburg (Thousand Islands Association) and his son, Harold Best, who became pastor of the church. The congregation became the association's northernmost outreach.

In 1986 the Miller Street Baptist Church in Utica petitioned for membership in the Davis Association. Following its affiliation with Southern Baptists, the inner-city congregation was effective in ministering to Vietnamese families being processed through Utica's refugee relocation center. Contacts through the Foreign Mission Board assisted the congregation in this ministry.

Another independent congregation, the Jewell Free Chapel, affiliated with Southern Baptists in 1989 through the influence of the Beacon Light Baptist Church in Verona. In 1988 the church assisted the Jewell Chapel in calling a new pastor, Arthur Burdick, a student at the Mid-America Baptist Theological Seminary, Northeast Branch.

In 1983 Waylen Bray led the Stamford Baptist Church to reach out to the village of Jefferson with a new chapel. Don Keller was the congregation's first pastor. He was followed in 1985 by Don DeGarmo who guided the church through a building program that involved teams of volunteers from Virginia, Georgia, and Louisiana. The Jefferson Baptist Church entered its new building and was constituted in 1988.

The Greater Syracuse Association

The family of seven churches which constituted the Greater Syracuse Association in 1980 relished the opportunity of advancing Southern Baptist work in the "heart" of the convention territory. Like the Davis Association, the Syracuse fellowship was a humble denominational structure, but this in no way was a source of discouragement—it was a missionary challenge. Guided by directors of missions Darwin Bacon (1982–1984) and Michael Anderson (1985–1993), the diverse churches worked together to create a meaningful network of fellowship and ministry for the Syracuse area.

The Bellewood Baptist Church was an early leader in mission outreach among Syracuse-area churches. The congregation sponsored a new work in Cortland that was constituted as the Emmanuel Baptist Church in 1980. Larry Badon was the church's first pastor. The Bellewood Church cosponsored a chapel in Syracuse with the Northside Baptist Church which was constituted in 1982 as the University Baptist Church. Steve Cosgrove, a Mission Service Corps volunteer, divided his time between campus ministry at Syracuse University and serving as pastor of the church.[2] Other new works the church attempted in Fayetteville, Camillus, Cicero, and Oswego were short-lived. The Central Baptist Church later revived work in Oswego with a Spanish-speaking chapel.

In the early 1980s, the Northside Baptist Church assisted pastor Seok Won Kim in cultivating a Korean congregation in Liverpool. Shortly after that mission dissolved, the church initiated new work in the community of Pennellville. Victor Stefanini came in 1987 as the first pastor of the Pennellville Baptist Church, which continues to develop as a mission of the Northside Church.

The Thousand Islands Association

The churches dotting the St. Lawrence Seaway region, though rooted deeply in the history of the Frontier, Central, and Adirondack Associations, exhibited from their founding a strong regional self-consciousness or, as one pastor put it, a "ferocious autonomy." With direction from leaders like associational moderator Roger Best, the Thousand Islands Association developed a missionary strategy to help the churches extend their witness to new communities.

Pastor Joe Blalock of the Gouverneur Baptist Chapel assumed responsibility in the late 1970s for developing a new work in Watertown. With the help of Georgia volunteers Allen and Debbie Baldwin, the pastor led the church to be constituted in 1980 as the First Southern Baptist Church of Watertown. Over the next few years, the church benefited from the support of the Fifth Avenue Baptist Church in Rome, Georgia, and from volunteer construction teams sponsored by the Floyd County Baptist Association in Georgia.[3]

In 1982 the Watertown Church launched the first new work in the territory of the Thousand Islands Association. The church supported the efforts of church planter Harry Maples, who became founding pastor of the Long Falls Baptist Church in Carthage.

Despite its early involvement in the BCNY's mission program, the First Southern Baptist Church of Watertown elected in 1986 to drop its denominational affiliation. By the end of the decade, however, the Richville Baptist Church had planted another church in Watertown—the New Hope Baptist Church (1989), where Marvin Mullinax was founding pastor. The New Hope Church was soon one of the stronger churches of the association.

In 1987 the Thousand Islands Association welcomed its first non-English language church. The Korean Baptist Church of Watertown was begun in the mid-1980s by a group of Korean women whose husbands were stationed at Fort Drum. Through the leadership of pastor Bong Dok Suh, the congregation affiliated with Southern Baptists.

The Southern Tier Association

The 1980s proved to be a productive decade for new church starts in the Southern Tier Association. For the first time since the organization of the association in 1968, the churches had the undivided, sustained leadership of a director of missions. John Simmons brought to the Southern Tier Association the lessons he had learned in church starting while serving as a pastor in the Adirondack Association.

The failure of two previous attempts at starting new work in Ithaca did not discourage church planter Gene Henderson. Appointed by the Baptist Convention of New York in 1979, Henderson was asked to start a new church, and to initiate campus ministry at Cornell University. In January 1980, he began a Bible study in his home which became the nucleus of the Ithaca Baptist Church, constituted in May 1983. The new work was sponsored by the Owego Southern Baptist Church. Bob Finnis, who twenty-five years before as a layman in the Central Baptist Church, Syracuse, had been involved in an effort to start a church in Ithaca, returned as pastor of the congregation in 1986.[4]

Pastor Harold Lefler, who, like John Simmons, gained his church-starting experience in the Adirondack Association, helped instill in the Owego Church a heart for missions which led the congregation to become a leading sponsor of new churches in the Southern Tier Association. In 1981 Lefler resigned to become leader of "Tri-Town Baptist Ministries," a project to launch new work in the Bainbridge, Sidney, and Unadilla areas. Under the sponsorship of the Owego Church, the ministry resulted in the formation of the First Southern Baptist Church of Sidney in 1985. Pastor J. David Turner also led the Owego Church to sponsor new work in Norwich, which was constituted in 1984 as the Agape Baptist Church. The Owego Church later sponsored a mission in Elmira Heights which was constituted in 1986 as the Fellowship Baptist Church.

The Lincoln Avenue Baptist Church in Endicott, the "grandmother" church of the Southern Tier Association, assumed sponsorship in 1985 of a new work in North Fenton. Pastor John Garner led the mission to be constituted in 1992 as the North Fenton Baptist Church.

Several efforts were made in the 1980s to start a church in Binghamton, the largest city in the Southern Tier Association. The Lincoln Avenue and First Southern, Sidney, Churches attempted three new starts in the city, all of which disbanded after a few years. A discovery by a Praxis team in the summer of 1983, however, led to a surprising new development in church extension for the association. The team discovered a group of Korean students from the State University of New York at Binghamton who met regularly for Bible study. With assistance from John Simmons and the sponsorship of the Lincoln Avenue Church, the Korean fellowship launched a chapel in 1984. Woon Chul Kim was the first pastor of what later became the Korean Baptist Church of Susquehanna.

The association's diversity was also enhanced by the addition of the Friendship Baptist Church in Corning. The African-American congregation joined the association in 1983. With the disbandment of the Corning Baptist Church and its Havenvue Chapel by 1985, the Friendship Church became the only Southern Baptist congregation in the Corning area.

The Hudson Association

The defections of the Ballston Lake, Albany, and Adirondack Churches in the mid-1980s dealt a heavy blow to the Hudson Association. Without the New Hope and Grace Churches, which were developed through the mission programs of the Metropolitan and Adirondack Associations, the association would have been reduced to one church—the Trinity Baptist Church of

Schenectady, which for many years had been the eastern outpost of the Central Association. Three churches and a struggling mission at Catskill comprised the Hudson Association family of churches at mid-decade.

Things began turning around for the association in the latter half of the 1980s. The ministry of the Trinity Baptist Church was strengthened through the leadership of pastor James Guenther who arrived in August 1986. He led the congregation in 1988 to again launch out in mission, this time to the Ballston Spa area with the establishment of the Saratoga Baptist Chapel which was constituted in 1990 as the Praise Baptist Church. He also led the Trinity Church to cooperate with the Mid-America Baptist Theological Seminary in the school's efforts to establish a northeastern campus in the Capital District.

Mid-America President Gray Allison began dreaming in the late 1970s of establishing a seminary in the Northeast. When the Southern Baptist Convention balked at the idea of opening a traditional seminary facility in the region, he led the independent, Memphis-based school to pursue the possibility of beginning a branch campus. Allison believed the proposed school would greatly assist Southern Baptists in their efforts to impact the Northeast.[5]

In September 1987, professors Duane Garrett, Howard Bickers, and Al Shackelford began seminary extension classes at the Trinity Church with seven students. In August 1989, the school dedicated a 15,400-square-foot building to house classrooms, a library, administrative offices, and a chapel.

The seminary became a stabilizing force in the Hudson Association area and brought an influx of leadership for prospective new works. The churches also benefited from the arrival of James Arrant, a church planter/strategist who arrived in November 1989 to coordinate the association's mission program. He later assumed the role of director of missions. The Hudson Association was poised for a new day in the 1990s.

The Adirondack Association

If anyone had a sense of ownership for a ministry in a particular area, it was Norman Bell. His affection for the churches and the people of the Adirondack Association made it painful for him to say good-bye in 1982 when a heart condition necessitated his retirement. To honor their former director of missions and his wife, the churches established the "Norman and Lena Bell Offering for Associational Missions."

When James Perry became director of missions in December that year, he inherited a smaller association. His job assignment called for involvement with the new Thousand Islands Association along the St. Lawrence

Seaway, but living in Malone, his ministry was focused primarily in the eastern half of the Adirondack region. Perry served the churches of the North Country until in 1990.

Not all churches in the Adirondack Association were begun through a happy, cooperative process of church extension. The Bread of Life Church in Plattsburgh emerged out of a schism in the Sharron Woods Church. Primarily a church of Air Force personnel and their families, Sharron Woods had a limited local outreach. In 1980 those in the church wishing to create a more inclusive fellowship began holding their own worship service. John Sullivan, who left the Sharron Woods Church in 1980 to become pastor of the Lawrenceville Church, returned to Plattsburgh in 1982 to become pastor of the Bread of Life congregation.[6] James Bradley became pastor in 1984, leading the Bread of Life Baptist Church to be constituted in 1986.

Revival preaching and the harmony of a gospel quartet from Anderson, South Carolina, laid the groundwork for the founding of a church at Tupper Lake. Held at the local synagogue, the revival meeting helped members of the First Christian Church of Brushton establish rapport with the community. The Tupper Lake Chapel developed slowly, almost dying several times in the ten years preceding Tom Niswonger's arrival as pastor in 1984. Under his leadership the chapel was constituted as the Tupper Lake Baptist Church. The church shortly thereafter assumed sponsorship of another mission of the First Christian Church, the Powerhouse Baptist Chapel in the Star Lake area. Vernon Bissonette was founding pastor of this congregation which remains a mission of the Tupper Lake Church.

The commitment to missions demonstrated by the First Brushton Church produced more than just new chapels across the North Country. In 1983 church member Judith Richards was appointed for missionary service by the Foreign Mission Board.

The Greater Rochester Association

A clamor again arose among the churches of the Greater Rochester Association in the early 1980s, but this time the issue did not result in polarization. The thought of discontinuing the association's quarterly hymn sings had some alarmed! "This indicated a genuine desire for the true harmony such as a praise gathering inspires," wrote Gloria Stanton, a leading layperson in the association.[7]

The Greater Rochester Association rebounded remarkably well from the difficulties it experienced in the late 1970s. With the leadership of Norman Beckham, who guided the association as director of missions until 1985, and Robert Sumrall (Rusty), who succeeded him in July 1986, the association consistently added new churches, developed new ministries, and enhanced its fellowship.

Christian social ministries directors Tom Cairns (1981–1988) and Barbara Wallace (1989–1994) assisted churches with opportunities for involvement in inner-city ministry, rehabilitation programs, and personal counseling. Sally Taylor provided a unique "deaf" campus ministry at the National Technical Institute for the Deaf and the Rochester Institute of Technology. Herbert Wagner, founding pastor of the Newark Baptist Fellowship Church (1985), became the first-ever chaplain for the Finger Lakes Racetrack in 1987.

In the early 1980s, the Browncroft Church sponsored the efforts of lay pastor Jim Jones in starting a new work at Spencerport. A longtime member of the Rochester Church, Jones was a valuable asset to the association in helping to launch several other churches in the association. The Spencerport Church was constituted in 1982 under his leadership. Two years later the church sponsored the Hamlin Community Baptist Church, where Fred Durkin was founding pastor. The Spencerport, or Northwest Church as it later became, was disbanded in 1989.

In 1980 the only church outside of Monroe County in the Rochester Association was the Geneva Southern Baptist Church. By 1985 the work of the association had expanded to five counties. In March 1982, the Geneva Church initiated a chapel in Canandaigua which was constituted in October 1983 as the New Covenant Baptist Church. James Flanagan was the church's first pastor. The Pinnacle Road Church extended its ministry to the outlying community of Geneseo in 1983 with the establishment of a new work under the direction of mission pastor David Brown; the chapel was constituted in 1985 as the Pleasant Valley Baptist Church. The New Covenant Church reached out to the community of Newark (New York) with a mission that in 1985 became the Newark Baptist Fellowship Church.

In 1989 the Rochester Association celebrated the birth of a "new" Pittsford Baptist Church. This work, organized in an area where a church had been lost a decade before, was founded by pastor Alan Todd under the sponsorship of the Browncroft Church. In many ways it attested to the tenacity of Southern Baptists in the Rochester area.

The Long Island Association

For much of the 1980s, the Long Island Association functioned without a director of missions. Joseph Causey's tenure was brief, and David Leary did not arrive until 1989. As a consequence, the churches lacked a comprehensive mission strategy. Bob Sommer, founding pastor of the Washington Avenue Baptist Church in Brentwood (1978) and associational moderator in the mid-1980s, described the early years of the association as disappointing—certainly less than what the pastors' fellowship had envisioned in 1981 when it advocated that their churches withdraw from the Metropolitan New York Association to form their own association. The difficulties of losing a church and a mission, severe membership losses in some congregations, and a steady turnover of leadership made the churches eager—some would even say desperate—for a director of missions by the late 1980s.[8]

Despite these setbacks, positive developments did occur within the association. In the early 1980s, the Long Island Association welcomed a new non-English language congregation to its fellowship. The Grace Baptist Church in Lake Grove launched the association's first Chinese congregation in 1984—the Elim Chapel. Andrew Yu was the first pastor of the congregation. Timothy Wong came as pastor in 1985 and later joined Bob Brooks, pastor of the Grace Church, in ministering to students at the State University of New York at Stony Brook.

In December 1986, Jim Watson came as chaplain to Belmont Park, one of the nation's most famous horse-racing facilities. Employed by Racetrack Chaplaincy of America, a Christian group that provides chaplains to fifty-four tracks nationwide, Watson began ministering to families of the "back-stretch"—workers at the racetrack who live just above the poverty level. Not all fellow Southern Baptists on Long Island welcomed his coming. Some questioned his involvement with the seedy world of horse racing and gambling. He reminded them that Jesus asked his Father to forgive the gamblers who cast lots at the foot of the cross.[9] Watson became moderator of the association in 1993.

Shortly after David Leary became director of missions, the Farmingdale Baptist Church called him as interim pastor. Through his influence, the church transferred its affiliation from the Metropolitan Association to the Long Island Association. The church provided the association with an unused building for offices and living quarters for missionary personnel. Leary led the association to refurbish the building. More importantly, he provided direction that led to several positive developments in the 1990s.

The Frontier Association

Cliff Matthews continued to lead the Frontier Association into the 1980s with significant church planting efforts. Following his resignation in 1983 to accept a position with the Florida Baptist Convention, the Frontier Association called its youthful moderator, Terry Robertson, as director of missions. The twenty-nine-year-old pastor of the First Baptist Church of Grand Island exhibited an earnestness that brought to mind the pioneering spirits who had planted churches in the region in the 1950s and early 1960s. A native Alabamian, Robertson perpetuated a long-standing affinity between that state and Southern Baptist work in western New York, which was planted originally by an Alabama church. He was joined on staff by Mark and Lisa Cain, Christian social ministry directors, and Allen Baldwin, an early BCNY Mission Service Corps volunteer who after attending seminary, returned to New York as a church starter/strategist. He was joined in this ministry by his wife Debbie.

The French Road Baptist Church[10] began the expansion of the Frontier Association in the 1980s by launching a new work in Clarence. Begun in 1980, the chapel developed under the leadership of pastor James Rivers, with assistance from Cliff Matthews. The congregation was constituted in 1982 as the Clarence Baptist Church, but later changed its name to the Emmanuel Baptist Church. The Assurance Baptist Church in Williamsville was begun in the early 1980s by students from Auburn University who did religious survey work in the area. The Emmanuel Church and the Lakeview Baptist Church in Auburn, Alabama, sponsored the new work which was constituted in 1986. Noel Wilmoth was the first pastor. The congregation changed its name to the New Beginnings Baptist Church in 1994.

In 1984 the Frontier Association received by petition the Baptist Tabernacle Church of Belmont. Organized during World War II by a transplanted Southern Baptist pastor from North Carolina, the church joined the association after it called church planter Bob Hill as pastor.

The West Main Baptist Church in Fredonia maintained its tradition of missionary outreach in the 1980s with the development of a new chapel in Jamestown, and Spanish-speaking missions in Dunkirk and Buffalo. Begun in 1983, the Jamestown work was cultivated by mission pastor Ted Ward. He remained as pastor until 1991 when the congregation was constituted as the Southside Baptist Church. The West Main Church's Hispanic outreach was directed in two locations by pastor Gus Suarez. The *Mision Bautista Hispana*, Dunkirk, and the *Puente de Paz* (Peace Bridge) works remain as chapels of the church.

Despite the large black population of the greater Buffalo area, the Frontier Association remained a family of predominantly Anglo, suburban churches. But the Fillmore Avenue Church began seeing more black families join its membership in the early 1980s. The remnant of the once proud Polish congregation saw a mission opportunity and called Wilbert Martin, an

African-American, as pastor in 1982.[11] Martin guided the congregation to reach out to other parts of Buffalo, establishing chapels on the east and west side of the city. In 1989 a second predominantly black congregation in Buffalo united with the association: the First Timothy Baptist Church, led by pastor Kenneth Wilkerson.

Mission pastor Ed Stetzer succeeded in establishing the Buffalo Bible Fellowship in 1988 as a mission of the Amherst Church. The multiethnic downtown church was constituted in 1990 as the Calvary Christian Church.[12]

Church planter Allen Baldwin was successful in initiating new works in Tonawanda and Batavia in the late 1980s. He enlisted the LaSalle Church as sponsoring congregation of the Tonawanda work, begun in 1988 with the Terry Robertson family as its first members. Rob Saathoff was pastor of the Tonawanda Baptist Church, constituted in 1991. The Victory Baptist Church in Batavia, also begun in 1988, was sponsored by the Emmanuel Church in Clarence. The new church was constituted in the mid-1990s with Ralph Vick as the first pastor.

The University Baptist Church, Getzville, designated as a mission of the First Baptist Church of Grand Island, was launched in the Amherst home of Dale and Jean Meredith. With the help of US-2 campus minister Ginger Ward, the Merediths reached out to the international community at the University of Buffalo, where Dale taught civil engineering. The chapel immediately attracted students and faculty members whose lives had been touched through the influence of Southern Baptist missions in Asia.[13] Although the new work welcomed local members, it had from its inception a decidedly international focus. David Lam and Bob Freeman were instrumental in promoting this aspect of the church's ministry. The University Church was constituted in 1989 with Steve Whitten as the first pastor.

The Metropolitan New York Association

"Our ethnic churches" or "our black churches" were phrases that made Quinn Pugh wince. Whose were they? Such comments, made innocently enough and with genuine concern for inclusiveness, revealed, nevertheless, a subtle paternalism.

With no particular ethnic group (including Anglos) representing a majority of churches in the Metro Association, there were no true "owners" in control—at least not theoretically. Predominantly Anglo churches provided a disproportionate share of the association's financial base, and often were in the majority with their participation in associational functions. Yet black churches and "non-English language/culture" churches (as

Pugh chose to call the polyglot family of congregations) usually led the association in baptisms, mission outreach, and overall church vitality. All of the churches were offered a significant place in the life of the association. As director of missions, Pugh had a way of making each church feel it was the most important congregation in the association.

The Metropolitan Association further enhanced its image as an international community of churches when it called David F. D'Amico as director of missions in June 1985. A native of Argentina, D'Amico brought to the task a strong academic background and experience in missions both as a former professor and as director of ministry to internationals at the South Main Baptist Church in Houston.[14] Pugh and D'Amico, and an able staff of DeLane Ryals, Ray Gilliland, Nona Bickerstaff, and Michael Chance, led the association to experience continued growth in the 1980s with new churches, and with new people groups reached. D'Amico served the association until his resignation in 1989 to accept a teaching assignment at Southern Seminary.

In the early 1980s, immigration policies favorable to medical personnel brought an influx of Filipino doctors, nurses, and their families to the metropolitan area. Jaime Prieto, an itinerate evangelist from the Philippines, organized some of these new immigrants into the Bible Church International in November 1982. Because of his familiarity with Southern Baptist mission work in the Philippines, he led the group to affiliate with the Metropolitan Association and to participate in the BCNY's program of church extension. With the sponsorship of the Madison Baptist Church, Bible Church International (BCI) became the first predominantly Filipino congregation on the east coast to relate to Southern Baptists.

By the time Romy Manansala became pastor of the congregation in February 1984, BCI had developed an ambitious vision to plant new Filipino churches in the metropolitan area and in key cities along the east coast from Boston to Miami. Manansala was struck by the commitment of New York Baptists to share in the church's dream of founding a network of Filipino congregations.[15] He resigned his pastorate in 1988 to become a Filipino church growth consultant for the Baptist Convention of New York. Kenneth Tan became pastor of the church that same year.

By the end of the decade, the church and its daughter congregations had planted a total of fifteen new churches, chapels, and Bible studies in the metropolitan area. New churches were also begun in Boston, South Jersey, and Tampa. Not all of the new works survived or remained affiliated with Southern Baptists, but many did.

Among the chapels which constituted as churches or remain as chapels at this writing are Bronx Bible Church, Paul Ignacio, founding pastor; Queens

Romy Manansala, BCNY Filipino church growth consultant, ministers to members of the Bronx Bible Church.

Bible Church, Delfin Orendain, founding pastor; Brooklyn Evangelical Church, Gene Miraflor, founding pastor; Bergen Christian Fellowship, Romy Manansala, founding pastor; Westchester Bible Fellowship, Cicero Bailon, founding pastor; New Rochelle Christian Fellowship, Cicero Bailon, founding pastor; Living Word Fellowship in Queens, Norman Solis, founding pastor; and Agape Bible Christian Fellowship in Monmouth County, New Jersey, Romy Manansala, founding pastor. Felix Sermon was also instrumental in organizing and developing Filipino congregations in the late 1980s.

The Bible Church International became a sponsor in 1989 to the BCNY's first Indonesian congregation. Pastor Jacob Tjoa gathered fellow Indonesian Christians into what became the First Indonesian Baptist Church of New York in 1993.

The Metropolitan Association also experienced a proliferation of Korean congregations in the 1980s. Rather than follow the church sponsorship extension model common among Southern Baptists, Koreans typically practiced what DeLane Ryals calls a "free enterprise" or "entrepreneurial" model of church starting. Like a small business owner, a hard-working pastor and a core group of family and friends united in forming a congregation, independent of a sponsoring relationship with another church. Language missions consultants assisted the new churches in developing relationships with the association and state convention.[16]

In 1981 the association welcomed the Korean-American Baptist Church in Jackson Heights, Queens. An outreach of the short-lived Manhattan International Baptist Church, the congregation was led by pastor Esther Nahm. In the early 1990s, she was murdered while on vacation in Washington, D.C. Michael Chiew succeeded her as pastor. The Seh Moon Korean Baptist Church, also in Queens, was organized by pastor Chang Kun Behk, and admitted to the association in 1985. That same year the

Praxis team of Moses and Soo Park organized Korean Bible studies as a prelude to developing the New Life Korean Baptist Church (formerly Monmouth Korean) sponsored by the Calvary Baptist Church in Aberdeen, New Jersey. Suk H. Shin was the Korean congregation's founding pastor.

Four new Korean congregations joined the Metropolitan Association in 1989. Pastor Young Ho Lee was organizing pastor of the Divine Grace Baptist Church (formerly Bergen Korean Baptist Church) in Hackensack, New Jersey. The Hosanna Baptist Church (formerly the First Korean Baptist Church of Brooklyn) was founded by pastor Ki Il Park. The Korean Baptist Church of Queens, which later moved to the Bronx, and then to the Rockland Baptist Church with the name, New York Han Shin Baptist Church, was guided by pastor Calvin Chang. James and Martha Chun organized the New Hope Korean Baptist Church in Queens Village, New York.

The Han Maum Baptist Church in Flushing was begun by a senior pastor who had once been known as the "Bob Hope" of Korea. Kyu Suk Kwak was a nationally known comedian before he entered Christian ministry. Organized in 1985, the Han Maum Church formally united with the Metropolitan Association in 1990. Pastor Kwak was succeeded in 1992 by his son-in-law Michael Pak.

Several Haitian missions begun in the mid-1970s were admitted to the association in the 1980s. Most were missions of the French-speaking Baptist Church of Brooklyn. Other missions not previously mentioned which were started by the Brooklyn Church included the French-speaking Baptist Church of Mt. Vernon, Wesner Mondelus, pastor; Bronx Haitian Chapel, Aquilas Achille, pastor; and the French-speaking Baptist Church of Spring Valley, Tony Joseph, pastor. The French-speaking Church of Far Rockaway sponsored the French-speaking Baptist Mission—Boucan Siloe, Ismael Pierre, pastor.

The New Jerusalem French-speaking Church in Irvington, New Jersey, was organized by pastor Joseph Etienne in 1980, and admitted to the association several years later. Andre Leonard was founding pastor of the Evangelical Haitian Baptist Church in Newark. Constituted in 1981, the church was a mission project of the Ebenezer Church in Brooklyn. Pastor Jean A. Florival founded the Source of Life Church in Brooklyn, which joined the association in 1985. In 1985 the association recognized the Ammi Baptist Church, Brooklyn, begun by Lamartine St. Juste. The *Église Baptiste Bethesda*, also in Brooklyn, became a part of the associational family in 1989 under the leadership of Jean Francois.

Pastor Emmanuel St. Juste led the French-speaking Church of Stamford, Connecticut, to sponsor a large family of new Haitian churches in that state and in neighboring Westchester County, New York. New works initiated were the French-speaking Baptist Church of Norwalk, Joseph Michel, pastor; French-speaking Baptist Church of Bridgeport, Franz St. Pierre, pastor; and the French-speaking Baptist Church of White Plains, which St. Juste served as pastor.

The Evergreen Baptist Church in 1982 launched a predominantly West Indian work in Brooklyn which became the Good Hope Baptist Church, led by pastor Alex Morgan. In 1987 the Bronx Baptist Church initiated a new congregation in the Bronx under the direction of Delroy Reid-Salmon. He led the Grace Baptist Church to be constituted in 1993.

Numerous other predominantly African-American congregations became affiliated with the Metro Association in the 1980s. Those in Brooklyn were the Martyr's Cross Crusade Baptist Church, R. Nicholas Parent, pastor; Southern Baptist Church, Clarence Williams, pastor; Christ Temple United Baptist Church, Ernest Hall, pastor; and the Union Baptist Church, Don Ali, pastor. In the Bronx were the Word of God Hour Baptist Church, Morris Wooten, pastor; and the Spring Grove Baptist Church, Paul Williams, pastor. Two Queens churches were among the new African-American members of the association: the First Freedom Baptist Church, Sam Dixon, pastor; and the Shiloh Baptist Church, Alvin Mills, pastor. Pastor Fernando Morris led the Emmanuel Missionary Baptist Church of Newark to join the association in 1984.

After extensive study of community data, Sam Wong began the Chinese Promise Baptist Church in 1984 in a part of Brooklyn he predicted would become New York City's third "Chinatown" (after lower Manhattan and Flushing). Sponsored by the Evergreen Baptist Church, the Promise Church utilized a variety of creative community events like an annual Labor Day street fair to share the gospel with non-Christian Chinese. In Queens, pastor Paul T. C. Cheung organized the Flushing Chinese Baptist Church in the early 1980s. The congregation became a part of the Metropolitan Association in 1985.

The large family of Hispanic churches in the association expanded further with the addition of several new congregations in the 1980s. The *Nueva Vida* Baptist Church in Queens, formed as a mission in 1983, was sponsored by the Canaan Baptist Church, and led by pastor Henry Ortiz. In Brooklyn, the Spanish Calvary Baptist Church began the *El Mesias* Spanish Mission in 1984 under the direction of Jose Somarriba. The congregation was constituted several years later and admitted to the Metropolitan Association in 1992. Also joining the association that year were two churches developed in the late 1980s through the leadership of Herberto

Becerra, pastor of the First Spanish Church of Manhattan. The Maranatha Spanish Baptist Church of Yonkers was formally organized by Ezequiel Coca. The New Jerusalem Baptist Church in Manhattan grew out of a Bible study hosted by Albertina Quinonez. Boanerges Maldonado was the church's first pastor. His wife Zully was elected president of Woman's Missionary Union, BCNY, in 1994. In 1989 the First Spanish Baptist Church of Passaic, New Jersey, established the Alpha and Omega Baptist Church in Newark. Bivocational pastor Reinaldo Casabona, a veterinarian, was organizing pastor. The Ebenezer Spanish Baptist Church in Queens, led by pastor Eliseo Toirac, began in 1988 another Hispanic congregation in Queens: the Faro De Luz Baptist Mission. The new church was constituted in the mid-1990s under Toirac's leadership.

The small circle of MNYBA ministries directed toward Middle Easterners expanded in 1986 with the addition of the Arabic Egyptian Baptist Mission in Jersey City. Sabry Elraheb, who was involved in other Arabic works in the metropolitan area in the 1970s, organized the congregation.

The association welcomed its first deaf congregation with the addition of the Shelter Rock Church of the Deaf in the 1980s. Once a "hearing" church, the Garden City Park, New York, congregation became "bilingual" with a translation for sermons offered in American sign-language. One of the first deaf appointees of the Foreign Mission Board was a member of the Shelter Rock Church.

Anglo church extension led to the development of five new congregations in the association. In New York City, the City Church of New York was organized by Bob Saul in 1980 as a unique urban ministry. After a few years of holding Sunday morning services on the sidewalk in front of Radio City Music Hall, most of the group dispersed. In the meantime their mission, the West End Baptist Church, developed on the Upper West Side of Manhattan with the leadership of pastor Sam Barrett.

In the early 1980s, the Madison Church sponsored chapels in Franklin and Hackettstown, New Jersey, which developed slowly throughout the decade. The Lakeland Baptist Chapel in Franklin, led by pastor Bill Lynch, assisted a summer Praxis team in organizing the Hackettstown work in 1981. This congregation was constituted as the Cornerstone Community Baptist Church in 1991 with William Budd and Jim Norton serving as co-pastors. The Lakeland Church was constituted the same year with Larry Wood as pastor.

Pastor Darwin Bacon led the Colts Neck congregation in 1986 to launch a chapel in the southernmost area of the BCNY—Howell, New Jersey. A Praxis team paved the way for mission pastor Neal McGlohon to begin

The Howell Baptist Church got its start in a township rescue squad building. Neal and Joy McGlohon helped launch the church in 1987.

the new work in a rescue squad building. He led the group to be constituted as the Howell Baptist Church in 1991.

Praxis teams over several summers cultivated prospects in western New Jersey for a chapel initiated by the Bridgewater Baptist Church in October 1987. The church gave part of its membership away in forming the chapel, and for a time Bridgewater pastor Jamie Munro divided preaching responsibilities between the church and the chapel. The Central Hunterdon Baptist Church was constituted in 1990. Retired SBC foreign missionary David King was interim pastor of the congregation. In 1992 Edward Hatcher became the church's first full-time pastor.

CHAPTER THIRTEEN

Baptist Convention of New York

A NEW DAY FOR MISSION ADVANCE, 1990-1994

The 1990s ushered in an auspicious, yet anxious time for Southern Baptists. New opportunities for global ministry fell into the denomination's lap in a manner reminiscent of the post-World War II era. Eastern Europe and the reemerging nations of the former Soviet Union were seemingly a spiritual vacuum waiting to be filled with the evangelical witness of Southern Baptists and others.

Mission opportunities beckoned on the home front as well. After forty years of advance into the so-called "pioneer areas" of the country, Southern Baptists were well represented with state and area conventions in all fifty states. The establishment of these denominational infrastructures meant not that the work of pioneer missions was complete, but that Southern Baptists were poised in an unprecedented way to touch the whole nation with their witness.

The kind of confidence expressed by leaders in the late 1950s about the convention's opportunistic response to new frontiers was again being heard in the early 1990s. When Morris Chapman was installed as chief executive officer of the SBC Executive Committee, Adrian Rogers pointed to the lofty role he felt Southern Baptists had come to occupy on the global mission scene: ". . . I believe that the hope of the world lies in the West. I believe that the hope of the West lies in America. I believe that the hope of America is in Judeo-Christian ethics. I believe that the backbone of that Judeo-Christian ethic is evangelical Christianity. I believe that the bellwether or evangelical

Christianity is the Southern Baptist Convention. So I believe, in a sense, that as the Southern Baptist Convention goes, so goes the world."[1] Timothy George, dean of Samford University's Beeson Divinity School, saw the conservative resurgence in the convention as a "providential moving of God" to rescue the SBC from becoming "just another mainline denomination, bereft of missionary and evangelistic zeal."[2]

But others worried that the SBC by the early 1990s was not the kind of evangelical "bellwether" or missions-driven denomination some imagined it to be. They maintained that the controversy had distracted Southern Baptists from their foundational priorities, and eroded the confidence of the rank and file in national boards and agencies. The Executive Committee's own survey of SBC churches seemed to confirm the anecdotal evidence of a growing lethargy toward missions. The survey revealed that foreign and home missions ranked least important among seven selected areas of ministry.[3] This "snapshot" of the convention's sentiments, coupled with the threat of missionary dollars being siphoned off by the Cooperative Baptist Fellowship, was cause for concern—especially for state conventions heavily dependent upon support from the Home Mission Board.

A Prayerful and Deliberate Response

One response that seemed to offer hope for a reconciled and reunited Southern Baptist Convention was that of prayer for repentance and spiritual awakening. More than anyone else in the early 1990s, Henry Blackaby sensitized the denomination to the need for spiritual renewal. As the first director of the Home Mission Board's office of prayer and spiritual awakening, he promoted the Old Testament concept of "solemn assemblies" among the people of God for prayer and repentance.

In March 1990, Quinn Pugh called such an assembly for the Baptist Convention of New York. Along with convention president Roger Knapton and board chairman Larry Brown, he invited New York Baptists to gather in Albany prior to the annual evangelism conference to offer "extraordinary prayer for spiritual awakening and empowerment of believers and the church." Led by T. W. Hunt, a noted authority on prayer among Southern Baptists, ninety persons gathered for the event which was said to have brought a "quiet urgency" and the "very presence of God" to the evangelism conference.[4]

But Pugh also took pragmatic steps to help ensure the inclusiveness of the BCNY amid a growing SBC dispute over the nature of Cooperative Program gifts. In September 1990, he proposed a statement to the executive board which endorsed Southern Baptists' time-honored method of supporting convention causes, but also opened the door for the BCNY to forward gifts to the Cooperative Baptist Fellowship under the designation "Cooperative Program." "It is the practice of the Baptist Convention of New York," he wrote, "to honor any designations which may be assigned to monies sent through the treasurer of the Baptist Convention of New York, provided those designations are for causes supported by the budgets, respectively, of the Baptist Convention of New York and the Southern Baptist Convention."

Given that the Cooperative Baptist Fellowship at the time consisted of Southern Baptist churches supporting Southern Baptist causes, gifts made to the organization could be channeled through the BCNY as Cooperative Program funds. The executive director explained that the statement was more a description of what the BCNY had done for the past twenty-one years than a new policy.[5] The recommendation raised considerable discussion, but was adopted by the board with only three dissenting votes.

The Fallout of the "The Controversy" upon New York Baptists

While the SBC controversy did no direct damage to the fellowship or structure of the Baptist Convention of New York, it did impact the convention in other significant ways. The BCNY's heavy financial dependency upon the Home Mission Board meant that new SBC directives toward the board had a ripple effect that eventually reached the Northeast. After Larry Lewis became president of the Home Mission Board in 1987, he emphasized, almost exclusively, programs of direct evangelism and church planting. The Metropolitan Association subscribed to a broad-ranging, ministry-oriented, urban mission strategy that necessitated support from departments of the board deemphasized through budget and personnel cuts and restructuring. David D'Amico, director of missions for the Metro Association from 1985 to 1989, believes that the most demonstrable effect of the controversy on the BCNY was in the area of social ministry.[6]

Campus ministry also sustained significant budget reductions both from the Home Mission Board and the Baptist Sunday School Board. In his annual report to the BCNY in 1990, Chip Lockwood decried the fact that "at a time when universities and colleges are more open to a strong Christian witness and when students are willing to listen to the Gospel, available funding and personnel are decreasing."[7] Gone was any "growth capital" for expanding ministry to new campuses.

A less tangible and measurable effect of the controversy was its impact upon potential new missionary personnel for such diverse and "nontraditional" areas of the convention as metropolitan New York. Influenced by a majority of new trustees supportive of the SBC's conservative course correction, the Home Mission Board brought greater theological scrutiny to bear in screening candidates for missionary service. Whereas before the Baptist Faith and Message statement of 1963 had represented the broad parameters of Southern Baptist orthodoxy, now particular interpretations of the confessional statement were required of potential appointees. Metro Association leaders like DeLane Ryals believe this significantly diminished the pool of qualified and gifted candidates for ministry.[8]

The controversy was for New York Baptists a "crisis" in that it could be represented by the Chinese character indicating such—a danger juxtaposed with an opportunity. It could produce cynicism, bitterness, and a loss of vision, or it could instill a resolve among the churches and associations to be become more self-reliant. It could be a continual preoccupation, or it could make New York Baptists determined to demonstrate for the rest of the Southern Baptist Convention that unity in mission was possible without lockstep unanimity of thought.

Certainly the emphasis upon repentance, renewal, and spiritual awakening was a development all the churches could support regardless of political sympathies. Coming off a year when their convention had recorded its highest number of baptisms in five years, New York Baptists appeared to have their priorities in place. "Now our energies must be directed towards the ever-growing burden of the unsaved, unreached persons around us," wrote Quinn Pugh. ". . . Everywhere we sense that the Lord is mightily at work in the lives of people who are hungering for meaning and hope."[9]

Two years later Pugh called New York Baptists' attention to the bicentennial of the modern missions movement, launched in 1792 by William Carey. He exhorted messengers to the 1992 annual session at Albany to recognize "the fresh call of God upon his people." Like Carey's call to mission, he observed, the new day of mission advance demanded by dramatic new opportunities for sharing the gospel is "no casual moment." He offered a missions declaration that he hoped would become the credo of the Baptist Convention of New York throughout the 1990s:

An Albany Declaration

Every Baptist believer, a missionary
Every Baptist congregation, a missionary fellowship
Every Baptist member, a missionary in training
Every Baptist education program, a missionary training school
Every Baptist meeting house, a missionary outpost
Every Baptist ministry, a missionary outreach
Every Baptist budget, a cooperative missions budget.[10]

A New Partner in Ministry

After thirteen years of assisting New York Baptists through a sister-state relationship, the Georgia Baptist Convention concluded its partnership with the Baptist Convention of New York in November 1990. Quinn Pugh led the convention in expressing thanks to the Georgia body for its invaluable contributions of human and financial resources in advancing the work of Southern Baptists in the Northeast.

Waiting in the wings was the Baptist State Convention of North Carolina, prepared to enter into a five-year partnership with the BCNY. Roy Smith, executive director of the North Carolina Convention, was present for the 1990 annual session at Melville, Long Island, to co-sign with Quinn Pugh a covenant which formalized the new sister-convention relationship. The leaders were confident that the agreement would result in important benefits to both conventions.[11]

North Carolina volunteers Hank and Dorothy Greer helped initiate the linkage by touring the territory of the Baptist Convention of New York in 1992 to assess needs and opportunities for creative exchanges of resources. In 1993 alone, seventeen hundred North Carolina partners representing 112 churches assisted BCNY congregations and associations with evangelism crusades, WMU events, construction projects, and outreach efforts. The North Carolina Convention offered generous financial support and provided the BCNY one of its own employees, Beth Ward, as an assistant for WMU ministry and summer missions programs. She later became the partnership liaison for the two conventions.[12]

New York Baptists were able to give back to their North Carolina counterparts assistance such as consultation for ministry in multihousing projects, non-English language ministry support, and leadership for revival meetings, lay renewal weekends, and missions emphases.[13] The partnership proved to be a joyful, mutually rewarding undertaking for both conventions.

Serving the Churches, 1990–1994

In 1989 convention staff, associational leaders, and members of the executive board updated VISION 2000, the BCNY's long-range strategy plan, through a careful process of evaluation. The revised document became the convention's road map for mission and ministry in the 1990s.

Clayton Day, a familiar name in the beginnings of Southern Baptist work in the metro New York area, was the first new member added to the

BCNY staff in the 1990s. The pastor of the Clinton Road Baptist Church and retired Army chaplain became director of the evangelism division in September 1990. At the same time, he assumed responsibilities as assistant to the executive director. Day remained with the Baptist Convention of New York until his resignation in 1995 to pursue other ministry opportunities in his native Texas.

One of the evangelism division's first tasks of the 1990s was to prepare churches for revival meetings and other special events associated with the "Here's Hope: Jesus Cares For You" evangelism campaign. Associate director George Russ provided training for evangelistic outreach, including prison evangelism in Buffalo, multihousing evangelism in Rochester, home Bible study evangelism among Filipino churches, and discipleship development training among African-American churches. The division also helped New York Baptists prepare for Billy Graham Crusades in Albany, Northern New Jersey, Long Island, and Central Park, where more than 250,000 gathered on the Great Lawn for a rally in September 1991.

In September 1992, the evangelism division joined with the Salvation Army and the South Jefferson County Historical Association in sponsoring a bicentennial observance of Charles Finney's birth. The BCNY held its annual Finney Institute in conjunction with the event, welcoming as keynote speakers two of the Southern Baptist Convention's leading scholars in evangelism: Lewis Drummond and Roy Fish.[14]

The Baptist Convention of New York was host in May 1993 to the Home Mission Board's National School of Evangelism and Church Growth. Held in Parsippany, New Jersey, the event attracted more than four hundred participants. That same year the board sponsored "Crossover New York"— a major effort to provide resources for local evangelism programs and projects which included ministry to the World University Games in Buffalo, a Bible and literature distribution at the New York State Fair, and a "Celebrating Our Diversity" event in New York City's Central Park.[15]

The education division recorded impressive statistical gains in Sunday School enrollment for 1990. Director Daniel Paixao attributed the increase in part to effective educational leadership and training at the associational level. A revised format of regional and specialized training events in 1991 attracted a total of almost eight hundred registrants to five conferences. The educational ministry of BCNY churches also benefited in 1991 from the addition of staff consultants Claude McGavic and Mary Lois Sanders for the programs of discipleship training and church music, respectively. Sanders, a former missionary to Brazil, created a program that included an annual church music conference, associational choral workshops, and training opportunities for consultants in a variety of program areas.

Teenagers share a light moment at the BCNY youth convention. This one in 1992 was hosted by the Lincoln Avenue Baptist Church in Endicott.

Following Daniel Paixao's resignation in July 1992, Quinn Pugh assumed leadership of the education division with assistance from Claude McGavic. In January 1994, Mark A. Fischer became director of the education division. Having spent the previous eight years as a missionary in Ecuador, he was well equipped to respond to the diverse needs and challenges of the New York mission field. Of note in Fischer's first year of leadership was an especially successful youth convention in Lake Placid which attracted almost four hundred participants.

The 1990s brought numerous personnel changes in the program of campus ministry. Alton and Fairy Harpe—"fixtures" at the United States Military Academy at West Point—retired in 1992 after completing more than twenty years of compassionate ministry to students, officers, and their families. In January 1993, United States Naval Academy graduate Bill Blackwell became Baptist campus minister at West Point.

Former University of Buffalo campus minister and BCNY resort ministries consultant Robert Freeman became campus minister at Columbia University in March 1992. Working with Freeman in New York City was Susan Field, who reactivated a Baptist Student Union program at New York University. US-2 missionary Theresa Thompson became acting Baptist chaplain at Columbia after Freeman's resignation in August 1994.

The Baptist Chaplaincy at Princeton University was maintained during 1990–1992 by interim leaders Greg Faulkner, a Princeton Seminary student, and Susan Field, NYU campus minister. Michael Arges became director of the program in June 1992. A member of the first "official" Southern Baptist student group at Princeton University in the 1970s, Arges attempted to expand the program in the early 1990s to include ministry at Rutgers University.

Ministry to international students remained an important part of the BCNY's program of campus ministry in the 1990s. The ministry was strong at Columbia and at the University of Buffalo, and blossomed at other sites like SUNY Stony Brook, where Serena Lin began working with Chinese students in 1992. Michael and Michelle Dean's efforts with internationals at Syracuse University resulted in some students being baptized and involved in local churches.

Armetta Fields Wright, a member of the Ithaca Baptist Church, was a Mission Service Corps volunteer campus minister at Cornell University from 1991 to 1994. During this same time, Gay Cabral worked closely with pastor James Bradley of the Bread of Life Baptist Church in Plattsburgh to provide a program for students at SUNY Plattsburgh. Partnerships like these between churches and campuses enabled the BCNY to enlarge its outreach to students despite difficult financial constraints.

One of the most significant developments of the early 1990s in the missions division was the calling of the convention's first director of black church extension. Although funding for a director/consultant had been in place since 1986, it was not until August 1992 that the position was filled by Victor Ketchens, a former member of the Bronx Baptist Church. With cooperation from black leaders like Sam Simpson, extension strategist for the Bronx, Herbert Graves, Ernesto Robinson, Arnaldo Campbell, Wilbert Martin, and Ricky Armstrong, Ketchens developed a program focused upon new church starts, Sunday School and discipleship training leadership, and evangelism.

The missions division's program of Brotherhood also developed under the leadership of Peter John, a member of the Wake Eden Baptist Church in the Bronx. In 1994 the organization's goal of beginning a disaster relief ministry in the Northeast was realized when the Maryland/Delaware Convention donated its fully equipped disaster trailer for use in all the northeastern state convention areas. The BCNY Brotherhood accepted the gift with the understanding that the unit would be stored in Syracuse, while expenses for its upkeep would be shared through a "Northeast Disaster Relief Consortium" consisting of the Maryland/Delaware, Pennsylvania/South Jersey, New England, and New York Conventions.

Steven Diaz became director of multilanguage church extension in January 1991. Although serving only two years, Diaz made a significant contribution to this area of ministry by fostering an attitude of church growth among multilanguage congregations, and by recruiting effective leaders for new and existing congregations. Oscar Medina, a New Jersey native and member of the Emmanuel Spanish Baptist Church in Union City, succeeded Diaz in January 1994. Others serving on the multilanguage extension staff in the early 1990s were Soon Il (Robert) Kim, an experienced Korean pastor and church planter; David Phan, a Vietnamese pastor who helped start new works in Rochester, Binghamton, and Buffalo; and Romy

Glenn Igleheart, director of the BCNY missions division (left), discusses a proposal with George Russ, associate director of evangelism division.

Manansala, a Filipino church growth consultant who in 1994 became director of multilanguage extension for the Metropolitan Association.

Starting new churches remained a priority for the missions division in the early 1990s. Director Glenn Igleheart led the division to sponsor new work probes in Hispanic communities of central New Jersey in 1991 and within a four-county area of the lower Hudson Valley in 1993. Praxis teams sponsored through the BCNY's partnership with local churches worked to launch new works in the Syracuse area, Tonawanda, Niagara Falls, and North Greece. The annual Paul and Ava James Offering for BCNY Missions, totaling almost fifty thousand dollars for 1993–1994, was a vital resource for the division's program of church extension.

Personnel within the department of church and community ministries remained fairly constant in the early 1990s, with a corps of experienced missionaries assigned to four sites in the Metropolitan Association and as associational CCM directors for the Greater Rochester and Long Island Associations. In 1993 Michael Williams was reassigned from his position at the Harlem Ministry Center to become the first full-time AIDS ministry consultant appointed by the Home Mission Board.

Hunger ministry remained an important part of the BCNY's program of responding to human needs. Between 1990 and 1994, the Home Mission Board channeled almost forty thousand dollars per year through the Baptist Convention of New York to local churches and associations for hunger relief. Under the leadership of Liz Pearson, CCM workers ministered to meet physical and emotional needs, but also to respond to spiritual needs. Pearson's 1993 church and community ministries report included the following information: 1,502 volunteers utilized; 201 ministries offered; 71 professions of faith; and 15 baptisms.[16]

When messengers to the 1990 annual session at Melville, Long Island, received word of Ava James's death in Florida, they were reminded of her trademark advice for effective ministry: "If you want your church to grow, start a Woman's Missionary Union in your congregation." Mrs. James was an extraordinary example of sacrificial missionary service and witness. One

Liz Pearson, BCNY director of Woman's Missionary Union (front left), shares a Second Century grant certificate with Fairy Harpe, state WMU president. Behind them are Carolyn Miller, national WMU president, and Carroll Pharris, Second Century Fund committee chair.

of the highlights of the BCNY's program of WMU in the 1990s was the publication of June Andrews's book, *So Generations Will Remember: A History of Woman's Missionary Union, Baptist Convention of New York, 1969–1994*. Andrews chronicled the ministry of Ava James and a host of other women responsible for keeping the imperative of missions before BCNY churches.[17]

Quinn Pugh's support for WMU was boldly demonstrated in April 1993 when he joined four other SBC leaders in a national campaign to affirm the organization after it was harshly criticized for its decision to produce materials for the Cooperative Baptist Fellowship. Pugh wrote: "As a missions leader . . . I have leaned heavily upon the support of WMU. In the territory of the Baptist Convention of New York, our young churches serve a population center of 26 million persons. . . . At the forefront of training, church starting, community ministries, and missions support has stood WMU—a beautiful mosaic of committed women, young women, and girls of all races, cultures, and a dozen or more languages. . . . I am pleased to endorse WMU—this Christ-centered, God-given Baptist helper!"[18]

Personal Losses among the BCNY Family

The Baptist Convention of New York suffered a series of devastating personal losses in the mid-1990s. Within the span of one year, the spouses of three staff members died.

In January 1993, Junita Day (June), the wife of Clayton Day, director of the evangelism division, was killed in an auto accident near the couple's home in Fayetteville, New York. The Whitehouse, Texas, native was survived by her husband, two adult sons, and three grandchildren.

In July 1993, Patricia Lockwood, the wife of Chip Lockwood, director of the office of communications and campus ministry, died after an extended battle with cancer. Long the object of many prayers, "her brave, courageous spirit and her steadfast Christian commitment," wrote Quinn Pugh, "remained a bright encouragement to all who knew and loved her." She left behind three college and high school-aged sons.

On the evening of January 23, 1994, Theresa Losito, thirty-four, was killed when the van in which she and her family were riding was struck almost head-on by a drunk driver about one mile from the family's Liverpool, New York, home. Her husband, David Losito, BCNY accountant and business manager, and five children, ages six months to eight years old, were treated and released from the hospital.[19]

In each of these cases, the churches of the Baptist Convention of New York rallied to comfort the grieving families through prayer and other expressions of support. The impact was hardest among the convention staff. Quinn Pugh spoke of a "systemic grief" in the state office that only the hope of the gospel could transcend.

The BCNY also grieved collectively over the loss of a pastor who committed suicide in 1992. Amid reports of other pastors struggling with depression—some to the point of being hospitalized—the executive board appointed an ad hoc group to study the sources of stress in pastors' families, and to recommend ways for churches to provide support. Mark Lawson, pastor of the Bellewood Baptist Church, headed the study group which discovered the "lack of some resource" as the primary source of stress. Lack of funds for the church's ministry, lack of personal income for family support, or lack of people for the work of the church were the most commonly identified stress factors. Among other suggestions, the committee recommended that associations provide support group ministries for pastors and their spouses.[20]

Financial Struggles

The hope of financial growth in the 1990s comparable to what the convention had experienced in the latter half of the 1980s was not realized. A healthy increase of 10 percent over the previous year's Cooperative Program gifts brought 1989 receipts to $552,631. This was followed by growth of only 3 percent in 1990 to reach $569,853. By mid-1991, receipts had dipped to 24 percent below budgeted spending levels, and year-to-date

Larry Brown (paper in hand) meets with Phyllis Adams (left), church and community ministries director for the Long Island Association; David Leary, director of missions for the association; Larry Pridmore, 1994 convention president; and David Pope, executive board chair.

expenses over revenue stood at more than ninety thousand dollars.

The administrative committee of the executive board met in August for a special-called session to consider the problem. The committee concluded that more than anything else, the economic recession which had gripped the Northeast was to blame for the shortfall. Hopeful that the downturn in giving was a temporary aberration, convention president Larry Brown and board chair Keith Cogburn issued a statement acknowledging the financial struggles of New York Baptists and their churches. They also led the committee in devising a plan to help increase gifts in the last quarter of 1991. The plan resulted in stronger receipts to finish the year, but not strong enough to avert a decline in total gifts from the previous year to $561,342. Even so, the convention's deficit carried over from the 1980s remained constant at approximately seventy thousand dollars.[21]

Gifts rebounded only modestly between 1992 and 1994. Special receipts, however, generated for debt retirement through the convention's "Great Commission Endowment," and a sizable gift from North Carolina Baptists, contributed to a reduction in the deficit to $38,107 by the end of 1993. This improved financial status for the BCNY was short-lived. Unrealistic budget projections, deficiencies in financial reporting, significant overspending in some areas, and a shortfall in anticipated revenue resulted in an extraordinarily disappointing year financially for the convention. By the end of 1994, the deficit had mushroomed to $111,791. One of the greatest challenges facing the Baptist Convention of New York in the mid-1990s is to regain financial stability.

Celebrating a Rich Heritage

From their earliest days of ministry in Niagara Falls, Syracuse, and New York City, New York Baptists were aware of their historic role in Southern Baptists' advance toward becoming a national convention. "Making history" was the recurring theme for times when new churches were constituted, when associations and regional fellowships were organized, when the Baptist Convention of New York was born in 1969, and henceforth when the convention observed milestone anniversaries every five years in Syracuse. This historical consciousness made leaders aware of the need to create an archival collection to preserve and maintain materials related to the convention's rich heritage. By the time the convention celebrated its twentieth anniversary in 1989, the BCNY History Committee had established such a collection, and begun a campaign to secure materials.

As the convention approached its silver anniversary, the committee laid plans for a grand celebration—a New York Baptist family reunion—to be held in Syracuse in November 1994. The committee also led the BCNY to commission Keith Cogburn, pastor of the Raritan Valley Baptist Church in Edison, New Jersey, to author a comprehensive history of the convention.[22]

Recognizing the need for a permanent organization to encourage the study and preservation of Southern Baptist history in the Northeast, particularly in the territory of the Baptist Convention of New York, the committee helped organize what became in 1993 the John Gano Baptist History Fellowship. An eighteenth-century Baptist pastor, chaplain, educator, and missionary with roots in New Jersey and New York, Gano seemed to embody a spirit and missionary purpose the Baptist Convention of New York wished to emulate. DeLane Ryals, director of church extension for the Metropolitan Association, was elected the first president of the fellowship.[23]

The twenty-fifth anniversary session of the convention was a joyful time of recounting a rich missionary heritage and of contemplating the challenges of a "new day for mission advance." Present were former executive directors Paul James and Jack Lowndes, language missions leader Leobardo Estrada, staff members John Tubbs and Daniel Sanchez, directors of missions Arthur Walker and Norman Bell, and other pastors and laypeople who played a significant role in shaping the convention. Messengers paid special tribute to these leaders and to the first seventy and the last seventy churches to be constituted within the convention. Almost five hundred messengers and guests gathered for a closing missions rally which featured SBC president Jim Henry as the keynote speaker. Perhaps not since the 1969 annual session had New York Baptists been so moved with a sense of providential calling to ministry and mission.

New York Baptists and the Church Growth Movement

A number of BCNY churches in the early 1990s began adapting innovative church growth strategies in an attempt to reach "baby boomers"—that large segment of the population which many experts assessed as unresponsive to the traditional church. To appeal to those turned off by the formalities of litanies, hymn singing, and the general staidness of typical mainline Protestant worship, some churches adapted to a service of worship where a guitar substituted for an organ, upbeat praise choruses and hand-clapping replaced stately hymns, and casual dress was the order of the day. Cell group ministry also became popular as a substitute for traditional adult Sunday School.

Among the churches most successful in making the transition to contemporary worship was the Floyd Baptist Church which in June 1994 adopted a new name, "One Heart Church." Pastor David Pope, who led the church to experience significant growth in the early 1990s, explained that while the One Heart Church was warm, casual, and "seeker-friendly," it was also "high-commitment" in the expectations it had for those who wished to be members.[24]

Pastor Steve Hollaway led the Madison Baptist Church in October 1994 to begin a separate, alternative "contemporary" worship service at 8:30 A.M. on Sundays. The church utilized creative direct mail and publicity techniques to market the service to the unchurched population. The service was later moved to Saturday evenings to appeal to those with no church background or with marginal experience in the Roman Catholic tradition.

Like the Bergen Baptist Church which in 1991 adopted the name "Christ Community Church," the One Heart Church dropped "Baptist" from its name to widen its appeal. Both pastor Jack Mercer of the Christ Community Church and David Pope saw the denominational label as an unnecessary obstacle to their churches' witness. Mercer discovered through a series of community focus groups that Baptist churches were often presumed to be "overly emotional, legalistic, and out of sync with the culture." "We changed our name for one reason alone," he wrote, "to reach more people for Jesus Christ."[25]

While only a few churches took the kinds of bold steps described above, many have made adjustments to their worship style, Bible study format, outreach efforts, and overall philosophy of ministry based upon new church growth methodologies which had proven successful in many areas. In 1993 Michael Chance's staff assignment with the Metropolitan Association was redefined to include a focus upon educating leaders in church growth trends and ideas.

Growth in Associations and Churches

Although it lost yet another church through unusual circumstances, the Hudson Association grew steadily in the early 1990s with the planting of new mission chapels. In October 1993, pastor David Merrill led the Praise Baptist Church to drop its affiliation with Southern Baptists because of the national convention's failure to take a strong stand against the Masonic Lodge for its "secret rituals."[26] This left the association with only three churches, but by the end of 1994, these churches were sponsoring six new mission chapels. Students at the Northeast Branch of Mid-America Seminary provided pastoral leadership for almost all the new works.

To the north, the Grace Baptist Church, Whitehall, launched a chapel in Ticonderoga—the Calvary Baptist Church. Wayne Ferguson was mission pastor. With the help of church planter/strategist James Arrant, the Trinity Baptist Church in Schenectady began to sow seeds in the early 1990s for new churches with small "fellowships" in several locations. In Albany, the church sponsored the Crossroads Baptist Fellowship, which was begun in 1990 by Steve Ford. Students Ford reached at the State University of New York at Albany were instrumental in the establishment and growth of the Crossroads congregation. The next year the Trinity Church extended its witness to Duanesburg. In 1992 the Trinity Church started two additional fellowships in Galway and in the facilities of Mid-America Seminary. After interim leadership from James Arrant, the Galway Fellowship called Steve Cerny as pastor. The Open Arms Fellowship at the seminary was led initially by Rick Geeslin. Paul Schlett was organizing pastor of the Trinity Church's Hamilton Hill Fellowship in 1994.

The Southern Tier Association welcomed Terry Douglas as its new director of missions in January 1992. The former pastor of the First Baptist Church of Morgan City, Louisiana, assisted BCNY multilanguage associate David Phan that year in gathering a Vietnamese chapel in Endicott. Douglas enlisted the

Lincoln Avenue Church as the chapel's sponsor. The Korean Baptist Church of Susquehanna expanded its work in 1992 to include a program of campus ministry at the State University of New York at Binghamton.

The Southport Church in Elmira started several new works in the early 1990s. In Elmira, the congregation began the Hope Baptist Chapel in 1992, with David Ivy as pastor. The Hope congregation was later sponsored by the Ithaca Baptist Church. In Waverly, the Southport Church was involved in two church starts, the last resulting in the formation of Agape Life Bible Church in 1994, with Duane Arnold as founding pastor. The Southport Church reached across the state line into Pennsylvania to begin a new work at Sayre—the New Hope Baptist Chapel, with John Talada as pastor.

James Goforth, former pastor of the First Baptist Church of Rusk, Texas, became director of missions for the Adirondack Association in November 1991. The following fall he utilized his Texas connections to bring Bob Dixon, director of the state's Baptist Men's program, as guest speaker for an associational retreat. Focused upon spiritual renewal and revival, the highly effective retreat gave Goforth the idea of leading the association to host an annual northeastern conference centered around these themes. In September 1993, the Adirondack Association hosted its first "Maples Conference," welcoming as guest speaker one of Southern Baptists' foremost authorities on spiritual renewal and revival—Henry Blackaby.[27]

The Adirondack Association grew with the addition of three new mission chapels in the early 1990s. The First Christian Church of Brushton planted a new work in Massena in 1990. Pastor Joseph Burt led New York Baptists in their return to this site where pioneer missionary Zig Boroughs had first planted a new work more than thirty years before. In October 1991, the Shiloh Baptist Church in Malone began a chapel in Chateaugay—the Faith Baptist Church—under the direction of mission pastor Robert Sanders. John and Peggy Clark, laypeople in the Lake Placid Baptist Church, helped restart the Moriah Baptist Chapel in October 1994.

The fellowship and ministry of the Thousand Islands Association were enhanced by the able leadership of retired foreign missionaries who served as volunteer directors of missions. John Poe led the association in 1990–1991. He was followed in 1993 by Paul Stouffer, whom the North Carolina Baptist State Convention assisted.

The Greater Syracuse Association added a congregation to its family of churches in 1991 when the University Baptist Church became sponsor of the Manlius Family Fellowship. David Harris was founding pastor.

The churches of the neighboring Davis Association extended ministry outreach in a number of areas, including special programs for youth, prisoners, deaf persons, and senior citizens. In 1991 messengers adopted an ambitious long-range plan for doubling the number of congregations in the association by the year 2000.

The Greater Rochester Association was served well by a ministry team led by Rusty Sumrall, director of missions until his resignation in 1993. As director of church and community ministries, Barbara Wallace continued to sensitize churches to opportunities for responding to human need, while June Campbell provided ministry to the large community of deaf persons in the area associated with the National Technical Institute for the Deaf. She also was campus minister at the Rochester Institute of Technology. David Jackson, pastor of the Southport Baptist Church in Elmira, New York, became director of missions in 1994.

Among the new churches and ministries added to the association in the early 1990s was another church start in North Greece, sponsored by the Hamlin Community Church. The new work was launched in 1991 under the direction of mission pastor Charles Short. With the help of David Phan, the Rochester Baptist Church began an outreach to the Vietnamese community, forming the Rochester Vietnamese Mission in April 1992. The Browncroft Church revived a ministry among Rochester's Asian Indian population. Pastor Melootu Abraham oversaw this work. Barbara Wallace assisted the Pittsford Church in an outreach to the Pines of Perinton, a multihousing complex where the church ministered to the physical as well as spiritual needs of the residents.

The Long Island Association showed new signs of life in the early 1990s, welcoming several chapels and Bible study fellowships as missions of the Farmingdale Baptist Church. David Leary, director of missions and interim pastor of the Farmingdale Church, cultivated the involvement of two predominantly African-American congregations in the association. The Bibleway Mission in Wyandanch, led by William Glover, and the Open Door Christian Center in Farmingdale, led by Eugene Wright, affiliated with the association in 1993 as chapels of the Farmingdale Church. The church also launched a new Filipino congregation under the direction of Gene Miraflor, and provided a facility for the Seoul Korean Baptist Church of New York—a congregation that moved from Queens in 1992. Pastor Jae Yong Kim later relocated the church to Mineola.

New works resulting from church divisions also joined the Long Island Association in the early 1990s. The Victory Chapel, an offshoot of the Calvary Baptist Church, Medford, joined the association in 1990. The Long Island Bible Fellowship, led by pastor Brookins Taylor, became a mission of the Farmingdale Church in 1991.

Described by some as the most vibrant SBC church on Long Island, the Chinese Christian Gospel Church in Lake Grove was initiated in 1992 by campus minister Serena Lin. The new work grew out of her ministry to students at the State University of New York at Stony Brook. After a year as interim pastor, Lin became pastor of the congregation in 1993.[28]

Having prioritized ministry support as a primary need among the churches, the Long Island Association called Phyllis Adams in 1993 as director of church and community ministry. Among other work, she assisted the Chinese Christian Gospel Church in establishing English-language classes, and surveyed the churches to determine what ministry programs and outreach efforts were most needed in the association.

The Frontier Association continued to grow in the 1990s with the addition of new chapels sponsored by a wide cross section of churches. In 1990 the Calvary Christian Church in Buffalo initiated the Lancaster Baptist Fellowship. The congregation was led by mission pastor John Galda. Later, the church changed its name to the New Hope Fellowship. To the south, the First Baptist Church of Silver Creek extended its witness to Gowanda with the establishment of the Gowanda Baptist Chapel in 1992. Spencer Brown was the founding pastor.

The historic LaSalle Baptist Church in Niagara Falls was a sponsor to two new works in the northern region of the Frontier Association. In 1992 the church became involved in an effort to reestablish a congregation on Grand Island. Robert Dixon was pastor of the Grand Island Baptist Chapel. Two years later the LaSalle Church established the Youngstown Baptist Chapel, led by Denny Webb.

The Fillmore Avenue Church helped begin another church within the city limits of Buffalo in 1994. The church launched the multiethnic North Buffalo Community Church, led by pastor William Smith.

Following his resignation from the Southside Baptist Church in Jamestown, Ted Ward became the Frontier Association's "church starter liaison" in Alabama as a Mission Service Corps volunteer. His efforts on behalf of Southern Baptist work in western New York brought two mission pastors from Alabama to start new churches in the region. In 1993 Larry Summers came as pastor of the House of Prayer in Salamanca, a chapel of the Veteran's Park Church. Andrew Baril arrived the same year to lead the Wheatfield Baptist Chapel, begun by the Amherst Church.

Terry Robertson resigned as director of missions in 1992 to become pastor of the Amherst Baptist Church. In June 1994, the Frontier Association called Michael Flannery as its new director. A Pennsylvania native, Flannery was previously a church and community ministries worker in Indiana and North Carolina.

The Metropolitan Association welcomed several new staff members to its ministry team in the early 1990s. In 1990 the association called David

Dean, pastor of the First Baptist Church of Sudbury, Massachusetts, as director of missions. Rebecca Waugh succeeded Nona Bickerstaff as director of church and community ministries in 1993. New workers coming in 1994 to the church extension staff were Barbara Oden, multihousing strategist, and Romy Manansala, director of multilanguage church extension.

The Hope Baptist Church started the 1990s parade of new churches in the Metropolitan Association with a deaf ministry that resulted in the formation of the Hope Baptist Church of the Deaf. Pastor Leslie Bunn was a former member of the Shelter Rock Church of the Deaf.

In the early 1990s, the association added new groups to its long list of languages and cultures represented among the churches. The All Saints Baptist Church, a Bronx congregation consisting of immigrants from several African countries, became involved with the association during this time. The church was led by Charles McWhales of Liberia. In 1994 multi-language missionary Robert Kim helped cultivate a small Japanese fellowship in Queens. Azurma Suwabe was pastor of the group. The Park Slope Church in Brooklyn ministered to Russian immigrants through an English tutoring program, as well as to Spanish-speaking people through the Mount of Olives Mission. Miguel Humphreys was pastor of the mission.

In 1994 the Living Word (Filipino) Fellowship adopted the First Bangla Christian Church as a chapel. Pastor Sanford Bhowmik organized the congregation among fellow Bangladeshi Christians in Queens after coming to the United States in 1993 to seek medical treatment for his son.

New Chinese churches uniting with the association in the 1990s were the Mandarin Fellowship Baptist Church in Manhattan and the New Jersey First Chinese Baptist Church in Edison. The Mandarin Church was developed by pastor Andrew Yu, with sponsorship from the Vassar Road Baptist Church. The New Jersey First Chinese Church—the first Southern Baptist-affiliated Chinese congregation in the state—was organized by pastor Chung Wong, with cooperation from the Raritan Valley Church, which hosted the new work.

The French-speaking Baptist Church of Brooklyn continued to be a prolific mother of new Haitian congregations. Two new works begun under its sponsorship, the Sentinel Baptist Church in St. Albans (1992) and the French-speaking Church of New Rochelle (1994), were led, respectively, by pastors David Box and Rigaud Pierre. The French-speaking Baptist Church Elus in Queens, led by pastor Vercanne Davilus, became a part of the Metro Association in 1990. The El Shaddai Haitian Baptist Church and the New Bethlehem Haitian Baptist Church, both in Brooklyn, were admitted to the association in 1991. Withney Pierre was pastor of the El Shaddai Church; Norbert Philistin led the New Bethlehem Church. In

1992 the association welcomed the Ebenezer French-speaking Baptist Church of Irvington, New Jersey, Frederick Cheriscat, pastor. The French-speaking Church, Spring Valley, initiated the Haitian Community Chapel of Harlem in 1990, under the leadership of Tony Joseph.

In Connecticut and Westchester County, New York, Emmanuel St. Juste led the French-speaking Church of Stamford to launch two new works: the French-speaking Church of Danbury, Jacques Cailleau, pastor, and the First French-speaking Church of Yonkers, which he served as pastor.

A rich harvest of new Filipino congregations continued in the Metropolitan Association. With the exception of a fellowship begun in Harlem, all of the new starts in the early 1990s were in New Jersey, where the Filipino population grew rapidly, especially in areas near medical facilities. The new works were: City Chapel in Jersey City, Romy Manansala founding pastor; Living Stone Christian Fellowship in Livingston, Tim Barredo, founding pastor; Piscataway Bible Fellowship in Piscataway, David Sera-Josef, founding pastor; and the International Christian Church of Toms River, Jose Bulaun, founding pastor. By the mid-1990s, Felix Sermon and other members of the Metropolitan Southern Baptist Filipino Fellowship were making plans for an additional work related to international seamen passing through Port Newark.

Six new Korean congregations joined the association by petition in 1993–1994. In 1993 the association welcomed the First Korean Church of New Jersey in Rutherford, Henry Kwak, pastor; Central Korean Baptist Church, Long Island City, New York, Dong Suk Oh, pastor; The Savior's Korean Baptist Church of New York, Flushing, Chun Woo Lee, pastor; and the New York Antioch Korean Baptist Church, Woodside, Sun Il Lee, pastor. Korean congregations joining the association the next year were Korean Baptist Church of Northern New Jersey, Nam Kyu Cho, pastor; and the Westchester Korean Baptist Church, Yonkers, Yong Mok Kim, pastor. The Madison Korean Church, Youngje Han, pastor, later merged with the northern New Jersey Church; the combined congregation shares a building with the *Resurreccion* (Spanish) Baptist Church in Dumont.

In addition to these constituted churches which formally united with the association, several other Korean congregations began relating to the association during this time. These were: the Grace Korean Baptist Church in New Milford, New Jersey, Jong Hur, pastor; Korean Baptist Church of Chappaqua, Robert Kim, pastor; Dae Heung Korean Baptist Church, Tae-Jin Chung, pastor; First Korean Baptist Church of Long Island, Byung Woo Choi, pastor; and the Staten Island Korean Mission, Ou Soon Lee, pastor.

The Hispanic congregations continued outreach within their culture, establishing the Christ the Only Hope Baptist Church in Yonkers, Milton

Delgado, pastor; and the *Mision Christiana*, also in Yonkers, Edgar Morales, pastor. The churches also initiated a Fairview, New Jersey, fellowship. The First Spanish Baptist Church of Long Beach, New York, Solomon Orellano, pastor, began relating to the association. Increasingly, however, the Spanish-speaking churches were beginning to focus upon other language groups in mission. In 1993 the Canaan Baptist Church began an English-speaking chapel under the direction of church planter Larry Holcomb. The First Spanish churches of Manhattan and Passaic also began exploring ways to minister to Asian groups, and to English-speaking people living in their communities.

Three new Middle Eastern congregations were organized by Metro Association churches in 1992. Nagi Yousef was founding pastor of the First Arabic Baptist Church of Yonkers, a mission of the First Arabic Church of New Jersey. The Terrill Road Baptist Church in Scotch Plains, New Jersey, sponsored an Arabic fellowship led by pastor Abdalla Mikhail. The West End Church in Manhattan sponsored Assaad Eid in launching the Arabic Baptist Church in Brooklyn. Although few in number, the Arabic churches maintained several outreach fellowship groups among the large concentration of Middle Easterners living in the metro New York area.

In 1991 the African-American Mount Chapel Missionary Baptist Church of Irvington, New Jersey, joined the Metropolitan Association. Carnell Witherspoon is pastor of the church.

The First Portuguese-speaking Baptist Church of New Jersey was begun in 1992 as a mission of the First Portuguese-speaking Church of New York. The Newark congregation was constituted under the leadership of Daniel Paixao, the former director of the education division for the Baptist Convention of New York.

Baptist Convention of New York

LIKE THE BOOK OF ACTS

Albert McClellan was right. Southern Baptists' advance into the Northeast was in many ways "like the Book of Acts." He made that statement in 1960 when the pages of the book were just beginning to be written. Since then many more chapters have been completed.

Luke records in Acts that the early Christians were almost always an unwitting people of destiny, guided through seemingly mundane circumstances to cross racial and ethnic barriers with the gospel. They were not driven in the beginning by an intentional agenda to share the good news with everybody—the light for this imperative dawned slowly. Not even the miracle of Pentecost convinced Peter of the inclusiveness of a Christian family which knew no geographic or racial boundaries. Personal experience brought him to this realization.

Pentecost became a compelling metaphor for New York Baptists as the possibilities for a multicultural family of churches in an unlikely place for Southern Baptists were illuminated through moments of personal discovery. In 1954 some good citizens of Gantt, Alabama, needed a new church in Niagara Falls. Sure, it was an unorthodox idea, but why not establish a Southern Baptist work there? Forty years later people from a nation that did not even exist when these Alabamians arrived—Bangladesh—came calling at the door of the Metropolitan Association. Was the ethnic embrace of the convention wide enough to welcome them? Are you kidding? What a journey of discovery these past forty years have been for New York Baptists, and for Southern Baptists too, as they have followed our lead!

The Book of Acts also demonstrates that people of sincere faith did not always agree; they, in fact, sharply disagreed. Paul and Barnabas, Peter and Paul; conservative and progressive; merciful and exacting; traditional and innovative—these differences were apparent among early Christians; one can read between the lines other elements of diversity. Yet for all their differences, these believers were united behind what some call the church's earliest creed: "Jesus is Lord."

The Baptist Convention of New York is marked by differences which, if exploited, could lead to the convention's undoing. There seems, however, to be a remarkable core of constituents who feel that the reality of God's work of reconciling the world unto himself is far more important than any religio-political loyalty, organization, or theological interpretation. This center is very much intact within the convention.

Despite the Apostle Paul's best-laid plans of missionary advance, things did not always turn out the way he expected. His plans for ministry in Asia and Bithynia were thwarted by some pesky circumstance behind which he saw the guidance of the Spirit. A closed door opened another door for a fruitful ministry in Macedonia, which began by the riverside where Lydia and her friends prayed each Sabbath.

New York Baptists have been similarly perplexed and frustrated by failed mission efforts, only to discover some new opportunity in an unlikely place. Mission expansion was never surrendered to a random, serendipitous pattern, but many of the churches which today comprise the BCNY were not developed according to a predictable plan. They were some of God's good surprises.

Finally, the early chapters of Acts describe the church as offering a holistic response to human need. Goods were provided for those in need; widows received a special distribution of support (resulting in some dispute). BCNY churches, on the whole, strive to follow this pattern—sharing ministry in Jesus' name with those he called the "least of these my children."

The Baptist Convention of New York is the impressive testimony of more than forty years of missions, ministry, and evangelism. The BCNY remains an evolving historical entity, meaning, of course, that pages of the story are being written even now by the more than 350 churches and chapels that comprise the convention. May we write those pages with the same fervor and conviction of those who came before us. They were, for all their shortcomings, a people of faith and hope.

HISTORICAL RECORD OF THE
BAPTIST CONVENTION OF NEW YORK

Representatives of seventy churches met in the Central Baptist Church, Syracuse, New York, on September 26, 1969, and organized the Baptist Convention of New York which began operations January 1, 1970.

Date of Meeting	Place	President	Recording Secretary	Number of Churches	Total Members	Preacher of Annual Sermon
1970	Towne House Motor Inn, Rochester, NY	Ken Lyle	Curtis Porter	74	10,413	Leobardo Estrada
1971	Madison BC & Long Hill Ch., Madison, NJ	Gene Fant	Curtis Porter	78	11,155	R. Quinn Pugh
1972	Thruway Hyatt House, Albany, NY	Homer C. Schumacher	Curtis Porter	87	12,877	J. T. Davis
1973	Treadway Inn, Binghamton, NY	Homer C. Schumacher	Curtis Porter	92	14,213	Elias Gomes
1974	Hotel Syracuse, Syracuse, NY	Fred H. Boehmer	Billy Caine	101	15,684	
1975	Greenwich Baptist Church, Greenwich, CT	Fred H. Boehmer	Billy Caine	101	16,976	
1976	Treadway Motor Inn	Nelson Tilton	Billy Caine	122	18,164	
1977	Albany Thruway House, Albany, NY	Charles Jolly	C. Truett Smith	139	19,471	
1978	Americana Hotel, Rochester, NY	Ron Madison	C. Truett Smith	153	18,603	
1979	Hotel Syracuse, Syracuse, NY	Wallace Williams	C. Truett Smith	157	18,581	
1980	Greenwich Baptist Church, Greenwich, CT	Wallace Williams	David Platt	152	19,152	
1981	Albany Thruway House, Albany, NY	Curtis Porter	David Platt	173	21,830	
1982	Amherst Baptist Church, Tonawanda, NY	Curtis Porter	Andrew Lee	143	20,388	
1983	Lincoln Ave. Baptist Church, Endicott, NY	Wesley Ellis	Andrew Lee	159	19,918	
1984	Hotel Syracuse, Syracuse, NY	Wesley Ellis	L. Coleman	171	22,312	Heberto J. Becerra
1985	Rochester Hilton, Rochester, NY	J. Edwin Hewlett	L. Coleman	180	23,225	Donald J. Burke
1986	Calvary Baptist Church, Aberdeen, NJ	J. Edwin Hewlett	Jon F. Meek Jr.	172	22,409	Dale Meredith
1987	Howard Johnson Lodge, Plattsburgh, NY	Samuel G. Simpson	Jon F. Meek Jr.	185	24,562	Victor Tan
1988	Sheraton Inn, Utica, NY	Samuel G. Simpson	Jon F. Meek Jr.	196	24,418	Roger Knapton
1989	Sheraton Inn, Liverpool, NY	Roger Knapton	Jon F. Meek Jr.	208	27,606	Paul S. James
1990	Radisson Plaza Hotel, Melville, LI, NY	Roger Knapton	Jas. Guenther	217	25,940	Jon F. Meek Jr.
1991	Radisson Hotel, Niagara Falls, NY	Larry Brown	Robert Taylor	222	23,998	Romeo Manasala
1992	Holiday Inn Turf, Albany, NY	Larry Brown	Robert Taylor	231	22,740	Bruce Aubrey
1993	Corning Hilton, Corning, NY	Larry Pridmore	Steven Blake	247	18,089	David Dean
1994	Sheraton Inn, Liverpool, NY	Larry Pridmore	Steven Blake	237	21,342	Ken Lyle

ENDNOTES

Introduction

1. Edwin Scott Gaustad, *A Religious History of America*, 3rd ed. (San Francisco: Harper, 1990), 47–48; Jesse C. Fletcher, *The Southern Baptist Convention: A Sesquicentennial History* (Nashville: Broadman Press, 1994), 31; Robert A. Baker, *A Baptist Source Book, with Particular Reference to Southern Baptists* (Nashville: Broadman Press, 1966), 20.

2. Courts Redford, *Home Missions: USA* (Atlanta: Home Mission Board of the Southern Baptist Convention, 1956), 90; Arthur B. Rutledge, *Mission to America: A Century and a Quarter of Southern Baptist Home Missions* (Nashville: Broadman Press, 1969), 115. Robert Baker provides an excellent systematic survey of Southern Baptists' geographic expansion in the twentieth century in *The Southern Baptist Convention and Its People, 1607–1972* (Nashville: Broadman Press, 1974), 355–91. See also Thomas J. Nettles, "Southern Baptists: Regional to National Transition," *Baptist History and Heritage 16* (January 1981): 13–23; and G. Thomas Halbrooks, "Growing Pains: The Impact of Expansion on Southern Baptists Since 1942," *Baptist History and Heritage* 17 (July 1982): 44–55.

3. *Annual*, Southern Baptist Convention, 1951, 36.

4. Redford, 13.

Chapter One

1. Everett Hullum Jr., "They Went Thisaway, Too," *Home Missions,* October 1974, 13.

2. Source materials cited for the LaSalle Baptist Church story, including newspaper clippings, correspondence, remembrances, etc., can be found in the archives of the Baptist Convention of New York (hereafter cited as BCNY), under "LaSalle Baptist Church." Notes from my interviews with Zig Boroughs and charter members of the church are also found in the archives.

3. Ralph Zeigler Boroughs to R. Quinn Pugh, 24 November 1989; the attached notes from Boroughs's address, "What Are You Doing in Niagara Falls?"

4. Boroughs to "Mother and Dad," 19 December 1954.

5. See, for example, works by Samuel S. Hill Jr., *Southern Churches in Crisis* (New York: Holt, Rineheart, and Wilson Inc., 1967); and Kenneth K. Bailey, *Southern White Protestantism in the Twentieth Century* (New York: Harper and Row Publishers, 1964).

6. Quoted in Blake Smith, "The Southern Baptist Invasion: Right or Wrong?" *Foundations* 2 (October 1959): 324.

7. Boroughs, interview by author, 7 March 1994.

8. John and Martha Mathison, interview by author, 10 January 1995; Ettie Jo Gilmer, interview by author, 9 March 1994; Richard and Faustine Williamson, interview by author, 10 January 1995; unidentified newspaper clipping, "LaSalle Baptist Group Gets Own Home."

9. Boroughs, interview; "What Are You Doing in Niagara Falls?"

10. Boroughs to "Mother and Dad," 7 January 1955.

11. Boroughs, "History of the LaSalle Baptist Church," *Ohio Baptist Messenger,* April 1957, 8.

12. Central Baptist Church file, BCNY; Most citations documenting the beginnings of the Central Church are in a scrapbook Ferguson compiled throughout 1957 which includes correspondence, service bulletins, and newspaper clippings.

13. Dowis to Ferguson, 15 March 1957.

14. Boroughs to Ferguson, 26 April 1957; 7 June 1957.

15. Ferguson to Becker, 13 June 1957; Becker to Ferguson, 19 June 1957.

16. Paul Becker, interview by author, 15 March 1994; 29 January 1995.

17. Boroughs to Becker, 18 July 1957; Becker to Boroughs, 29 July 1957.

18. Becker, interview; Becker to Ferguson, 29 July 1957.

19. Becker, interview; Becker to Ferguson, 20 August 1957.

20. For an example of Becker's approach toward southerners, see his correspondence to Robert C. Burkett, n.d.; see also Becker to Ferguson, 20 August 1957; Becker to "Friends," 28 May 1958; "Rev. Becker Takes a New Pulpit Here," *Syracuse Herald Dispatch,* 5 October 1957.

21. Becker to "Friends," January 1958.

22. "Church Is a Center for Southerners," *The Post-Standard* (Syracuse), 16 June 1958, section 2, 1.

Chapter Two

1. F. C. Tuttle, "Southern Baptists' Obligation to the Great Industrial North," *Ohio Baptist Messenger,* June 1956, 9.

2. Solomon F. Dowis, "Statement on Our Cities," *Home Missions,* July 1957, 24; Smith, 322.

3. Bailey, 53–54; "Jubilee Advance Committee," *Annual,* Southern Baptist Convention, 1964, 259–62.

4. The remembrances of Cash and Dowis about this period are incorporated into John D. Raymond's thesis, "The Development of the Southern Baptist Convention in the Northeast, 1957–1966" (Th.M. thesis, Princeton Theological Seminary, 1967), 20–27.

5. Melba Aaron, interview by author, 26 October 1994.

6. "A Soldier of God in a Pentomic Age," typewritten manuscript in Manhattan Baptist Church file, n.d., BCNY; Chlocile Massey, interview by the author, 15 March 1994.

7. Pauline Robb, "History of the Manhattan Baptist Church," undated typewritten manuscript in the Manhattan Church file, BCNY; Saxon Rowe Carver, *James Robb—Pioneer* (Atlanta: Home Mission Board, 1963), 69.

8. Robb, "History;" Ray E. Roberts, "How It All Began," *Maryland Baptist,* March 1958, 6; "History and Minutes of the Manhattan Baptist Church of New York City," undated typewritten manuscript in Manhattan Church file, BCNY.

9. Charles Jolly, interview by the author, 2 November 1994.

10. Charles A. Jolly, "Enter College Avenue," *Maryland Baptist,* March 1958, 7.

11. See correspondence in the Manhattan Church file, BCNY, Charles Jolly to Roland Smith, 6 May 1993.

12. Francis A. Davis, "One Layman's View," *Maryland Baptist,* April 1958, 5; Jolly to Smith, 6 May 1993.

13. Jolly to Smith, 6 May 1993.

14. The arrangement was as follows: 1) All missionaries in the Northeast are to be considered missionaries both of the Home Mission Board and the Maryland Convention; 2) The Home Mission Board is to have administrative and financial responsibility for mission work in the Northeast; and 3) All work in the Northeast is to be related directly to the Maryland Convention, and all missionary money is to be so channeled. See *Maryland Baptist,* 1 January 1960, 7; Ibid., 2 February 1967, 1.

15. "New Mission in New York City," *Ohio Baptist Messenger,* August 1957, 1

16. Paul James, interview with the author, 4 November 1994; 12 January 1995.

17. Ibid.; Ava L. James, "The Hand of God: The History of Manhattan Baptist Church," undated typewritten manuscript in the Manhattan Church file, BCNY.

18. Ibid.

19. Paul James to Members of the Southern Baptist Chapel, New York City, 12 September 1957, in Manhattan Church file, BCNY.

20. Ibid.; Jolly to Smith, 6 May 1993.

21. Paul and Ava James, "Where Families Live in Layers," *Home Life,* September 1959, 18–21.

22. "Report of the Home Mission Board Meeting," *Maryland Baptist,* 1 January 1958, 2.

23. Paul S. James, "The New York Story," pamphlet published in 1967 to commemorate Southern Baptists' tenth anniversary in New York.

24. Paul James, interview, 12 January 1995.

Chapter Three

1. R. Eugene Puckett, "Personal Paragraphs," *Ohio Baptist Messenger,* 15 August 1959, 2.

2. *The Frontier Baptist News* (hereafter cited as *Frontier News*), July 1958, 1.

3. Boroughs, interview by author, 9 April 1995; *Frontier News,* September 1958, 1.

4. Arthur Walker, "The Unfolding of God's Work in Western New York and Pennsylvania," typewritten manuscript in Frontier Association file, BCNY; Boroughs, interview.

5. Esther Heilig, interview by author, 6 April 1995.

6. Ibid.; Walter Heilig, "The High Cost of a Mission," *Home Missions,* January 1960, 2; Bernard Foor, interview by author, 7 April 1995.

7. Frontier Baptist Association, *Minutes,* 23 September 1958.

8. In 1954 the State Convention of Baptists in Ohio was constituted with thirty-nine churches and ten missions. By August 1962, the numbers had increased to 266 churches and 107 missions, which included work in West Virginia, Pennsylvania, and New York.

9. Walker L. Knight, "Area Missionary: The Modern Pioneer," *Home Missions,* January 1960, 8.

10. J. T. Davis, interview by author, 5 April 1995.

11. Paul Becker, "Work That Began Because of Interest of a Southern Baptist Layman," *Maryland Baptist,* 14 May 1964, 9.

12. Davis, interview, 5 April 1995.

13. Upon Davis's retirement in 1982, the Central Association was renamed the Davis Association.

14. "New Mission at Utica, New York," *Ohio Baptist Messenger,* 5 April 1960, 12.

15. "Clinton Road Church in New York Constitutes," *Maryland Baptist,* 16 May 1968, 4.

16. Shirley Bove, interview by author, 19 April 1995.

17. Charles E. Magruder, interview by author, 24 May 1995.

18. Knight, "Modern Pioneer," 7.

19. Walker, "The Unfolding of God's Work."

20. Knight, "Modern Pioneer," 8.

21. Gloria Stanton, "Rochester Baptist Church History," in Rochester Baptist Church file, BCNY.

22. Walker, "The Unfolding of God's Work."

23. Charles E. Magruder, "An Analysis of Southern Baptist Work in Upstate New York and Northwest Pennsylvania," January 1963, 3–5. Document in Frontier Association file, BCNY.

24. Garland Sparks to Darty Stowe, 20 June 1961, Frontier Association file, BCNY.

25. Charles E. Magruder to Arthur L. Walker, 11 August 1965, Frontier Association file, BCNY.

26. Charles E. Magruder, "Memo to Associational Missions Committees and Moderators," 18 February 1963, Frontier Association file, BCNY.

27. Gloria Stanton, "History of the Greater Rochester Baptist Association," in Greater Rochester Association file, BCNY.

29. *Annual*, Central New York Baptist Association, 1963, 17.

30. "SBC Polish Work Grows With Buffalo Mission," *Ohio Baptist Messenger*, 9 January 1964, 5; Michael Odlyzko, interview by author, 2 June 1995.

31. Eva B. Magruder, "New York, Southern Baptists in Upstate," *Encyclopedia of Southern Baptists*, Vol. 3 (Nashville: Broadman Press, 1978), 1870.

32. Charles E. Magruder to E. L. Golonka, 1 May 1967, Frontier Association file, BCNY.

Chapter Four

1. Gene Fant, interview by author, 31 May 1995; Norman S. Bell, *A History of the Adirondack Baptist Association, 1954–1983* (privately printed, 1984), "New Associations," 1.

2. Garland Sparks to Darty Stowe, 20 June 1961, Frontier Association file, BCNY.

3. Charles E. Magruder, interview by author, 24 May 1995; *Annual*, Central New York Baptist Association, 1964, 10.

4. Paul Becker, interview by author, 27 May 1995.

5. J. T. Davis, interview by author, 30 May 1995.

6. "New York Churches Re-Align with Maryland," *Ohio Baptist Messenger*, 9 January 1964, 5.

7. John Tollison, interview by author, 25 May 1995.

8. "Once Over Lightly," typewritten script for the 1970 annual Home Mission study filmstrip, in the BCNY general history file, 4–5; John Tollison, "Where Others Have Failed," *Maryland Baptist*, 29 August 1968, 7.

9. J. T. Davis, interview by author, 5 April 1995.

10. John Tollison, interview by author, 25 May 1995; "A History of the Trinity Baptist Church," in Trinity Baptist Church file, BCNY.

11. *Frontier News,* April 1959, 3.

12. "Convention Clippings," *Ohio Baptist Messenger,* 10 November 1960, 2.

13. Paul Becker, "A New Light on the Northern Border," *Ohio Baptist Messenger,* 1 October 1959, 4.

14. Boroughs, interview by author, 7 March 1995; Walker, "The Unfolding of God's Work," 4.

15. Bell, *History,* "A Man of God at Bay," 1–4.

16. Ibid., "The Beginning," 1.

17. Becker, "Work that Began," 9.

18. Bell, "Emmanuel, God Is With Us," 6; "First Christian Church, Brushton," 1.

19. Bell, "Emmanuel, God Is With Us," 6.

20. Bell, "New Associations," 2.

21. "Southport, Elmira, Constitutes," *Ohio Baptist Messenger,* 31 October 1963, 2–4.

22. Mary Knapton, interview by author, 5 May 1995.

23. "Kansas Pastor Accepts Call to Native New York," *Ohio Baptist Messenger,* 27 March 1962, 2; "Church Constituted, Endicott, NY," *Ohio Baptist Messenger,* 5 July 1962, 3.

24. Roger Knapton, interview by author, 5 June 1995; Paul Becker, interview by author, 22 April 1995.

25. Roger Knapton, interview.

Chapter Five

1. "New Mission in New York City," *Ohio Baptist Messenger,* August 1957, 1; A. B. Cash to Charles A. Jolly, 10 July 1957, Manhattan church file, BCNY.

2. Samuel S. Hill, Jr. and Robert G. Torbet, *Baptists North and South* (Valley Forge: Judson Press, 1964), 61.

3. *Tabernacle Tidings,* newsletter of the Tabernacle Baptist Church, Atlanta, 17 October 1957, in Manhattan Church file, BCNY.

4. W. B. Lipphard, "As I See It," *Missions,* December 1957, 12.

5. John W. Bradbury, "Southern Baptist Expansion," *The Watchman-Examiner,* 17 July 1958, 615.

6. "American Baptists Discuss Southern Baptist Invasion," *Maryland Baptist,* 15 June 1959, 5.

7. Blake Smith, "The Southern Baptist Invasion: Right or Wrong?" *Maryland Baptist,* 1 July 1959, 4–5; 8 July 1959, 4–5.

8. R. G. Puckett, "Southern Baptists in the North, Why?," *Ohio Baptist Messenger,* 15 July 1958, 2; "Comity or Commission?" *Ohio Baptist Messenger,* 15 August 1959, 2.

9. "Concerning the Southern Invasion," unidentified newspaper clipping in Manhattan church file, BCNY.

10. "Northward Ho," *Newsweek,* 28 August 1961; "SBC Goes Nationwide," *Home Missions,* November 1961, 6; M. Dean Goodwin to Arthur B. Rutledge and Rutledge to Goodwin in Raymond, 96–97; "'Competing with the Devil' Says Rutledge," unidentified newspaper clipping in Manhattan church file, BCNY.

11. Paul James, interview by author, 4 November 1994.

12. Joseph Heartburg, "North of the South," *Ohio Baptist Messenger*, 3 May 1963, 4; Glenn Igleheart, memo to author, 22 September 1993, in General History file, BCNY.

13. "Report from New York," *Baptist Messenger,* 9 April 1959, 2.

14. Buryl Red, interview by author, 29 November 1994; Paul James, interview, 4 November 1994; "Manhattan Choir Records for Others," *Maryland Baptist,* 30 September 1965, 4; "New York Church Reaches Youth Through Music," *Maryland Baptist,* 11 July 1968, 3; "Christmas Eve TV Service Produced by Baptists," *New York Baptist,* 15 December 1970, 6.

15. James, interview.

16. Ibid., "The Establishment and Extension of Southern Baptist Work in the Greater New York Area—Statement Recommended by the Deacons and Adopted by the Church September 11, 1958," typewritten document in Manhattan church file, BCNY.

17. "Albany Church Supports Pastor Amid Race Issue," *Maryland Baptist,* 6 September 1962, 3; "FBC Richmond Admits Nigerian," *Maryland Baptist*, 28 January 1965, 1.

18. James, interview.

19. Ibid.; Norman Watson, interview by author, 16 July 1995.

20. Norvell Jones, interview by author, 3 November 1994.

21. Sherman secured the Miller Chapel for worship after a fire destroyed Murray-Dodge Hall on the Princeton University campus. When he approached James McKay about using the facility, the seminary president replied: "If I consent to this, some of my trustees will be angry at me. But if I don't, that Baptist lassie Mrs. McKay will be very unhappy with me." The McKays met at a student gathering sponsored by an Edinburgh, Scotland, Baptist church. Cecil E. Sherman, interview by the author, 30 November 1994.

22. Ibid.; Gene Maston, interview by author, 1 July 1995.

23. Paul S. James, "Manhattan Baptist Church—A Witness on Spiritual Frontiers, Its Present and Future," typewritten address dated 23 July 1961, in Manhattan Church file, BCNY.

24. Shirley Johnson, "Baptist Students in New York," *Maryland Baptist,* 15 July 1961, 3; William Pennington Vann, interview by author, 14 July 1995.

25. Maston, interview.

26. Milton A. Webb, interview by author, 17 July 1995.

27. The Home Mission Board's US-2 program places recent college graduates in strategic places of ministry for a two year appointment. "Eugene Maston Is Appointed Student Director for New York," *Maryland Baptist*, 10 May 1962, 3; "BSU Organizes at Syracuse University," *Maryland Baptist*, 11 July 1968, 4; Eugene Maston, "New York, Baptist Student Work in," *Encyclopedia of Southern Baptists*, Vol. 3 (Broadman Press, 1978), 1867.

Chapter Six

1. Paul S. James, "A Beachhead in the Northeast," *The Sunday School Builder*, October 1961, 20–21.

2. O. K. McCarter, interview by author, 16 August 1995; "Fulfilling the Dream—Madison Baptist Church, 1960–1985," typewritten manuscript in Madison church file, BCNY, 2.

3. "Fulfilling the Dream," 3.

4. Gainer E. Byran, "Southern Baptists at Work in Greater New York," *Maryland Baptist*, 12 July 1962, 4.

5. Ibid.

6. "Fulfilling the Dream," 7–12.

7. Vivian Cochran, interview by author, 30 November 1992.

8. "A Brief History of Monmouth Baptist Church," in Monmouth church file, BCNY; "Lincroft Baptist Chapel is Constituted," *Maryland Baptist*, 8 October 1964, 6.

9. "New Pastor at Calvary Chapel, Matawan," *Maryland Baptist*, 19 June 1969; "Calvary Baptist Church: Our Heritage," in Calvary church file, BCNY.

10. "Hope Baptist Church History," in Hope church file, BCNY.

11. "Historical Sketch of Terrill Road Baptist Church," in Terrill Road church file, BCNY.

12. Historical sketches in Somerset Hills church file, BCNY.

13. "Twin County Chapel Calls its First Pastor," *Maryland Baptist*, 23 January 1968.

14. "History of the Bergen Baptist Church," *Annual*, Metropolitan New York Baptist Association, 1970, 23–24.

15. R. Quinn Pugh, interview by author, 5 September 1995.

16. Ibid.

17. *Annual*, 1970, 24.

18. Donald L. Davidson, "A History of Southern Baptists in the Northeastern United States: 1950–1972" (Ph.D. dissertation, Southwestern Baptist Theological Seminary, 1974), 129–30.

19. "History of the Farmingdale Baptist Church," *Annual*, Metropolitan New York Baptist Association, 1968, 20.

20. Ibid.

21. Don McGregor, "Macedonia in the Northeast," *Baptist Standard*, 10 August 1960, 10–11.

22. "Migrant Missions Begun on Long Island," *Maryland Baptist*, 30 October 1962, 4.

23. Don Miller, "How Churches Grow Through Home Fellowships," *Home Missions*, January 1962, 12; personal interview cited in Davidson, 120.

24. "History of Farmingdale," 21.

25. "Grace Chapel, Oak Grove, NY, Constitutes," *Maryland Baptist*, 25 January 1968, 4; "History of the Emmanuel Baptist Church," *Annual*, Metropolitan New York Baptist Association, 1971, 23.

26. Van H. Savell, "'A Stupid Feeling Inside,'" *Home Missions*, September 1968, 29.

27. Ibid.

28. "History of the Ridgecrest Baptist Church," *Annual*, Metropolitan New York Baptist Association, 1968, 21.

29. "History of the Vassar Road Baptist Church," *Annual*, Metropolitan New York Baptist Association, 1969, 23.

30. "Southern Baptists Establish a Colony on the Hudson," *Maryland Baptist*, 1 August 1963, 5.

31. Davidson, 123; *Annual*, Metropolitan New York Baptist Association, 1970, 73.

32. "Southern Baptists Establish a Colony," 8.

33. "Twenty-five Years on a Walk of Faith, 1963–1988," history of Greenwich Church in Greenwich Church file, BCNY.

34. "Connecticut Fellowship Looks for Members," *Maryland Baptist*, 7 February 1963, 5.

35. H. Lawrence Martin, interview by author, 3 September 1995.

36. "Westchester Baptist Church Constituted at Hartsdale," *Maryland Baptist*, 7 December 1967, 4; "WMU President Joins Husband in Project 500," *Maryland Baptist*, 2 May 1968, 8; "A History of the Westchester Baptist Church," in Westchester Church file, BCNY.

37. "Wilton Baptist Church Historical Chronology," in Wilton Church file, BCNY.

38. "A Short History of the Rockland Baptist Church," in Rockland Church file, BCNY.

39. "Staten Island Survey," *Metropolitan New York Baptist Bulletin*, February 1966, 2.

40. The fifth church aligned with the association was the Park Baptist Church in Irvington, New Jersey—a congregation that developed independently of the Manhattan Church. The Park Church was disfellowshiped from the association in 1962 due to the pastor's "illegal activities" and lack of contact with the association. The church never played any significant role in the development of Southern Baptist work in the Northeast. Davidson, 45; *Minutes*, Northeastern Baptist Association, 1960, 3; "Northeastern District Association Organized," *Maryland Baptist*, 15 May 1960, 7.

41. *Minutes*, Northeastern Baptist Association, 1962, 10.

42. Ibid.

43. "City Evangelism Studied by Dr. Chafin," *Metropolitan New York Baptist Bulletin,* November 1965, 3.

Chapter Seven

1. A. B. Cash to Charles Jolly, 10 July 1957, Manhattan Church file, BCNY; Don McGregor, "Macedonia in the Northeast," *Baptist Standard,* 10 August 1960, 10–11.

2. Basil Hewitt, interview by author, 16 September 1995; David Morgan Jr., interview by author, 14 September 1995.

3. David Morgan Jr., interview.

4. Eileen Morgan, interview by author, 15 September 1995.

5. David Morgan Jr., interview.

6. Gainer Bryan, "Southern Baptists at Work in New York," *Maryland Baptist,* 12 July 1962, 3.

7. "First Baptist Church of Brooklyn Girds for International Ministry," *Maryland Baptist,* 7 February 1963, 3; "Pastor, Family Robbed in Brooklyn Parsonage," *Maryland Baptist,* 7 February 1963, 3.

8. "Historical Review of First Baptist Church of New York," in Evergreen Baptist Church file, BCNY, 10.

9. "British diplomat calls discrimination 'evil' in talk before Brooklyn Church," *Maryland Baptist,* 13 May 1965, 4.

10. "Board Names Language Director for New York," *Home Missions,* January 1962, 22; Leobardo Estrada, interview by author, 5 November 1994.

11. Estrada, interview.

12. Ibid.

13. "History of the First Baptist Church of Manhattan," in First Spanish Manhattan Church file, BCNY; "Into New York—Puerto Ricans," *Home Missions,* February 1963, 10; Bertha Maza Walker, interview by author, 3 October 1995.

14. "Spanish Church Constituted in New York," *Maryland Baptist,* 20 August 1964, 4.

15. "Queens Mission," *Maryland Baptist,* 6 June 1963; Jaime Santamaria, interview by author, 3 October 1995.

16. "Templo Bautista dedicates property acquired recently," *Maryland Baptist,* 16 July 1964; "History of Hispanic Work in New State," in Language Ministries file, BCNY.

17. "Revival or Else, SBC President Tells Area Church," *Maryland Baptist,* 2 July 1964, 1.

18. *Metropolitan New York Baptist Bulletin,* January 1966, 3.

19. "Two Spanish Chapels Become Churches," *Metropolitan New York Baptist Bulletin,* May–June 1969, 2; Nicomedes Flores, interview by author, 3 October 1995.

20. "Leobardo Estrada Second Vice-President of SBC," *Metropolitan New York Baptist Bulletin,* September 1965, 2.

21. "Evangel Chapel Becomes a Church," *Metropolitan New York Baptist Bulletin,* September 1965, 1; "Evangel Chapel in NYC Bronx is Constituted," *Maryland Baptist,* 22 July 1965, 5.

22. Cleveland Henry, interview by author, 9 October 1995.

23. Samuel Simpson, interview by author, 21 August 1995.

24. "Two Ordained by the Brooklyn Church," *Maryland Baptist,* 26 September 1963, 11; "Bronx Baptist Church—A Brief History," in Bronx Church file, BCNY.

25. Estrada, interview.

26. "Bronx Baptist Church—A Brief History."

27. "Southern Baptists in Harlem," *Metropolitan New York Baptist Bulletin,* April 1966, 1; "Harlem Has a New Church," *Maryland Baptist,* 25 July 1968, 4.

28. "A Need for New Methods, Constructive Cooperation, and Federal Money," *Home Missions,* December 1966, 19; "Couples Serving in Weekday Ministry," *Metropolitan New York Baptist Bulletin,* November–December 1968, 2.

29. Jean Baptiste Thomas, "Historical Foundation of the Haitian Community in New York City," in French-speaking Church, Brooklyn, file, BCNY; "New Work Started," *Metropolitan New York Baptist Bulletin,* April 1965, 3.

30. Estrada, interview.

31. "French Church is Constituted in Brooklyn," *Maryland Baptist,* 7 July 1966, 2.

32. Jean-Baptiste Thomas, interview by author, 9 October 1995.

33. Leonard Hill, *Mission: The Northeast,* 70; "Kasa Directs Pioneer Polish Work," *Metropolitan New York Baptist Bulletin,* September 1963; Gainer Bryan, "Now Southern Baptists Have a Polish Church in Brooklyn," *Maryland Baptist,* 19 December 1963.

34. Lloyd Burrus, "Why Southern Baptists Can and Should Act Now," *Home Missions,* June 1968, 24.

35. Davidson, "A History of Southern Baptists in the Northeastern United States," 146.

36. Ibid., 152; "Historical Sketch of the Highland Avenue Baptist Church," *Annual,* Metropolitan New York Baptist Association, 1973, 38–39.

37. "Historic Building Changes Hands," *Maryland Baptist,* 25 April 1968, 4.

Chapter Eight

1. "Our Northern Expansion," *Maryland Baptist,* 15 September 1960, 5.

2. *Annual,* Baptist Convention of Maryland, 1963, 33–36.

3. *Annual,* 1964, 37; "Southern Baptists in Northeast Plan Three Conventions," *Maryland Baptist,* 14 May 1964, 4.

4. *Annual,* 1964, 36–37.

5. "New York-New Jersey Convention Planned," *Ohio Baptist Messenger*, 15 October 1964, 5; "NY-NJ Area Convention Planned for '67," *Maryland Baptist*, 15 October 1964, 1.

6. *Annual*, 1964, 61–62.

7. Paul Becker to Curtis Porter, 13 June 1966, in Northeastern Fellowship file, BCNY.

8. "Minutes of the Steering Committee," 22 September 1966, in Northeastern Fellowship file, BCNY.

9. *Annual*, 1966, 51–55.

10. *Metropolitan New York Baptist Bulletin*, March–April 1968, 1.

11. See correspondence, 1 August 1967, "To the Churches of the Metropolitan New York Association," in Metropolitan New York Association file, BCNY.

12. See document "Requirement for State Convention" in Metropolitan New York Association file, BCNY.

13. Gresham to James, 2 August 1967, in Baptist Fellowship of New York file, BCNY.

14. James to Gresham, 7 August 1967, in Baptist Fellowship of New York file, BCNY.

15. "Action of the Metropolitan New York Baptist Association," 18 September 1967, in Baptist Fellowship of New York file, BCNY.

16. "Recommendation Regarding the Northeastern Regional Fellowship," in Baptist Fellowship of New York file, BCNY.

17. "Northeast Fellowship Splits," *Maryland Baptist*, 12 October 1967, 1.

18. Wendell Belew, interview by author, 27 January 1996.

19. "Convention Name," document in Baptist Fellowship of New York file, BCNY.

20. "Voices from Endicott," *New York Baptist*, May–June 1968, 3.

21. "Annual Meeting of the Baptist Fellowship of New York, First Baptist Church of Brooklyn, New York, September 27, 1968," in Baptist Fellowship of New York file, BCNY; see also, "New York Work 'Most Encouraging' in Eleven Years," *Maryland Baptist*, 25 July 1968.

22. "SBC Leaders Express Confidence in BFNY," *New York Baptist*, 15 March 1969, 1.

23. "State WMU to Organize in September at Syracuse," *New York Baptist*, 21 June 1969.

24. "Before you . . . an open door," season of prayer guide in Baptist Fellowship of New York file, BCNY.

25. "Annual Meeting," 5–7.

26. Ben Patterson, interview by author, 3 February 1996.

27. "Site Selection Committee," *Annual*, Baptist Convention of New York, 1979, 34.

28. Fred H. Boehmer to Paul S. James, 4 October 1968, in Baptist Fellowship of New York file, BCNY.

29. See notes, "Phone Call from David Morgan," 22 May 1968, in Baptist Fellowship of New York file, BCNY.

30. Curtis Porter, interview by author, 3 February 1996; Fred Boehmer, interview by author, 5 February 1996.

31. Paul S. James to Roger Knapton, 17 April 1969, in Baptist Fellowship of New York file, BCNY; "James Elected N.Y. Secretary," *New York Baptist*, 21 June 1969, 1.

32. "John M. Tubbs Elected New York Education Director," *Maryland Baptist*, 2 October 1969, 1.

33. "Ten Short," *New York Baptist*, 21 June 1969, 4.

34. "New York Becomes 31st State Convention," *Maryland Baptist*, 2 October 1969, 1.

35. *Minutes*, Baptist Convention of New York, 1969, 25.

36. Ibid., 26–30.

Chapter Nine

1. *Annual*, Baptist Convention of New York, 1970, 38–40.

2. Ibid., 1973, 58–63.

3. "From the Chairman of the Board," *New York Baptist*, 15 March 1970, 3.

4. "Two Leaders Begin Ministries in Missions Division of Baptist Convention of New York," *New York Baptist*, 15 January 1971.

5. "Retiring WMU Executive to Help New York Convention," *New York Baptist*, 15 May 1971, 8.

6. June Andrews, *So Generations Will Remember: A History of Woman's Missionary Union, Baptist Convention of New York, 1969–1994* (Syracuse: published privately by the Baptist Convention of New York, 1994), 124–25.

7. "International Missionary," *Royal Service*, July 1975, 2–3; Judy Touchton, "Christian Ambassador to Ambassadors," *Contempo*, March 1978, 20–22; Elaine Furlow, "Our Man at the UN," *Home Missions*, September/October 1979, 19–26.

8. "First BCNY Youth Convention Held in Syracuse," *New York Baptist*, 15 May 1970, 7.

9. M. Ray Gilliland, interview by author, 12 February 1996.

10. "Harpes Come to Leadership at West Point," *New York Baptist*, 15 February 1971, 6.

11. "William Dunning Assumes Staff Duties," *New York Baptist*, 15 March 1975, 1; *Annual*, Baptist Convention of New York, 1976, 47.

12. "Walsh Accepts Princeton," *New York Baptist*, August 1977, 5.

13. *Annual*, 1974, 52.

14. Jack P. Lowndes, "Editorial," *New York Baptist*, 15 April 1975, 1.

15. "Has God United Georgia and New York?" *New York Baptist*, October 1977, 2.

16. "Mission Service Corps To Enlist 5,000 Missionaries," *New York Baptist,* July 1977, 1.

17. "New York MSC Volunteers Undergo Orientation," *New York Baptist,* October 1978, 2.

18. "Million Dollar Budget Is Proposed," *New York Baptist,* June 1976, 1.

19. "Southern, National Baptists Cooperate in Harlem Revival," *Maryland Baptist,* 30 November 1967, 4; *Annual,* 1977, 54.

20. *Annual,* 1978, 55.

21. Ibid., 1973, 39; 1974, 43.

22. Ibid., 1976, 38

Chapter Ten

1. Gloria Stanton, "History: Greater Rochester Baptist Association," in Greater Rochester Association file, BCNY; "Beckhams named Baptist missionaries," *New York Baptist,* February 1980, 5.

2. Royce Denton, interview by author, 5 June 1995; Gloria Stanton, interview by author, 16 February 1996.

3. Norman Bell, *History,* "Grace Baptist Church, Ogdensburg."

4. A pastor with an Assembly of God background led the church to stop supporting the Cooperative Program and the work of the Adirondack Association. See Bell, *History,* "Sharron Woods Baptist Church."

5. Richard Graves, interview by author, 20 February 1996; Bell, *History,* "Philadelphia—Theresa."

6. "A Brief History of North Russell, New York Baptist Chapel of the Good Shepherd," in Adirondack Association file, BCNY.

7. Bell, *History,* "Bangor Baptist Chapel."

8. "History of the Ithaca Baptist Church," in Ithaca Baptist Church file, BCNY.

9. "Celebrating 20 Years of Ministry," booklet in Bellewood Baptist Church file, BCNY.

10. Ozie Bodner, "Central/Davis Association History, 1961–86," in Davis Association file, BCNY.

11. Larry Pridmore, interview by author, 24 February 1996; Wayne Dyer, interview by author, 24 February 1996.

12. Waylen Bray to Jon Meek, 8 December 1976, in Central Association file, BCNY.

13. Barbara Joiner, "Go Forward! Planting New Churches," *Royal Service,* March 1981, 25.

14. Ibid., 27.

15. "Alien immersion" typically refers to baptism by immersion practiced by a non-Baptist church. Some argue that such a baptism is invalid for membership in a Baptist church. See correspondence, James Bullis to "Whom it Concerns," 9 September 1970, in Frontier Association file, BCNY.

16. Chapels not sponsored locally by an existing church within the association usually enter the association through a membership process known as "petitioning." The Grossman Church was originally a part of the Pittsburgh, Pennsylvania, Association.

17. Joiner, "Go Forward," 26–27.

18. "The Village Difference," *Missions USA*, March–April 1990, 31.

19. "Association Youth Corps on the March!," *Metropolitan New York Baptist Bulletin*, January–February 1972, 1; "Over 600 Attend Two Youth Retreats," *Metropolitan New York Baptist Bulletin*, January–February 1974, 1.

20. Fletcher, 226; DeLane Ryals, interview by author, 25 October 1995.

21. Davidson, 165.

22. "Association Buys Mid-Town Building," *Metropolitan New York Baptist Bulletin*, March–April 1973, 1.

23. Todd Deaton, "School—a Tool for Christ," *New York Baptist*, February 1985, 1.

24. Praxis teams are typically seminarians who work through the summer doing door-to-door surveys in communities to discover persons who are interested in joining a Bible study or in forming a new church.

25. "Our First Ten Years," in Bridgewater Baptist Church file, BCNY.

26. See Paul James's final editorial in the *New York Baptist*, 15 February 1975, 2.

Chapter Eleven

1. "New association formed for Syracuse area," *New York Baptist*, September 1980, 4; "New association formed for Hudson area," *New York Baptist*, October 1980, 4.

2. Robert M. Sommer, "Southern Baptist work on Long Island resulting in the formation and growth of the Long Island Baptist Association," in Long Island Association file, BCNY.

3. *Annual*, Baptist Convention of New York, 1981, 50; 1982, 55; 1983, 54.

4. An audit of 1982 financial records revealed that the convention was in arrears $49,566 to the Foreign Mission Board and Home Mission Board for gifts not forwarded over the course of several years.

5. "Lowndes resigns; Gresham is interim," *New York Baptist*, January 1983, 1; Minutes of the Executive Board, Baptist Convention of New York, 30 November, 1 December 1982; Jack P. Lowndes, interview by author, 5 March 1996; "Appreciation Expressed," *New York Baptist*, November 1983, 5.

6. Jack Parrott, "A personal word—Roy Gresham," *New York Baptist*, January 1984, 2.

7. Quentin Lockwood, Jr., "Being obedient to the Lord's will," *New York Baptist*, November 1983, 4.

8. Ibid.

9. Paul James, interview by author, 4 November 1994.

10. "Pursuing the Vision," *New York Baptist*, November 1985, 3; see also "Strategy planning involves large numbers in process," *New York Baptist*, December 1984, 3; "BCNY: VISION 2000 to be presented," *New York Baptist*, October 1985, 1.

11. "Convention votes to purchase building," *New York Baptist*, April 1986, 1.

12. "Georgia, S.C. volunteers move BCNY into new headquarters," *New York Baptist*, August 1986, 1.

13. "Center dedicated to Glory of God," *New York Baptist*, April 1987, 1. The debt on the building was retired earlier than anticipated—in May 1996.

14. *Annual*, Baptist Convention of New York, 1986, 27; 1993, 51; see also, "Executive board reports on budget, foundation, and convention items, *New York Baptist*, October 1986, 1.

15. Marv Knox, "'Context' to be key for ministry school," *New York Baptist*, January 1988, 7.

16. "Ken Medema in the Baptist Convention of New York," in First Baptist Church of Montclair file, BCNY; "Igleheart named Missions director," *New York Baptist*, September 1984, 1.

17. "Executive Board fills two staff vacancies," *New York Baptist*, January 1989, 1.

18. "Daniel Paixao called as education director," *New York Baptist*, September 1985, 1.

19. "Board calls director, realigns assignments," *New York Baptist*, September 1985, 1.

20. Stanley Stamps, "Honduras-New York partnership results in 991 professions of faith," *New York Baptist*, July 1985, 1; "New York Baptists adopt England partnership," *New York Baptist*, December 1986, 3.

21. R. Quinn Pugh, "After Kansas City, what?" *New York Baptist*, June/July 1984, 2.

Chapter Twelve

1. Ozie Bodner, "Central/Davis Association History, 1961–1986."

2. "History of Bellewood Baptist Church," in Bellewood church file, BCNY.

3. Bell, *History*, "First Southern Baptist Church, Watertown."

4. "History of the Ithaca Baptist Church," in Ithaca Baptist Church file, BCNY.

5. B. Gray Allison, interview by author, 28 March 1996; Mid-America seminary defines its affiliation as follows: "The seminary is committed in purpose and curriculum to Southern Baptist churches, the Cooperative Program, missions programs, and doctrinal beliefs. However, the seminary is neither owned by nor controlled by, nor has any formal affiliation with the Southern Baptist Convention."

6. Bell, *History*, "Bread of Life, Plattsburgh."

7. Stanton, "History," 5.

8. Sommer, "Southern Baptist work on Long Island," 2.

9. Anita Bowden and others, *Going Where Others Cannot Go: Chaplains Doing the Work of Home Missions* (Alpharetta, Georgia: The Home Mission Board of the Southern Baptist Convention, 1995), 51–54.

10. This church itself reverted back to a chapel in 1985. After restarting, the congregation was "re-constituted" in 1989 under the leadership of pastor Tim Bissell.

11. Terry Robertson, interview by author, 9 September 1995.

12. Mark Wingfield, "Buffalo church starters offer Bible, not bingo," *New York Baptist,* February 1989, 4.

13. "International missions comes home to University Baptist Church," *New York Baptist,* December 1989, 5.

14. "D'Amico installation set for June 24," *New York Baptist,* June 1985, 5.

15. Romy Manansala, "Filipino Church Growth: Metropolitan New York Baptist Association, 1982–1994," in Bible Church International file, BCNY.

16. DeLane Ryals, interview by author, 2 April 1996.

Chapter Thirteen

1. Fletcher, *The Southern Baptist Convention*, 333–34.

2. Ibid., 347.

3. Ibid.

4. "A CALL TO AN ASSEMBLY OF PRAYER AND INTERCESSION," *New York Baptist,* March 1990, 1; "Call to Prayer and Evangelism Conference help change lives," *New York Baptist,* April 1990, 1.

5. "A statement concerning the Cooperative Missions Program" and "Executive Board elects Evangelism director," *New York Baptist,* October 1990, 1.

6. David F. D'Amico, interview by author, 9 April 1996.

7. *Annual,* Baptist Convention of New York, 1990, 37.

8. DeLane Ryals to Keith L. Cogburn, 9 April 1996, in Metropolitan New York Baptist Association file, BCNY.

9. "Decade marks growth in BCNY," *New York Baptist,* February 1990, 7.

10. Quentin Lockwood Jr., "New York Baptists focus on missions," *New York Baptist,* December 1992, 1.

11. "Executive Board enters into new partnerships," *New York Baptist,* November 1990, 1.

12. *Annual,* Baptist Convention of New York, 1993, 65–68.

13. See, for example, "North Carolina-New York partnerships developing," *New York Baptist,* October 1991, 5.

14. "Bicentennial celebration of Finney's birth held," *New York Baptist,* September 1992, 1.

15. "Pursuing the vision," *New York Baptist,* June 1993, 3.

16. *Annual*, Baptist Convention of New York, 1993, 66.

17. *New York Baptist*, November 1994, 20.

18. Greg Warner, "Vestal, Pugh, and others want to rally grass-roots support for WMU," and "Statement affirming Woman's Missionary Union," *New York Baptist*, April 1993, 1.

19. "Wife of Convention Evangelism Director killed in auto accident," *New York Baptist*, January/February 1993, 1; "Patricia Lockwood, wife of *New York Baptist* editor, dies," *New York Baptist*, June 1993, 1; "Theresa Losito dies in auto accident," *New York Baptist*, January 1994, 1.

20. "Executive Board receives report of stress in ministry," *New York Baptist*, March 1993, 1.

21. "Administrative Committee meets in special session," and "A letter to the churches of the Baptist Convention of New York," *New York Baptist*, September 1991, 1; 6; "Executive board receives NC gifts, addresses budget shortfall," *New York Baptist*, January 1992, 1.

22. Michael and Patricia Arges, "The time is now to tell the story of BCNY history," *New York Baptist*, August 1993, 2.

23. "New Baptist history organization will choose name in Corning," *New York Baptist*, September 1993; "History Committee," *New York Baptist*, November 1994, 12.

24. David Pope, interview by author, 17 April 1996.

25. "Bergen Baptist to become Christ Community Church," *New York Baptist*, March 1991, 8.

26. In 1992 Larry Holly, a trustee of the Baptist Sunday School Board, succeeded in getting the Southern Baptist Convention to launch an inquiry into the membership practices of the Masonic Lodge, which he claimed were contrary to the Scriptures. His concern was that a number of Southern Baptists, including prominent leaders, were Masons.

27. James Goforth, interview by author, 4 April 1996.

28. Michael Chance, interview by author, 10 April 1996.

INDEX

Photo page numbers are in bold type.

A

Aaron, James, 31–32
Aaron, Melba, 31
Aaron family, 31–32, 79
Abundant Life Baptist Church, 51
Achille, Aquilas, 196
Ackley Avenue Chapel, 63, 151
Adams, Frank, 153
Adams, Ira, 84, 118
Adams, Phyllis, **211**, 217
Adirondack Baptist Association, 61, 64, 124–26, 140–41, 149–51, 164–65, 185–89, 215
Adirondack Church, 154, 187
Agape Baptist Church, 187
Agape Bible Christian Fellowship, 195
Agape Life Bible Church, 215
Alabama Baptist State Convention, 22
Alaska Baptist Convention, 125
Albany Chapel, 154. *See also* Albany Church

Albany Church, 154, 187. *See also* Albany Chapel
Alexandria Bay Baptist Church, 149
Alexandria Bay Chapel, 58, 61
Alexandria Bay Church, 63, 150
Ali, Don, 197
Allen, Dean, 154
Allison, Gray, 188
All Saints Baptist Church, 218
Alonso, Manuel, 136, 167, 176
Alpha and Omega Baptist Church, 198
American Baptist Churches, U.S.A., 19
American Baptist Churches of New Jersey, 69
American Baptist Convention, 19, 66–67
America Board of Missions to the Jews, 159
American Legion Hall, 93
Amherst Baptist Church, 42, **43**, 47, 50–51, 82, 119,

180–81, 193, 217. *See also* Erie Baptist Chapel and Erie Baptist Church
Ammi Baptist Church, 196
Ammons, Chris, 84
Ammons, Elmer, 83
Ammons, Hazel (Mrs. Elmer), 83
Ammons, Pam (Mrs. Chris), 84
Anderson, Howard, 161
Anderson, Michael, 165, 185
Anderson, Monnie, 177
Andrews, June, 15, 182, 209
Annie Armstrong Offering, 121
Annuity Board, 136
Arabic Baptist Church in Brooklyn, 220
Arabic Egyptian Baptist Mission, 198
Arena, The, 89
Arges, Michael, 139, 206
Armstrong, Ricky, 207
Arnold, Duane, 215
Arrant, James, 188, 214
Arrubla, Roberto, 113
Association of Baptists in New York/New Jersey, 124

Assurance Baptist Church, 192. *See also* New Beginnings Baptist Church
Atlanta Baptist Pastors Conference, 36
Atonement Baptist Church, 110, 158
Aubrey, Bruce, 150, 182
Aubrey, David, 151
Auburn University, 192
Au-Yeung, H. C., 159

B

Bacallao, Xiomara, **106**
Bacon, Darwin, 83, 165, 185, 198
Badon, Larry, 172, 185
Bailon, Cicero, 195
Bair, Nancy, 138
Baldwin, Allen, 182, 186, 192–93
Baldwin, Debbie (Mrs. Allen), 186, 192
Baldwin Chapel, 87
Ballston Lake Baptist Church, 154, 165, 187
Bangor Baptist Church, 151
Baptist Book Store, 166, 172
Baptist Church of Ellington, 157

243

Baptist Church of the Good Shepherd, 150
Baptist Convention of Maryland, 34–35, 38, 55, 57, 61, 77, 87, 97, 103, 117–18, 122–24, 130, **131**, 133, 135, 138, 168
Baptist Convention of New York Center for Missions and Ministry, **173**
BCNY Foundation, 174
BCNY History Committee, 9, 212
Baptist Faith and Message statement, 203
Baptist Fellowship of New York, 125–27
Baptist General Association of New York, 122
Baptist General Convention of Texas, 136
Baptist Hour, 104
Baptist Joint Committee on Public Affairs, 181
Baptist Men, 136, 176, 215
Baptist Messenger, 69
Baptist Press, 65
Baptists in Western New York, 50
Baptist State Convention of North Carolina, 204, 215
Baptist Students of Princeton, 75
Baptist Student Union (BSU), 75, 78, 138–39, 206
Baptist Sunday School Board, 71, 77, 132, 137–38, 141, 166, 171, 179, 182, 202
Baptist Tabernacle Church of Belmont, 192
Baptist Tabernacle, Atlanta, 36
Baptist World Alliance, 34
Bard, Paul, 34, 156
Baril, Andrew, 217
Barnes, Clifton E., 88
Barnett, John, 184
Barredo, Tim, 219
Barrett, Sam, 198
Barron, Charles, 45–46
Basantes, Aixa (Mrs. Guillermo), 105
Basantes, Guillermo, 105

Baylor University, 256
Bayview Baptist Chapel, 47. *See also* Bayview Baptist Church and Jackson Road Baptist Church
Bayview Baptist Church, 48, 147. *See also* Bayview Baptist Chapel and Jackson Road Baptist Church
Beacon Light Baptist Church, Verona, 153, 184. *See also* Beacon Light Chapel
Beacon Light Chapel, 153. *See also* Beacon Light Baptist Church
Becerra, Herberto, 197–98
Becker, Paul, 24–28, **28**, 40, 45, 54–55, 58, 61–63, 119, 132
Becker, Ruth (Mrs. Paul), 25
Becker family, 27
Beckham, Norman, 148, 189
Bedford Avenue YMCA, 101, **102**
Belew, Wendell, 119–21, 124, 129
Bell, Albert, 78
Bell, Betty Jo, 78
Bell, Bob, 84, 158, 161
Bell, Norman, 59–60, **60**, **72**, 149, 165, 188, 212
Bellevue Baptist Church, 179
Bellewood Baptist Church, 153, 165, 185, 210. *See also* Bellewood Chapel
Bellewood Chapel, 153. *See also* Bellewood Baptist Church
Belmont Park, 191
Bennett, Donald, 48, 51
Benson, James, 136
Benton, Ann (Mrs. Jim), 162
Benton, Jim, 162
Bergen Baptist Chapel, 85. *See also* Bergen Baptist Church and Christ Community Church
Bergen Baptist Church, 85–86, 95, 106–07, 117–18, 157, 162, 169–70, 213. *See also* Bergen Baptist Chapel and Christ Community Church

Bergen Christian Fellowship, 195
Bergen Korean Baptist Church. *See* Divine Grace Baptist Church
Bernardsville Chapel, 84. *See also* Somerset Hills Baptist Church
Berry, Bill, 163
Beshear, Bill, 52
Beshear family, 46, 52
Besler, André, 113
Best, Harold, 184
Best, Roger, 150, 165, 184–85
Bethany Baptist Church, 99–100
Bethany Baptist Church, Jamaica, 161
Bethel Baptist Church, 113
Bethel Baptist Church, 56. *See also* Community Baptist Chapel and Bethel Chapel
Bethel Chapel, 56. *See also* Community Baptist Chapel and Bethel Baptist Church
Bethlehem Baptist Church, 107. *See also* First Spanish Baptist Church of Elizabeth
Bethsaida Baptist Church, 94
Bethune, Larry, 180
Bhowmik, Sanford, 218
Bible Church International (BCI), 194–95
Bibleway Mission, 216
Bickers, Howard, 188
Bickerstaff, Nona, 167, 176, 194, 218
Bidgood, J. Herbert (Herb), 86, **96**
Billy Graham Crusade, 36, 205
Birchwood Tabernacle, 61
Bissonette, Vernon, 189
Black, Ondra, 182
Blackaby, Henry, 201, 215
Blackwell, Bill, 206
Blake, Steve, 177
Blalock, Joe, 185
Boehmer, Fred, 91, 128–29, 132, 135, **140**, 144

Boisture, Bill, 84
Boisture, Bob, 139
Boisture, Mildred (Mrs. Bill), 84, 127, 136
Bold Mission Thrust, 141
Bolin, W. Eugene, 163
Bong Dok Suh, 186
Book, David, 140
Boroughs, Mary (Mrs. Ralph), 22, 44
Boroughs, Ralph Zeigler (Zig), 18–26, 40, 42, **42**, 44, 55, 57–60, 132, 149, 215
Boroughs family, 22
Bourne, Thomas, 93
Bove, Shirley, 46
Bowden, Ernest J., 28
Box, David, 218
Boyer, Charles, 90
Boyer family, 90
Bradley, James, 189, 207
Bratcher, Wes, 158
Bray, Waylen, 63, 151, 154, 170, 184
Bread of Life Baptist Church, 189, 207
Brighton/Pittsford Chapel, 148. *See also* Metropolitan Baptist Church and Browncroft Baptist Church
Bridgewater Baptist Church, 162, 180, 199
Bridgewater 4-H Club Center, 162
Broadway Baptist Church, 24
Bronx Baptist Chapel, 109. *See also* Bronx Baptist Church
Bronx Baptist Church, 109, 161, 181, 197, 207. *See also* Bronx Baptist Chapel
Bronx Bible Church, 194, **195**
Bronx Haitian Chapel, 196
Brooklyn Chapel, 101. *See also* First Baptist Church of Brooklyn
Brooklyn Chinese Baptist Church, 159, **159**
Brooklyn Evangelical Church, 195
Brooks, Bob, 191
Brooks, James, 84
Brooks, Robert, 165, 182
Brotherhood, 136, 176, 207

Brown, David, 190
Brown, Larry, 172, 182, 201, 211, **211**
Brown, Spencer, 217
Browncroft Baptist Church, 148, 181, 190, 216. *See also* Brighton/Pittsford Chapel and Metropolitan Baptist Church
Bruce, E. Maisie, 161, 176
Brushton Baptist Chapel, 61
Bryant, Phil, 45
Buchanan, Jerrell, 127
Buck, David, 175, **178**
Budd, William, 198
Buffalo Bible Fellowship, 193
Bulaun, Jose, 219
Bullis, Jim, 51, 124, 127, 155–56
Bullis, Mary (Mrs. Jim), 156
Bullis, Stanley, 51, 127
Bullock, Robert, 158
Bunn, Leslie, 218
Burdick, Arthur, 184
Burns, Carlos, 93
Burns, Jean (Mrs. Carlos), 93
Burrus, Lloyd, 112
Burt, Joseph, 215
Button, David, 182
Byrne, Caby, 78
Byung Woo Choi, 219

C
Cabral, Gay, 207
Cailleau, Jacques, 219
Cain, Lisa (Mrs. Mark), 177, 192
Cain, Mark, 177, 192
Cairns, June (Mrs. Tom), 176
Cairns, Tom, 176, 190
California Southern Baptist Convention, 102
Callender, J. D., 158
Calvary Baptist Church, Aberdeen, 83, 136, 144, 160, 162, 172, 196. *See also* Calvary Baptist Mission
Calvary Baptist Church, Bel Air, 157
Calvary Baptist Church, Canton, 150
Calvary Baptist Church, Matawan, 131

Calvary Baptist Church, Medford, 88, 162, 216
Calvary Baptist Church, Ticonderoga, 214
Calvary Baptist Mission, 83. *See also* Calvary Baptist Church, Aberdeen
Calvary Christian Church, 193
Calvary Christian Church, Buffalo, 217
Calvary New Covenant Church. *See* Sheridan Park Baptist Church
Campbell, Arnaldo, 207
Campbell, June, 140, 216
Campers on Mission, 176
Camp Iron Bell, 156–57
Canaan Baptist Church, Corona, 160, 197, 220
Capelozza, Paulo, 163
Caradon, Lord Hugh, 103
Carey, William, 203
Carlyle, Thomas, 132
Carroll, B. H., 12
Carroll, Bernice, 141
Carroll, Eulas, 141
Carter, President Jimmy, 141
Carteret Fellowship, 83
Casabona, Reinaldo, 198
Cash, A. B., 26–27, 31–34, 39, 50, 55, 65, **87**, 99, 115–16, 119, 132
Castrillon, Orlando, 113
Caulkins Road Baptist Church, 48. *See also* Henrietta Baptist Chapel and Pinnacle Road Baptist Church
Causey, Joseph, 165, 190
Cazenovia College, 178
Cedar Grove (New Jersey) Chapel, 176
Celebrate Life, 71
Center for Theological Studies in New York City, 166
Central Baptist Association, 54–57, 60–61, 64, 118, 122–26, 149, 152–53, **154**, 155, 164–65, 183, 185, 188

Central Baptist Church of Syracuse, 55–56, 78, 131, 138, 153, 166–67, 185–86. *See also* First Southern Baptist Church of Syracuse
Central Harlem Association of Neighborhood Churches Endeavor (C.H.A.N.C.E.), 157–58
Central High School, 73
Central Hunterdon Baptist Church, 199
Central Korean Baptist Church, 219
Central Nassau Baptist Church, 87–88, **88**, 89, 132
Central New York Area, 64
Central Spanish Baptist Church, 85
Cerny, Sherri, 182
Cerny, Steve, 214
Chafin, Kenneth, 97
Champlain Valley Baptist Chapel, 58. *See also* Champlain Valley Baptist Church
Champlain Valley Baptist Church, 61, 123–24, 149. *See also* Champlain Valley Baptist Chapel
Chance, Michael, 177, 194, 214
Chang, Calvin, 196
Chang Kuhn Behk, 195
Chaparro, Ernesto, 160
Chapman, Morris, 200
Chappell, C. L., 171
Cheriscat, Frederick, 219
Cheung, Paul T. C., 197
Chiew, Michael, 159, 176, 195
Chinese Christian Gospel Church, 216–17
Chinese MasterLife workshop, 177
Chinese Promise Baptist Church, 197
Christ Community Church, 86, 162, 213. *See also* Bergen Baptist Chapel and Bergen Baptist Church

Christ the Only Hope Baptist Church, 219
Christ Temple Baptist Church, 158
Christ Temple United Baptist Church, 197
Christy, Harriet, 59
Chung Wong, 218
Chun Woo Lee, 219
Chun, James, 159, 196
Chun, Martha (Mrs. James), 159, 196
Church Women United, 81
City Chapel, 219
City Church of New York, 198
City University of New York, 111
Civil War, 12
Clarence Baptist Church, 192. *See also* Emmanuel Baptist Church, Clarence
Clark, Harold, 151
Clark, John, 215
Clark, Peggy (Mrs. John), 215
Clark Baptist Chapel, 84. *See also* Terrill Road Baptist Chapel and Terrill Road Baptist Church
Clerk, Osbern, 87
Clinton Road Baptist Church, 46, 153, 155, 205. *See also* Utica Baptist Chapel
Coble, Darrell, 57
Coca, Ezequiel, 198
Cochran, Vivian, 82
Cogburn, Emily Anne, 10, 256
Cogburn, John Leland, 10, 256
Cogburn, Keith, 10, 211–12, 256
Cogburn, Laura, 10, 256
Coleman, Larry, 165
College Avenue Baptist Church, Annapolis, 33–35, 39, 82
Collins, Arlene, 177
Colorado Baptist General Convention, 153
Colts Neck Baptist Church, 163, 198
Columbia Bible College, 25
Columbia Presbyterian Hospital, 76

Columbia University, 75–76, 80–81, 109–10, 138–39, 178, **178**, 206
Comesanas, George, 160
Community Baptist Chapel, 56. *See also* Bethel Chapel and Bethel Baptist Church
Community Baptist Church, 148
Connally, Dan, 52, 124
Conservative Baptist Association, 19
Continuing Witness Training, 167
Controversy, The, 179
Cooper, Owen, 132
Cooperative Baptist Fellowship, 181, 201–02, 209
Cooperative Program, 116, 122–25, 132, 135, 141, 171, 201–02, 210
Corder, Loyd, 104
Cornell University, 171, 186, 207
Cornerstone Community Baptist Church, 198
Corning Baptist Church, 152, 187. *See also* Corning Chapel
Corning Chapel, 152. *See also* Corning Baptist Church
Corti, José Juan, 106
Cosgrove, Sally (Mrs. Steve), 141
Cosgrove, Steve, 141, 185
Courtney, Ragan, 70
Cowell, Ben, 57
Cox, Alvin, 83
Cox, James W., 96
Craig, Robert, 50, 56
Cranford, Valera, 166
Crawford, Donna (Mrs. Jimmy), 141, 150
Crawford, Jimmy, 141, 150
Criswell, Wally Amos, 36
Criswell Bible Institute, 148
Crossover New York, 205
Crossroads Baptist Fellowship, 214
Crow, Jim, 100
Crum, Don, 162

Cruz, Eloy, 107
Culpepper, Joe, 82
Couso, Juan, 160
Cutchogue Labor Camp, 87

D
Dae Heung Korean Baptist Church, 219
D'Amico, David F., 194, 202
David Livingstone Baptist Church, 107
Davilus, Vercanne, 218
Davis, Bertie Mae (Mrs. John Thomas), 44–45, **154**
Davis, Frances A., 34–35
Davis, John Thomas (J. T.), 44–45, 57–58, 117, 124, 126, 132, 153, 154, **154**, 165, 183–84
Davis Baptist Association, 165, 183, 185, 215
Davis family, 45, **154**
Day, Clayton, 72, 85–86, 101, 204–05, 209
Day, Junita (June), 209
Dean, David, 217–18
Dean, Michael, 207
Dean, Michelle (Mrs. Michael), 207
DeBerry, Nana, **178**
DeGarmo, Don, 184
Dehoney, Wayne, 106–07
Delaware Avenue YMCA, 41
Delaware Valley Association, 95
Delaware Valley Baptist Church, 94
Delgado, Milton, 219–20
Denham, Hardy, 72
Dennis, Alwyn, 113
Dennis, Miriam (Mrs. Alwyn), 113
Densmoore, Tommy, 42
Denton, Royce, 48, 148
Diaz, Steven, 207
Dick, Glen, 62–63
Dilday, Jesse, 83
Dinzler, Steve, 150
Divine Grace Baptist Church, 196
Dixon, Bob, 215
Dixon, Robert, 217
Dixon, Sam, 197
Donald, Grady, 158
Dong Suk Oh, 219

Doster, Reid, 162
Douglas, Terry, 214
Dowis, Solomon F. (Sol), 23, 26–27, 30, 34, 39
Downtown YMCA, 40, 47
Drew University, 81, 83–84, 256
Driggers, Carlisle, 171
Drummond, Lewis, 205
Drumwright, Huber, 33
Duke family, 80
Dunning, William R. (Bill), 139, 166, 174
Dutchess Valley Baptist Church, 162
Duvalier, Francois, 110
Dyer, D. Wayne, 165, 183

E
East Brunswick Baptist Church, 83, 160. *See also* Edison Church
Eastern Suffolk Baptist Chapel, 88. *See also* Emmanuel Baptist Church
East Seventh Baptist Church, 163. *See also* Graffiti/East Seventh Chapel
Ebenezer Baptist Church, 106. *See also* Highland Avenue Baptist Church
Ebenezer French Baptist Church, 161, 196
Ebenezer French-speaking Baptist Church of Irvington, 219
Ebenezer Spanish Baptist Church, 198
Edison Church, 82–83. *See also* East Brunswick Baptist Church
Edwards, J. W., 172
Edwards, John, **60**, 61, 151
Église Baptiste Bathesda, 196
Église Baptiste Française (French-speaking Baptist Church) of Brooklyn, 110–11
Eid, Assaad, 220
Elam, George, 152
Elim Chapel, 191
Ellington Odd Fellows Lodge, 157

Elliott, Bernice, 127
Elliot, Odus, 77
Ellis, Wesley, 170, 181
El Mesias Spanish Mission, 197
Elmira Church, 62
Elraheb, Sabry, 160, 198
El Shaddai Haitian Baptist Church, 218
Emmanuel Baptist Church, Clarence, 192–93. *See also* Clarence Baptist Church
Emmanuel Baptist Church, Cortland, 172, 185
Emmanuel Baptist Church of Potsdam, 59–61, 88, 140, 149–50, 180. *See also* Eastern Suffolk Baptist Church
Emmanuel Baptist Church, Riverhead, 87, 112, 167
Emmanuel Missionary Baptist Church of Newark, 197
Emmanuel Spanish Baptist Church of Union City, 160, 207
Enge, Siegfried, 112
Erie Association, 22, 24, 41
Erie Baptist Chapel, 41, 42. *See also* Amherst Baptist Church
Erie Baptist Church, 46. *See also* Amherst Baptist Church
Estrada, Isabel (Mrs. Leobardo), 104
Estrada, Leobardo (Leo), **96**, 104–06, **106**, 107–11, 136, 212
Estrada family, 104
Ethetton, Jim, 150
Ethetton, Peggy (Mrs. Jim), 150
Etienne, Joseph, 196
Evangel Baptist Church, 108
Evangelical Haitian Baptist Church, 196
Evangelical Reform Baptist Church of Newark, 161
Evergreen Baptist Church, 197
Evergreen German Baptist Church, 102–03

F

Fain, Maurice, 93, 96, 175

Fairleigh Dickinson University, 162

Faith Baptist Chapel of Waverly, 152

Faith Baptist Church, Chateaugay, 215

Faith Baptist Church, Niagara Falls, 156

Fant, Gene, 52, 132, 139, 143

Farmer, Lloyd, 180

Farmingdale Baptist Church, 87, **87**, 88, 95, 165, 191, 216. *See also* Long Island Chapel

Faro De Luz Baptist Mission, 198

Faulkner, Greg, 206

Fellowship Baptist Church, 152

Fellowship Baptist Church, Elmira Heights, 187

Fellowship Baptist Church, Irvington, 161

Fellowship Baptist Church, Staten Island, 161

Fellowship of Greenwich Clergy, 91

Ferguson, Beulah (Mrs. Wilburn), 23, **28**

Ferguson, Tommy, **28**

Ferguson, Wayne, 214

Ferguson, Wilburn C. (Wil), 23–25, 27, **28**, 31

Ferguson family, 24–25

Fernandez, Humberto, 160

Field, Susan, 163, 176, 206

Field, Taylor, 163, 175–76

Fifth Avenue Baptist Church, Rome, 186

Fillmore Avenue Baptist Chapel, 51. *See also* Fillmore Avenue Baptist Church

Fillmore Avenue Baptist Church, 51, 156–57, 167, 192, 217. *See also* Fillmore Avenue Baptist Chapel

Findsen family, 25

Finger Lakes Racetrack, 190

Fink, Henry, 42

Finney, Charles Grandison, 179, 205

Finney Institute, 179, 205

Finnis, Bob, 62, 186

First Arabic Baptist Church of Jersey City, 160

First Arabic Church of New Jersey, 220

First Arabic Baptist Church of Yonkers, 160, 220

First Bangla Christian Church, 218

First Baptist Chapel, 161

First Baptist Church, Albany, 154

First Baptist Church, Augusta, 100

First Baptist Church, Charleston, 12

First Baptist Church of Brooklyn, 98, 101, 102, **102**, 103, 107–10, 120, 126, 144. *See also* Brooklyn Chapel

First Baptist Church of Frankfort, 183

First Baptist Church of Grand Island, 51, 170, 192–93

First Baptist Church of Jena, 57

First Baptist Church of Lancaster, 172

First Baptist Church of Manhattan, 198

First Baptist Church of Montclair, 59, 145, 161

First Baptist Church of Morgan City, 214

First Baptist Church of Morristown, 68

First Baptist Church of Orchard Park, 46

First Baptist Church of Palatka, 42

First Baptist Church of Richmond, 74

First Baptist Church of Rusk, 215

First Baptist Church of Silver Creek, 52, 156, 217. *See also* Fredonia-Dunkirk Chapel and West Main Baptist Church

First Baptist Church of Sudberry, 218

First Baptist Church of Waverly, 32

First Baptist Church of Wellsburg, 63

First Brooklyn Church, 95

First Christian Church of Brushton, 59–60, 149–52, 189, 215

First Freedom Baptist Church, 197

First French-speaking Church of Asbury Park, 161

First Great Awakening, 12

First Indonesian Baptist Church of New York, 195

First Korean Baptist Church of Brooklyn. *See* Hosanna Baptist Church

First Korean Baptist Church of Long Island, 219

First Korean Church of New Jersey, 219

First Polish Baptist Church of Brooklyn, 111–12, 160

First Portuguese-speaking Church of New Jersey, 220

First Portuguese-speaking Church of New York, 160, 220

First Romanian Baptist Church of Ridgewood, 160

First Southern Baptist Church of Endicott, 62–63. *See also* Tri-Cities Chapel and Lincoln Avenue Baptist Church

First Southern Baptist Church of Sidney, 187

First Southern Baptist Church of Syracuse, 27, 28, **28**, 29, 41, 45, 53–55, 58, 61–62, 116. *See also* Central Baptist Church of Syracuse

First Southern Baptist Church of Tucson, 23

First Southern Baptist Church of Watertown, 186

First Southern Churches, 42

First Spanish Baptist Church of Elizabeth, 107. *See also* Bethlehem Baptist Church

First Spanish Baptist Church of Hackensack, 131

First Spanish Baptist Church of Long Beach, 220

First Spanish Baptist Church of Los Angeles, 104

First Spanish Baptist Church of Passaic, 107, 198

First Spanish Baptist Church of Rochester, 148

First Spanish Baptist Church of Rockaway, 160

First Timothy Baptist Church, 193

Fis, Heliodoro, 107

Fischer, Mark A., 206

Fish, Roy, 205

Flanagan, James, 190

Flannery, Michael, 217

Fleming, Karl, 68

Fling, Helen (Mrs. Robert), 92, 136, 144

Fling, Robert, 92

Flores, Alfonso, 106

Flores, Nicomedes, 106

Florida Baptist Convention, 179, 192

Florida State University, 138

Florival, Guy Jean, 161

Florival, Jean A., 196

Flowers, Harold, 100

Floyd Baptist Chapel, 57. *See also* Floyd Baptist Church and One Heart Church

Floyd Baptist Church, 57, 131, 213. *See also* Floyd Baptist Chapel and One Heart Church

Floyd County Baptist Association, 186

Flushing Chinese Baptist Church, 197

Follett, John, 150

Foor, Bernard, 42

Foor family, 23

Forbes, R. M., 63

Ford, Steve, 214

Fordham, Drucillar, 158

Foreign Mission Board. *See* Southern Baptist Foreign Mission Board

Fosdick, Harry
Emerson, 69
Fox, Arnold, 161
Francis, Hyacinth, 109
Francois, Jean, 196
Frazier, S. H., 76
Fredonia-Dunkirk
Chapel, 52. See also
West Main Baptist
Church and First
Baptist Church of
Silver Creek
Freeman, Bob, 176, 193
Freeman, Robert, 206
French Haitian Baptist
Church of
Manhattan, 161
French Road Baptist
Church, 156, 192
French-speaking
Baptist Church of
Bridgeport, 197
French-speaking
Baptist Church of
Brooklyn, 160, 196,
218
French-speaking
Baptist Church Elus,
218
French-speaking Baptist
Church of Far
Rockaway, 161, 196
French-speaking
Baptist Church of
Mt. Vernon, 196
French-speaking
Baptist Church of
Norwalk, 197
French-speaking
Baptist Church of
Spring Valley, 196
French-speaking
Baptist Church of
Stamford, 161, 196,
219
French-speaking
Baptist Church of
White Plains, 197
French-speaking
Baptist Mission,
Boucan Siloe, 196
French-speaking
Church of Danbury,
219
French-speaking
Church of New
Rochelle, 218
French-speaking
Church, Spring
Valley, 219
French-speaking
Church of Yonkers,
219

G

Gainey, Leroy, 167
Galda, John, 217
Galway Fellowship,
214
Gambrell, Ansel, 56
Gantt Baptist Church,
18–21
Garner, John, 187
Garrett, Carol S., 109
Garrett, Duane, 188
Garrett, James Leo, 75
Garrison, Searcy S., 141
Geeslin, Rick, 214
Georgetown (Kentucky)
College, 74
Georgia Baptist
Convention, 141,
172, 174, 177, 204
Genesis Baptist Church,
Newark, 161
Geneva Baptist Chapel,
63. See also Geneva
Southern Baptist
Church
Geneva Southern
Baptist Church, 64,
147, 176, 190. See also
Geneva Baptist
Chapel
George, Timothy, 201
Gera, George, 162
Getsemane Baptist
Church, 113
Gibson, A. J., 56
Gilliland, M. Ray,
138–39, 158, 163, 194
Gilmer, Ettie Jo, 21
Glass, Betty, 135
Glenn, George, 138
Glens Falls Chapel. See
Adirondack Church
Glorietta Conference
Center, 36
Glover, William, 216
Goforth, James, 215
Golden Gate Baptist
Theological
Seminary, 175, 182

Golonka, Elias, 51, 111,
137
Gomes, Elias, 162
Gooch, 77
Good Hope Baptist
Church, 197
Good Shepherd Baptist
Church, 158, 161
Goodwin, R. Dean, 68
Gouverneur Baptist
Chapel, 185
Gowanda Baptist
Chapel, 217
Grace Baptist Church,
Bronx, 197
Grace Baptist Church,
Centereach, 88
Grace Baptist Church,
Lake Grove, 165, 191
Grace Baptist Church,
Ogdensburg, 150,
165, 184. See also
Ogdensburg Chapel
Grace Baptist Church,
Rome, 45, 54, 56–58,
153, 154. See also
Rome Chapel
Grace Baptist Church,
Whitehall, 151, 214
Grace Church, 187
Grace Korean Baptist
Church, 219
Graffiti, 163
Graffiti Baptist
Ministry, 176
Graffiti/East Seventh
Chapel, 163. See also
East Seventh Baptist
Church
Graham, Billy, 163, 179
Grand Island Baptist
Chapel, 217
Grand Island Chapel, 48
Graves, Herbert, 161,
207
Graves, Mona (Mrs.
Richard), 150
Graves, Richard, 150
Graves family, 150
Great Commission
Endowment, 211
Great Depression, 12
Greater File Chapel
Baptist Church, 158
Greater New Hope
Baptist Church, 161
Greater New Jerusalem
Baptist Church of
Morristown, 161
Greater Rochester
Baptist Association,
50, 64, 147–48, 177,
181, 189, 208, 216

Greater Syracuse
Baptist Association,
165, 185, 215
Greater Universal
Baptist Church, 158
Greater Victory Baptist
Church, 158
Greenwich Baptist
Church, 91–92, 92,
124, 129, 140, 161,
163
Greenwich YMCA, 90
Greer, Dorothy (Mrs.
Hank), 204
Greer, Hank, 204
Gresham, Roy, 55, 103,
115, 120, 122–23, 125,
129, 131, 131, 132,
168–69
Grogan, Gloria, 137, 167
Gross, Heriberto, 113
Grossman Avenue
Baptist Church, 156
Guenther, James, 188
Gulfshores Conference
on Associationalism,
50
Guy, Cal, 132, 158

H

Haines Road Baptist
Church, 117
Haire, Marvin, 82–83,
124
Haitian Community
Chapel of Harlem,
219
Halbrook, John, 163
Hall, Bennett F., 84
Hall, David C., 82, 124
Hall, Ernest, 197
Hamilton Hill
Fellowship, 214
Hamlin Community
Baptist Church, 190,
216
Hamm, Sarah, 178
Han Maum Baptist
Church, 196
Hanson Place YMCA,
110
Hardy, Gladys, 80
Harlem Educational
Services Mission,
110, 112
Harlem Ministry
Center, 176, 208
Harpe, Alton, 138–39,
178, 206
Harpe, Fairy (Mrs. Alton),
138, 177, 206, 209
Harris, David, 215
Harrison, Coley, 58, 63

Hartsdale Chapel, 92. *See also* Westchester Baptist Church
Harvard University, 78
Hatcher, Edward, 199
Havenvue Chapel, 187
Heartburg, Joseph, 69
Heilig, Esther (Mrs. Walker), 42
Heilig, Walter, 42, **42**, 82, 117
Heilig family, 42
Henderson, Eugene, 170, 186
Henderson, Genny, 135
Henrietta Baptist Chapel, 48. *See also* Caulkins Road Baptist Church and Pinnacle Road Baptist Church
Henry, Cleveland, 108
Henry, Jim, 213
Hewitt, Basil, 99–100
Hewitt family, 99
Hewlett, Edwin, 141, 148, 181
Hewlett, Mildred (Mrs. Edwin), 141, 148
Highland Avenue Baptist Church, 106, 112–13, 160. *See also* Ebenezer Baptist Church
Hildreth, Robert (Bob), 89–90, **96**
Hill, Bob, 192
Hill, Katie, 177
Hiott, John, 21
Hobbs, Herschel H., 36
Hokit, Linda, 176
Holcomb, Larry, 220
Holiman, Maggie Leece, 70
Hollaway, Stephen (Steve), 139, 175, 178, **178**, 213
Hollis, Earl, **72**
Home Mission Board. *See* Southern Baptist Home Mission Board
Home Missions, 68, 113
Home Missions U.S.A., 23
Honeywell Avenue Baptist Church, 109
Hope Baptist Church, 83, 131, 176, 215, 218. *See also* Roxbury Baptist Chapel
Hope Baptist Church of the Deaf, 218
Hope Church, Flanders, 162
Hora Bautista, La, 104

Horta, Efraim, 105
Hosanna Baptist Church, 196
Hotel New Yorker, 39
House of Prayer, 217
Hovde, Carole, 81
Hovde, Howard, **72**, 80–81, 84, 94
Howell Baptist Church, 199, **199**
Hudgins, J. Scott, 178
Hudnall, Lomita, 78
Hudson, Deal, 139
Hudson Baptist Association, 165, 177, 187–88, 214
Hudson Valley Church, 124
Hughston, John, 120
Hui, Florence (Mrs. Mark), 159
Hui, Mark, 159, **159**
Huisinga, Glenn, 152
Humphreys, Miguel, 218
Hunt, Joe H., 158
Hunt, T. W., 201

I
Igleheart, Glenn, 69, 137, 175–76, 208, **208**
Ignacio, Paul, 194
Indian River Baptist Church, 150
Inlet Community Church, 184
Interfaith Witness, 69, 137, 176
International Christian Church of Toms River, 219
Ithaca Baptist Church, 171, 186, 207, 215
Ithaca/Caroline Chapel, 152
Ivy, David, 215

J
Jacks, Robert (Bob), 58, 61, 124
Jackson, David, 216
Jackson, Fred, 161
Jackson Hill Baptist Church, 85
Jackson Road Baptist Church, 48, 147–48. *See also* Bayview Baptist Chapel and Bayview Baptist Church
Jae Yong Kim, 216
James, Ava Leach (Mrs. Paul), 15, 37–38, **38**, 66, 69, 130, 140, **140**, 170, 208–09

James, Edward, 88, 93
James, Paul S., 15, 36–38, **38**, 39, 55–57, 65–66, 68–72, **72**, 73–76, 80–82, 85, 94–96, **96**, 97, 99–101, 104, 112, 119–24, 126–31, **131**, 132–35, 140, **140**, 145, 157, 163, 169, 170, **170**, 212
James, Sandy (Mrs. Edward), 88
James family, 38–39, 170
James Robb–Pioneer, 32
Jefferson Baptist Church, 155, 184
Jemmott, David, 109
Jerusalem Baptist Chapel, 107
Jewell Free Chapel, 184
Jin Chung, 219
John, Peter, 207
John Gano Baptist History Fellowship, 212
Johnson, William, 63
Jolly, Charles, 33–35, 39, 82, **140**, 144
Jolly, Dorothy, **140**
Jones, Eldon, 64, 126
Jones, Janice (Mrs. Jerry), 157
Jones, Jerry, 157
Jones, Jim, 47–48, 190
Jones, Norvell, **72**, 74, 84, 94
Jones, Peter Rhea, 96
Jones, Ron, 178
Jong Hur, 219
Jordan, Bob, 84
Joseph, Karnest, 161
Joseph, Tony, 196, 219
Judson, Adoniram, 37

K
Kasa, John, 111
Keller, Don, 184
Kentucky Baptist Convention, 125
Ketchens, Victor, 207
Kever family, 23
Khalil, William, 160
Ki Il Park, 196
Killinger, John, 82
Kim, H. M., 159
King, Kenneth, 84, 127
Kinney, Jack, 83
Kirby family, 46
Knapp, Donald, 57
Knapton, James, 153
Knapton, Mary (Mrs. Roger), 62, 127, 171

Knapton, Roger, 62–63, 117, 124, 126–27, 169, 174, 181–82, 201
Knapton, Warren, 63–64
Knapton, Mrs. Warren, 63
Knight, Francis, 89
Knight, Lonnie, 86
Korean-American Baptist Church, 195
Korean Baptist Church of Chappaqua, 219
Korean Baptist Church of New York, 159
Korean Baptist Church of Northern New Jersey, 219
Korean Baptist Church of Queens, 196. *See also* New York Han Shin Baptist Church
Korean Baptist Church of Susquehanna, 187, 215
Korean Baptist Church of Watertown, 186
Kratz, C. W., 80
Kung, Peter, **159**
Kyu Suk Kwak, 196, 219

L
Lakeland Baptist Chapel, 198
Lakeland Baptist Church, Franklin, 162
Lake Placid Baptist Church, 215
Lakeview Baptist Church, Auburn, 192
Lam, David, 193
Lancaster Baptist Fellowship, 217. *See also* New Hope Fellowship
Langley, James, 75
Langley, Ralph, 75
LaSalle Baptist Church, 22–26, 41–42, **42**, 44, 51, 57, 131, 156, 193, 217
LaSalle Baptist Mission, 21–22
LaSalle YMCA, 21
Laurel Baptist Church, 62
Lawrenceville Baptist Church, 151, 189
Lawson, Mark, 210
Lay, David, 152
Leamer, Elsie, 144

Leary, David, 165, 190–91, **211**, 216

Lee, Andrew, 175

LeFevre, Rosemary, 135

Lefler, Harold, 151, 187

Leonard, Andre, 196

Leonidas, Pierre, 161

Lewis, Larry, 202

Liesmann, R. P., 83

Lin, Serena, 207, 217

Lincoln Avenue Baptist Church, 62–63, 125, 127, 152, 171, 182, 187, **206**, 215. *See also* Tri-Cities Baptist Chapel and First Southern Baptist Church of Endicott

Lincroft Baptist Church, 82

Lindsay, Florence (Mrs. Maurice), 59, 61, 150

Lindsay, Maurice, 59, 150

Lindsay family, 59

Lindsey, John, 163

Lingelbach, Charles, 56

Lipphard, W. B., 66

Living Gospel Baptist Church, 162. *See also* Rutherford Baptist Church (ABC) and Living Gospel Chapel

Living Gospel Chapel, 162. *See also* Living Gospel Baptist Church and Rutherford Baptist Church (ABC)

Living Proof campaign, 143

Living Stone Christian Fellowship, 219

Living Word (Filipino) Fellowship, 218

Living Word Fellowship, Queens, 195

Lockport Chapel, 48

Lockwood, Patricia (Mrs. Quentin, Jr.), 210

Lockwood, Quentin, Jr. (Chip), 139, 178, 202, 210

Loney, Roderick, 109–10

Long, Charles, 181

Long Falls Baptist Church, 186

Long Island Baptist Association, 165, 190–91, 208, **211**, 216–17

Long Island Baptist Chapel, 86–87, 124. *See also* Farmingdale Baptist Church

Long Island Bible Fellowship, 216

Long-range Action Committee, 134

Losito, David, 168, 210

Losito, Theresa (Mrs. David), 210

Lowe, Lewis, 94

Lowndes, Doris (Mrs. Jack), **140**, 166

Lowndes, Jack P., 140, **140**, 141–43, 145, 167–68, 212

Lutz, Byron, 51, 155–56

Lyle, Kenneth, 88, **88**, 89, 97, 124, 132–33, 143, 157

Lynch, Bill, 198

Lynn, Robert, 154

M

M. Wile Suit Company, 52

Madison Avenue Baptist Church, 32

Madison, Ron, 144

Madison Baptist Church, 81–84, 86, 89, 94–95, **140**, 144, 162, 168, 172, 177, 194, 198, 213

Madison Korean Church, 219

Magruder, Charles, 48–52, 54, 124, 126

Maher, Herb, **72**

Maldonado, Boanerges, 198

Maldonado, Zully (Mrs. Boanerges), 198

Mallory Baptist Church, 56

Malone, Dennis, 83

Malone, Marilyn, 144

Manansala, Romeo, 176

Manansala, Romy, 182, 194–95, **195**, 207–08, 218–19

Mandarin Fellowship Baptist Church, 218

Manhattan Baptist Chapel, 94–95

Manhattan Baptist Church, 39, 57, 65–66, 69–72, **72**, 73–80, 82–86, 89–90, 93–98, 100–01, 105, 112, 115, 163

Manhattan International Baptist Church, 195

Manhattan YMCA, 104

Manlius Family Fellowship, 215

Maples, Harry, 186

Maples, Robert, 159

Maples Conference, 215

Maranatha Spanish Baptist Church of Yonkers, 198

Marshall, Daniel, 12

Marshall, Edna (Mrs. Glen), 174

Marshall, Glen, 174

Marshall, Martha Stearns, 12

Martin, H. Lawrence, 91

Martin, Isaac, 158

Martin, Wilbert, 192–93, 207

Martinez, Jesus, 160

Martyr's Cross Crusade Baptist Church, 197

Mary, Come Home, 156

Maryland Baptist, 34, **38**, **106**

Maryland Baptist Church, 155

Maryland/Delaware Convention, 174, 207

Maryland State Convention. *See* Baptist Convention of Maryland

Masonic Hall of Westhampton Beach, 88

Massachusetts Institute of Technology, 78

Massena Baptist Chapel, 44, 58, *See also* Massena Baptist Church

Massena Baptist Church, 54, 59–60. *See also* Massena Baptist Chapel

Massey, Chlocile (Mrs. Clarence), 31

Massey, Clarence, 31

Massey family, 31–32, 79

MasterLife, 166

Maston, Freda (Mrs. Gene), 76

Maston, Gene, 75–78, 96–97

Mathison, John, 156

Mathison, Martha (Mrs. John), 156

Mathison family, 23

Matthews, Austin, 124

Matthews, Clifford (Cliff), 46, 124, 153–55, 191–92

Matthews, Peggy (Mrs. Clifford), 155

Mauriel, Lena, 82

Mauriel, Ralph, 82

Mayo, Ernest, 36

McBurney YMCA, 33, 35

McCarter, Matrel, 80, 97

McCarter family, 80

McCarty, Doran, 175

McClellan, Albert, 115, 221

McCormick, Wallace, 81

McDearmon, George, 154, 165

McFadden, Vol, 41

McGavic, Claude, 176, 205–06

McGavic, Martha, 9

McGlohon, Joy (Mrs. Neal), **199**

McGlohon, Neal, 198, **199**

McKelvey, John, 41

McKinney, J. C., 48

McLeod, Kenneth, 59

McWhales, Charles, 218

Medema, Ken, 145, 164, 176

Medina, Oscar, 207

Meek, Charles, 80, 89

Meek, Jon F., Jr., 83, 136, 172, 182

Memorial Baptist Church, Arlington, 140

Meola, Jim, 151

Mercer, Jack, 170, 213

Merck, Jimmy, 150

Meredith, Dale, 155, 170, 193

Meredith, Jean (Mrs. Dale), 155, 193

Merrill, David, 214

Metropolitan Baptist Church, 148, 163. *See also* Brighton/ Pittsford Chapel and Browncroft Baptist Church

Metropolitan Baptist Ministries, 159

Metropolitan Baptist Mission (Spanish), 163

Metropolitan Brazilian Baptist Mission, 163
Metropolitan New York Baptist Association, 9, 55, 95, **96**, 97, 107, 110, 112, 114, 118–19, 122–30, 136, 138–39, 143, 157–63, 165, 167, 169, 174–77, 179, 181, 187, 191, 193–97, 202–03, 208, 212, 214, 217–21
Metropolitan Southern Baptist Filipino Fellowship, 219
Miami University, 138
Michael, Katie, 46
Michael, Mike, 46
Michel, Joseph, 197
Mid-America Baptist Theological Seminary, Northeast Branch, 184, 188, 214
Middlebury College, 139
Mikhail, Abdalla, 220
Miller, Carolyn, **209**
Miller, Don, 87, **87**, 88, **96**, 117, 142
Miller Chapel, 75
Miller Street Baptist Church, 184
Mills, Alvin, 197
Minchow-Proffitt, Terry, 178, **178**
Miraflor, Gene, 195, 216
Mision Bautista Hispaña, 156
Mision Christiana, 220
Missions, 66
Mission Service Corps, 141, 148, 150, 166, 174–75, 178, 181, 185, 192, 207, 217
Mississippi Baptist Convention, 137
Mohawk Valley Chapel, 56–57. *See also* Trinity Baptist Church
Monday, Curtis, 156
Mondelus, Wesner, 196
Monk, Raymond, 45
Monk, Sharon, 45
Monmouth Baptist Church, 82–83
Monmouth Church, 163
Monmouth Korean Baptist Church. *See* New Life Korean Baptist Church

Montalvo, Walter, 163
Montclair State University, 162
Moody, Robert, 161
Moore, John, 32, 36
Morales, Edgar, 220
Morgan, Alex, 197
Morgan, David, **96**, 98–102, **102**, 103–04, 108, 110, 114, 120, 124–27, 132, 144
Morgan, David, Jr., 99–100
Morgan, Eileen (Mrs. David), 97, 100–01, 103
Morgan, Rodwell, 113
Morgan, Rodolph, 109, 158
Morgan family, 103
Moriah Baptist Chapel, 215
Morris, Fernando, 197
Motor Cities Association, 36
Mount Chapel Missionary Baptist Church, 220
Mount Hope Missionary Baptist Church, 158
Mount of Olives Mission, 218
Mount Zion Baptist Church of Christ, 158
Mullinax, Marvin, 186
Munro, Jamie, 180, 199
Munro, Joyce, 175, 180

N

Nahm, Esther, 195
Nam Kyu Cho, 219
National Baptist Convention, 158, 161, 167
National Council of Churches, 81, 88, 109
National School of Evangelism and Church Growth, 205
National Technical Institute for the Deaf, 190, 216
Navarro, Conrad, 174–75
Nazareth Baptist Church, 85, 106–07
Neighbor, Ralph W., Jr., 95
Nesmith, Barbara, 167
Nevels, Paul, 24, 41
Newark Baptist Fellowship Church, 190

New Beginnings Baptist Church, 192. *See also* Assurance Baptist Church
New Bethlehem Haitian Baptist Church, 218
Newburgh Baptist Chapel, 89. *See also* Ridgecrest Baptist Church
New Covenant Baptist Church, 190
New England Baptist Association, 79, 95, 122
New England Convention, 174, 207
New England Fellowship, 123
New Hope Baptist Church, Kingston, 162
New Hope Baptist Chapel, Sayre, 215
New Hope Baptist Church, Watertown, 186
New Hope Church, 187
New Hope Fellowship, 217. *See also* Lancaster Baptist Fellowship
New Hope Korean Baptist Church, 196
New Jersey Baptist Chapel, 80
New Jersey Convention, 39
New Jersey First Chinese Baptist Church, 218
New Jersey Southern Baptists, 80
New Jerusalem Baptist Church, 198
New Jerusalem French-speaking Church, 196
New Life Korean Baptist Church, 196
New Orlean's Baptist Theological Seminary, 18, 21, 42, 44, 159, 182
New Rochelle Christian Fellowship, 195
New Salem Baptist Church, 162
Newsweek, 68
New York Antioch Korean Baptist Church, 219

New York Baptist City Mission Society, 111
New York Baptist Fellowship, 125
New York City Baptist Student Union, 76–77
New York Han Shin Baptist Church, 196. *See also* Korean Baptist Church, Queens
New York/New Jersey Fellowship, 118–19, 123
New York Baptist, 127, 131, 135, 137, 142, 171, 178, 180
New York Times, 39
New York University, 138, 206
Niagara Falls Southern Baptist Mission, 21
Nieto, Luis, 182
Niswonger, Tom, 189
Norman, Ron, 182
Norman and Lena Bell Offering for Associational Missions, 188
North American Baptist Fellowship, 86
North Buffalo Community Church, 217
Northeast Baptist Convention, 116
Northeast Baptist Educational Consortium (NeBEC), 175
Northeast Disaster Relief Consortium, 207
Northeast Emphasis Committee, 121
Northeast Evangelism Thrust campaign, 167
Northeastern Baptist School of Ministry (NEBSM), 175
Northeastern Bible College, 108
Northeastern District Association, 94–95, 98, 104
Northeastern Regional Fellowship, 115–17, 119–21, 123
Northeast Thrust, 121
Northeast Task Team on Theological Education (NTTE), 174

North Fenton Baptist Church, 187
North Shore Baptist Church, Kings Park, 87, 162
North Shore Church, Long Island, 142
Northside Baptist Chapel, 56. *See also* Northside Baptist Church
Northside Baptist Church, 56, 165, 185. *See also* Northside Baptist Chapel
North Tonawanda Baptist Church. *See* Abundant Life Baptist Church
North Tonawanda Church, 156. *See also* Friendship Baptist Church
Norton, Frank, 52
Norton, Jim, 198
Nueva Vida Baptist Church, 197

O

Oates, Wayne, 76
Oden, Barbara, 218
Odlyzko, Michael, 51
Officer's Christian Union (OCU), 77
Ogdensburg Chapel, 150. *See also* Grace Baptist Church, Ogdensburg
Ohio Baptist Messenger, 40
Ohio Convention. *See* State Convention of Baptists in Ohio
Oliver, Joe, 48
One Heart Church, 57, 213. *See also* Floyd Baptist Chapel and Floyd Baptist Church
Open Arms Fellowship, 214
Open Door Christian Center, 216
Orchard Park Chapel, 44. *See also* Orchard Park Church
Orchard Park Church, 52. *See also* Orchard Park Chapel
Orellano, Solomon, 220
Orendain, Delfin, 195
Orr, J. Edwin, 143
Ortiz, Henry, 197
Oswampke, Chris, 74

Ou Soon Lee, 219
Outreach Baptist Church, 108
Owego Chapel, 152. *See also* Owego Southern Baptist Church
Owego Southern Baptist Church, 152, 186–87. *See also* Owego Chapel

P

Pack, Forrest Neal, 91–92
Paige, James, 161
Paixao, Daniel, 177, 205–06, 220
Pak, Michael, 175, 196
Parent, R. Nicholas, 197
Park, Moses, 196
Park Slope Baptist Church, 113, 218
Park, Soo (Mrs. Moses), 196
Parker, A. Wilson, 152
Parrott, Jack, 167, 179
Partin, James, 41
Pascu, Cornel, 160
Patmos Baptist Church, 109–10
Patterson, Benton, 91
Patterson, Larry, 113
Patterson, Pat (Mrs. Benton), 91
Paul and Ava James Offering for BCNY Missions, 170, 208
Pearson, Elizabeth (Liz), 177, 208, **209**
Pennellville Baptist Church, 185
Pennsylvania/South Jersey Convention, 118, 174, 207
Pennsylvania/South Jersey Fellowship, 125
Perry, James, 165, 188–89
Phan, David, 207, 214, 216
Pharris, Carroll, **209**
Philistin, Norbert, 218
Phillips, Arthur, 161
Pierre, Ismael, 161, 196
Pierre, Rigaud, 218
Pierre, Withney, 218
Pike, H. T., 35
Pinnacle Road Baptist Church, 48, 147–48, 190. *See also* Henrietta Baptist Chapel and Caulkins Road Baptist Church

Pinson, William, 132
Pioneer and Western Missions, 36
Pioneer Missions Movement, 18
Pittsburgh Association, 118
Pittsburgh (Pennsylvania) Baptist Church, 82
Pittsford Baptist Church, 190, 216
Pittsford Church, 149
Piscataway Bible Fellowship, 219
Pleasant Valley Baptist Church, 190
Poe, John, 215
Pollard, Ramsey, 20, 30
Pope, David, **211**, 213
Popesku, Aureliam, 160
Porter, Curtis, 50, 119, 124, 126–27, 131–32, 155, 180–81
Post-Dispatch, 28
Potsdam Church, 60
Powerhouse Baptist Chapel, 189
Praise Baptist Church, 188, 214. *See also* Saratoga Baptist Chapel
Prather, Bill, 82
Pressler, Paul, 75
Price, Bertram, 158
Pridmore, Larry, 151, **211**
Prieto, Jaime, 194
Primero Iglesia Bautista de Manhattan, 106
Princeton Theological Seminary, 10, 33, 82, 84–85, 96, 139, 178, 206, 256
Princeton University, 75, 139, 178, **178**, 206
Project 500, 47–48, 52, 82, 93, 121
Puckett, R. G., 40–41, 46, 68
Pugh, Norma (Mrs. R. Quinn), 10, 85, 169, **170**, 182
Pugh, R. Quinn, 10, 85, **96**, 97, 117, 119, 126–27, 143, 157, 169, **170**, 172–74, 182, 193–94, 201, 203–04, 206, 209–10

Q

Queens Bible Church, 194–95

Queens College, 138
Quinonez, Albertina, 198

R

Racetrack Chaplaincy of America, 191
Raper, William H., 47
Raritan Valley Baptist Church, 10, 82, 84, 159, 161, 212, 218, 256
Rattray, Hervin (Mrs. Pat), 109
Rattray, Pat, 109
Ray, Juanita (Mrs. Marion), 93
Ray, Marion, 93
Red, Buryl, 70
Redford, Courts, 14, 34, 36, 103, 132
Reeves, Carroll, **72**
Reformed Baptist movement, 154
Reid-Salmon, Delroy, 197
Resurreccion (Spanish) Baptist Church, 219
Resurrection Baptist Church, Bergenfield, 160
Rhymes, Donald, 113
Richards, Judith, **60**, 189
Richboro Baptist Church, 94. *See also* Staten Island Chapel
Richville Baptist Church, 150–51, 186. *See also* Richville Chapel
Richville Chapel, 150. *See also* Richville Baptist Church
Rickman, Calvin, 47
Rickman, Irene (Mrs. Calvin), 47
Rick's Institute, 81
Ridgecrest Baptist Church, 89–90, 95, 103. *See also* Newburgh Baptist Chapel
Ridgecrest Conference Center, 138
Ridgedale Avenue School, 80
Ridgeway, Richard, 94
Rivers, James, 192
Robb, James, 31
Robb, Pauline (Mrs. James), 31–32
Robb family, 31–32, 79
Roberts, Ray, 22, 33–34, 36, 41, 43, 49, 53–55, 115, 119, 129, 131, **131**

Roberts, Richard, 132
Robertson, Terry, 9, 192–93, 217
Robinson, Cecelia, 108–09
Robinson, Doris (Mrs. Ernesto), 161
Robinson, Ernesto, 161, 207
Robinson, Edith (Mrs. James), 92
Robinson, Edwina, 137
Robinson, James, 92
Rochester Association, 173, 190
Rochester Baptist Church, 47–48, 144, 147–48, 190, 216
Rochester Institute of Technology, 139, 190, 216
Rochester Vietnamese Mission, 216
Rockland Baptist Church, 93, 131, 175, 196
Rodriguez, Reyes, 157
Rogers, Adrian, 179–80, 200
Rome Chapel, 44–45. *See also* Grace Baptist Church
Rose, Lloyd, 108
Roundtree, Malachi, 157
Routh, Porter, 67
Roxbury Baptist Chapel, 83. *See also* Hope Baptist Church
Royal Ambassadors, 32, 136
Ruiz, José, 105–06
Russ, George, 167, 179, 205, **208**
Russell, Ralph, 151
Rutgers University, 138, 206
Rutherford Baptist Church (ABC), 162. *See also* Living Gospel Baptist Church and Living Gospel Chapel
Rutledge, Arthur, 68, 116, **131**, 132
Ryals, DeLane M., 9–10, 83, 87, **96**, 158, 175, 181, 194–95, 203, 212
Ryals, Nancy, 157

S

Saathoff, Rob, 193
St. Juste, Emmanuel, 161, 196–97, 219

St. Juste, Lamartine, 196
St. Phard, Emma (Mrs. Pierre), 110–11
St. Phard, Pierre Ludovic, 110–11
St. Pierre, Franz, 197
Salvation Army, 205
Samford University's Beeson Divinity School, 201
Sam Simpson: Architect of Hope, 109
Samuelson, Gil, 156
Sanchez, Daniel R., 142–43, 166, 175, 212
Sanchez, José, 106
Sanders, Mary Lois, 205
Sanders, Robert, 215
Sanders, William L., 174
Sandy Creek Church, 12
Santamaria, Jaime, 106
Saratoga Baptist Chapel, 188. *See also* Praise Baptist Church
Saturday Evening Post, 91
Saul, Bob, 143, 198
Saul, Nancy, 143
Savior's Korean Baptist Church of New York, 219
Sayer, Avery, 113, 176
Sayer, Myra (Mrs. Avery), 176
Scalise, Charles, 139
Scarpeta, Marcelena, 105
Schlett, Paul, 176, 214
Schoonmaker, Bruce, 163
Schumacher, Homer C. (Bud), 143
Scott, Noel Henry, 144
Screven, William, 12
Screven Memorial Baptist Church, 79, 94
Scruggs, Jerry, 88–89
Second Baptist Church of Auburn, 36
Second Century Fund, **209**
Segura, Luis, 107
Seh Moon Korean Baptist Church, 195
Sentinel Baptist Church, St. Albans, 218
Seok Won Kim, 185

Seoul Korean Baptist Church, 216
Sera-Josef, David, 219
Sermon, Felix, 195, 219
Seventh Day Adventist Church, 86
Shackelford, Al, 188
Sharp, Charles, 153
Sharper, Horace P., 161
Sharron Woods Baptist Church, 149, 189
Shelter Rock Church of the Deaf, 198, 218
Sheridan, George, 137, 176
Sheridan Park Baptist Church, 50
Sherman, Cecil, 75
Shiloh Baptist Church of Malone, 151, 215
Shiloh Baptist Church, Queens, 197
Shin, Suk H., 196
Shirkey, David, 148
Short, Charles, 216
Simmons, J. Kelly, 68
Simmons, Jasper, 158
Simmons, John, 149, 152, 186–87
Simpson, Lola (Mrs. Sam), 108–09
Simpson, Sam, 108–09, 161, 174, 181, 207
Sims, Tom, 89
Sizemore, Elmer, 94, 117
Skelton, Beverly, 91
Skelton, Jack, 90–91
Skelton family, 90
Slade, Becky, 175
Smith, Bailey, 180
Smith, Blake, 67–68
Smith, Roy, 204
Smith, William, 217
Sochia, Tom, 150–51
So Generations Will Remember: A History of Woman's Missionary Union, Baptist Convention of New York, 1969–1994, 15, 209
Solis, Norman, 195
Somarriba, Jose, 197
Somerset Baptist Church, 161
Somerset Hills Baptist Church, 84, 131, 181. *See also* Bernardsville Chapel
Sommer, Robert (Bob), 162, 191

Soon Il Kim (Robert), 175, 207, 218–19
Sorrell, Sam, **72**, 74, 94
Source of Life Church, 196
Southern Baptist Annuity Board, 182
Southern Baptist Brotherhood Commission, 182
Southern Baptist Chapel of New York City, 33, 35, 37
Southern Baptist Christian Life Commission, 182
Southern Baptist Church, Brooklyn, 197
Southern Baptist Convention, 12, 20, 30, 50, 71–72, 74, 86, 94–95, 97–98, 100–01, 106–07, 112, 116, 125–26, 132, 135, 143, 148, 158, 166, 174, 177, 180–81, 188, 201–03, 205, 209, 213, 216
Southern Baptist Convention Executive Committee, 67, 115, 132, 182, 200–01
Southern Baptist Convention Seminary Presidents' Council, 175
Southern Baptist Foreign Mission Board, 21, 31, 145, 162, 182, 184, 189, 198
Southern Baptist Historical Commission, 182
Southern Baptist Home Mission Board, 14, 17, 22–24, 26–27, 30–37, 39, 47, 49, 51, 55–58, 62, 66, 68–69, 72, 75, 78, 81–82, 85–87, **87**, 89, 93–94, 100–06, 108–17, 119–21, 124, 129, **131**, 132, 134, 136–37, 139–43, 149, 154–55, 157, 159, 167, 171, 175–76, 182, 201–03, 205, 208
Southern Baptist Radio and Television Commission, 40, 178, 182

Southern Baptist Stewardship Commission, 182
Southern Baptist Theological Seminary, 36, 46, 76, 174
Southern District Association, 35
Southern Seminary, 97, 194
Southern Seminary's Boyce Bible School, 177
Southern Tier Association, 64, 126, 147, 149, 151–52, 154, 164, 182, 186–87, 214
South Hill Baptist Church, 79
South Jefferson County Historical Association, 205
South Main Baptist Church, 80, 194
Southport Church, Elmira, 62–63, 119, 152, 215–16
Southport Church, Waverly, 215
Southside Baptist Church, Columbus, 47
Southside Baptist Church, Jamestown, 192, 217
Southside Baptist Church, Kingsport, 90,162
Southwestern Baptist Theological Seminary, 33, 132, 143, 158, 182
Spanish Baptist Church of Paterson, 107
Spanish Calvary Baptist Church, 107, 197
Sparks, H. Garland, 46
Spencerport (Northwest) Church, 190
Speers, Theodore, 77
Spring Grove Baptist Church, 197
Stamford Baptist Church, 155, 184
Stanton, Gloria, 189
State Convention of Baptists in Ohio, 22, 24, 27, 32–33, 40–41, 43, 46–47, 49–51, 54–55, 57, 118–19, 124–25, 131, 133, 135

Staten Island Chapel, 93. See also Richboro Baptist Church
Staten Island Korean Mission, 219
State University of New York, Albany, 214
State University of New York, Binghamton, 187, 215
State University of New York, Fredonia, 139
State University of New York, Stony Brook, 191, 217
Stearns, Shubal, 12
Stefanini, Victor, 185
Stetzer, Ed, 193
Stewart, Leroy, 124, 140
Stewart Air Force Base, 90
Stouffer, Paul, 215
Stowe, Darty, 54
Strange, James, 84
Styerses, 80
Suarez, Gus, 192
Suburban Baptist Church, 86, 95, 107
Sullivan, Hartman, 131
Sullivan, John, 189
Sullivan, Maurice, 127
Sullivan Road Baptist Church, 156
Summers, Larry, 217
Sumrall, Robert (Rusty), 190, 216
Sun Il Lee, 219
SUNY Stony Brook, 207
Suwabe, Azurma, 218
Suzukawa, Henry, 88
Syracuse University, 45, 78, 155, **178**, 185, 207

T
Tabernacle Baptist Church, 157
Talada, John, 215
Tan, Kenneth, 194
Taylor, Betty (Mrs. Bob), 153
Taylor, Bob, 153
Taylor, Brookins, 216
Taylor, Howard, 90
Taylor, Sally, 190
Temple Baptist Church, 153
10/90 Challenge, 177

Terrill Road Baptist Chapel, 84. See also Clark Baptist Chapel and Terrill Road Baptist Church
Terrill Road Baptist Church, 84, 127, 144, **178**, 220. See also Clark Baptist Chapel and Terrill Road Baptist Chapel
Theresa Hotel, 109
Thirty Thousand Movement, 30, 43, 67, 99
Thomas, C. C., 34
Thomas, Jean-Baptiste, 111, 160
Thompson, Theresa, 206
Thompson, Truett, 62
Thousand Islands Baptist Association, 165, 184–86, 188, 215
Thurston, Elizabeth, 84
Tillich, Paul, 77
Tilton, C. Nelson, 144, 148
Tjoa, Jacob, 195
Todd, Alan, 182, 190
Toirac, Eliseo, 106, 198
Tollison, John, 55–57, 61, 63, 118, 124
Tolton, W. William, 158
Tom, Ken, 159
Tomlinson, Jim, 148
Tonawanda Baptist Church, 193
Total Operations for Neighborhood Environment (T.O.N.E.), 158
Training Union, 25, 70, 80, 130
Treigle, Norman, 70
Tri-Cities Baptist Chapel, 62. See also First Southern Baptist Church of Endicott and Lincoln Avenue Baptist Church
Tri-County Baptist Ministries, 154
Triennial Convention, 12
Trinity Baptist Church, 162
Trinity Baptist Church, 57. See also Mohawk Valley Chapel
Trinity Baptist Church, 63. See also Windsor Chapel

Trinity Baptist Church, Schenectady, 153–54, **154**, 171, 187–88, 214
Trinity Chapel, 113. See also United Trinity Baptist Church
Tri-Town Baptist Ministries, 187
Trust in God Baptist Church, 159
Trust in God Chinese Baptist Church, 175
Tubbs, John M., 130, 137–38, 212
Tupper Lake Baptist Church, 189. See also Tupper Lake Chapel
Tupper Lake Chapel, 189. See also Tupper Lake Baptist Church
Turner, Ellis B., 148, 155
Turner, J. David, 187
Tuttle, F. C., 30
Twelfth Street Reformed Church, 113
Twin County Baptist Church, 84, 131

U
Union Baptist Church, 197
United States Coast Guard Academy, 78
United States Merchant Marine Academy, 78
United States Military Academy at West Point, 76–78, 138, **178**, 206
United States Naval Academy, 206
United Trinity Baptist Church, 113. See also Trinity Chapel
Unity Freedom Baptist Church, Newark
University Baptist Church, Getzville, 193
University Baptist Church, Austin, 67
University Baptist Church, Syracuse, 185, 215
University of Buffalo, 176, **178**, 193, 206
University of Chicago, 75
Urdaneta, Rafael, 107
Utica Baptist Chapel, 46. See also Clinton Road Baptist Church

V

Vacation Bible School, 24, 41, 51, 59, 63, 80, 86, 137, 153, 156

Vann, William Pennington (Penny), 76

Vassar College, 78

Vassar Road Baptist Church, 90, 95, 181, 218

Venable, Frank, 90

Verrazano Narrows Bridge, 93

Veteran's Park Baptist Church, 156, 217

Vick, Ralph, 193

Victory Baptist Church, 151

Victory Baptist Church, Batavia, 193

Victory Chapel, 216

Virginia Commonwealth University, 139

VISION 2000, 171, 173, 176, 204

W

Wagner, Herbert, 190

Wake Eden Academy, 161

Wake Eden Community Baptist Church, 161, 181, 207

Wake Eden Community Center, 176

Walker, Arthur L., 41–42, **42**, 43–43, 47–48, 61, 119, 132, 212

Walker, Joy, 109

Walker, Larry, 88

Walker Missionary Baptist Church, 158

Wallace, Barbara, 177, 190, 216

Walsh, John, 139

Waltz, Joe, 117–18

Ward, Beth, 9, 204

Ward, Ginger, **178**, 193

Ward, Ted, 192, 217

Washington Avenue Baptist Church, 162, 191

Washington D.C., Convention, 174–75

Wassily, George, 160

Watson, Betty (Mrs. Harry), 89, 162

Watson, Harry, 89, 162

Watson, Jim, 191

Watson, Norman, **72**, 74–75, 84

Watt, Howard and Francis, 57

Waugh, Rebecca, 218

Webb, Art, 77

Webb, Denny, 217

Webb, Rodney, 137

Wellsburg Baptist Chapel, 63

Welsh Neck Baptist Church, 46

West, Ross, 51

Westchester Baptist Church, 92–93, 180. *See also* Hartsdale Chapel

Westchester Bible Fellowship, 195

Westchester Korean Baptist Church, Yonkers, 219

West End Church Baptist, Manhattan, 198, 220

West Main Baptist Church, 52, 131, 143, 156, 192. *See also* Fredonia-Dunkirk Chapel and First Baptist Church of Silver Creek

West Monmouth Baptist Chapel, 83

West Monmouth Baptist Church, 158, 163

West Point Baptist Church, 139

West Point Baptist Student Union, 77

West Pomona Community Church, 93

West Side Baptist Church, 150–51

West Virginia Fellowship of Southern Baptists, 125

Wheatfield Baptist Chapel, 217

Wheaton College, 36–37

Whitehall Chapel, 165

White Plains YMCA, 92

Whittaker, Fermin, 101, 103

Whitten, Steve, 193

Wilkerson, Kenneth, 193

Wilkinson, Sonny, 59

William Carey Baptist Church, 160

Williams, Clarence, 197

Williams, Glendora (Mrs. Michael), 176

Williams, Michael, 176, 208

Williams, Paul, 197

Williams, Thad, **72**

Williams, Wallace A. C., 144, 168, 174, 181

Williamson, Faustine (Mrs. Richard), 21

Williamson, Richard, 21

Williamson family, 23

Wilmoth, Noel, 192

Wilson, Fred, 139

Wilson, Jack, 92

Wilson, Mary (Mrs. Jack), 92

Wilton Baptist Church, 93, 124, 144, 162, 181. *See also* Wilton Baptist Fellowship

Wilton Baptist Fellowship, 93. *See also* Wilton Baptist Church

Windsor Baptist Chapel, 63. *See also* Trinity Baptist Church

Wingate, James, 162

Witherspoon, Carnell, 220

Woman's Missionary Union (WMU), 15, 80, 84, 86, 92, 97, 127, 135–37, 139, 144, 148, 152, 167, 177, 198, 208–09, **209**

Wong, Sam, 197

Wong, Timothy, 191

Wood, Larry, 162, 198

Woodside Spanish Baptist Church, 160

Woolbright, Robert, 158

Woon Chul Kim, 187

Wooten, Morris, 197

Word of God Hour Baptist Church, 197

Work Related to Non-Evangelicals, 69

World War II, 13

Wright, Armetta Fields, 207

Wright, Bob, 41

Wright, Eugene, 216

Wright, James, 88, 112–13

Y

Yale University, 70, 78

Yong Mok Kim, 219

Young Ho Lee, 196

Youngje Han, 219

Youngstown Baptist Chapel, 217

Yousef, Nagi, 220

Youth Corps, 157

Yu, Andrew, 191, 218

Z

Zion Temple Baptist Church, Brooklyn

Zurheide, Jeffrey, 175

ABOUT THE AUTHOR

Keith L. Cogburn has served as pastor of the Raritan Valley Baptist Church in Edison, New Jersey, since 1983. After graduating from Baylor University, he earned graduate degrees from Baylor, Princeton Theological Seminary, and Drew University. He was pastor of two Texas churches from 1977 to 1983. He served as chairman of the Executive Board of the Baptist Convention of New York (1990–1991), and has been a field education supervisor for the Princeton Theological Seminary Department of Field Education since 1989. He and his wife Laura, a preschool teacher, have two children: Emily Anne and John Leland.